29205

OXFORD STUDIES IN AFRICAN AFFAIRS

General Editors
JOHN D. HARGREAVES *and* GEORGE SHEPPERSON

SOURCES OF YORUBA HISTORY

SOURCES OF YORUBA HISTORY

EDITED BY

S. O. BIOBAKU

CLARENDON PRESS · OXFORD

1973

Oxford University Press, Ely House, London W.1

GLASGOW NEW YORK TORONTO MELBOURNE WELLINGTON
CAPE TOWN DELHI IBADAN NAIROBI DAR ES SALAAM LUSAKA ADDIS ABABA
BOMBAY CALCUTTA MADRAS KARACHI LAHORE DACCA
KUALA LUMPUR SINGAPORE HONG KONG TOKYO

PRINTED IN GREAT BRITAIN
BY WILLIAM CLOWES & SONS, LIMITED
LONDON, BECCLES AND COLCHESTER

Preface

IN 1956, an imaginative scheme—the YORUBA HISTORICAL RESEARCH SCHEME—was launched by the Government of the then Western Region of Nigeria, with the present writer as its Director. The aim was to write an authentic history of the Yoruba peoples from the earliest ascertainable time to the present, using all the modern techniques of recapturing the history of a non-literate society. Trained historians, practitioners of allied disciplines such as archaeology, ethnography, anthropology, and sociology were to play their part no less than traditional local historians and celebrated authorities on the traditions, the customs and *mores* of the Yoruba peoples. A small staff of full-time historians and anthropologists co-operated with part-time visiting scholars such as William Fagg of the British Museum and Professor Frank Willett, the archaeologist of Ifẹ; local dignitaries and associates included Chief I. O. Delanọ, the Yoruba lexicographer, and Adeniji, the seemingly inexhaustible fountain of Iwo and general Yoruba traditions. Of the full-time officers, Peter Morton Williams, now of the University College, London, and Dr I. A. Akinjogbin, now Professor of History at the University of Ifẹ, did much spade work during the early stages of the Scheme to enhance its academic standards.

Inevitably, the Scheme lost much of its initial momentum for, despite the generous endowment by the Western Region Government, it had to rely more and more upon part-time direction of a dwindling number of full-time workers; and the hope of producing concrete results within a few years did not materialize. By 1966–67, however, the Director, now at the University of Lagos, was fortunate in securing the services of Dr Robin Law as his Research Assistant and with amazing ease and facility Dr Law plunged into the task of helping to assemble, collate and write materials which have gone into the making of the present volume, the first in a three-volume series, which deals with the various sources that any historian of the Yoruba must consult. It occurred to the Director that a treatise on sources of Yoruba History was the logical first step in the unfolding of the history of such non-literate societies. A disquisition on the various sources, stating them, analysing them critically and showing that like all sources from which historical evidence must be fashioned, they must be checked and cross-checked, and neither received as "gospel truths" nor rejected as fantasies or "old wives' tales"—that is a pre-requisite to the understanding of the expertise which the historian of non-literate societies must these days bring to bear on his task.

The result is indeed a collaborative effort of many writers and varied experts but through the variegated pattern must run the synthesizing thread of the deftly trained historian working upon his historical sources. As editor of the volume and the series, the present writer owes an incalculable debt to Dr Robin Law for his invaluable help, without which this volume would never have been written. Immense thanks also go to all the contributors to the volume for their painstaking efforts and their patience in awaiting the inevitably laborious birth of the volume. To Mrs Mary Eke, who read the proofs and assisted the editor in her spare time in addition to her duties as his official secretary, goes deep and sincere appreciation. To the successive Governments of the Western Region (now Western State) the editor reserves his undying gratitude for the confidence reposed in him that the history commissioned so long ago would eventually see the light of day, and to the Government and people of the Western State, represented by His Excellency, Brigadier Oluwọle Rotimi, the present Military Governor, this first volume, 'Sources of Yoruba History' is hereby humbly dedicated, as the harbinger of two more volumes which will record that history as far as our knowledge goes at the time of their appearance.

SABURI O. BIOBAKU

26th March 1972   *Vice-Chancellor, University of Lagos*
and
Director, Yoruba Historical Research Scheme

Contents

List of Illustrations

TEXT FIGURES

PLATES

List of Abbreviations

J.A.H.   *Journal of African History*

J.H.S.N.   *Journal of the Historical Society of Nigeria*

Odu   *Odu, A Journal of Yoruba and Related Studies*

Odu, n.s.   *Odu, University of Ifẹ Journal of African Studies*

W.A.A.N.   *West African Archaeological Newsletter*

CHAPTER I
Introduction

THE name 'Yoruba' is applied to a linguistic group, numbering several millions, which occupies a large area extending through the Kwara, Lagos, and Western States of the Federation of Nigeria and the Republics of Dahomey and Togo. Besides their common language, the Yoruba are united, to a large extent, by a common culture, and by traditions of a common origin in the town of Ile Ifẹ in the Western State of Nigeria. It does not seem, however, that they have ever constituted a single political entity,[1] and it is even more doubtful whether, before the nineteenth century, they referred to each other by a common name.[2] Before the imposition of European rule and the establishment of the present political boundaries, the Yoruba were divided into numerous independent kingdoms. To a great degree, the history of the Yoruba has to be studied as the history of these various kingdoms.

The Yoruba language was not reduced to writing until the nineteenth century, mainly through the efforts of Christian missionaries.[3] Before this, it is possible, even probable, that the kingdom of Ọyọ, the most northerly of the Yoruba states, had adopted the practice of writing in Arabic from its islamized neighbours to the north.[4] But the Arabic records of Ọyọ, if they existed, have not survived. For practical purposes the history of the Yoruba up to the nineteenth century is the history of a wholly non-literate

---

[1] See, however, the suggestion put forward by I. A. Akinjogbin that Ifẹ before the nineteenth century exercised an effective suzerainty over the kingdoms derived from her (*Dahomey and its Neighbours, 1708–1818* (Cambridge, 1967), pp. 14–17).

[2] The name 'Yoruba' originally applied only to the Ọyọ. Its extension to the whole linguistic group occurred only in the nineteenth century, at the hands of Christian missionaries engaged in the study of the language. The first use of the word in this general sense seems to have been by J. Raban, *The Eyo Vocabulary* (1832).

[3] See J. F. A. Ajayi, 'How Yoruba was reduced to writing', *Odu*, no. 8 (1960).

[4] In about 1786 Landolphe met in the Benin area some ambassadors from the inland kingdom of 'les Ayeaux' (Ọyọ?) who 'savaient écrire et calculer en arabe' (*Memoires du Capitaine Landolphe* (Paris, 1823) ii, p. 86).

people. The reconstruction of the history of such peoples, in the absence of the kind of written documentation on which conventional history depends, presents obvious problems. In this book an attempt will be made to assess the various categories of source material available for the reconstruction of Yoruba history. While attention is restricted to the case of the Yoruba, it is hoped that the problems discussed and the methods of approach suggested will also have some general relevance for the history of other non-literate peoples.

In the first place, there is a limited amount of written documentation available for the historian of the Yoruba. This consists of records left by literate neighbours of and visitors to Yorubaland. To the north of the Yoruba, as has been observed, were peoples literate in Arabic, and individuals from these areas certainly visited and lived in Qyǫ and other Yoruba towns. Yet the amount of contemporary Arabic documentation of Yoruba history so far recovered is negligible.[1] For contemporary written evidence we are almost entirely dependent upon the European nations—Portuguese, Dutch, French, and English—who from the late fifteenth century established contacts by sea with the West African coast which forms the southern limit of Yoruba country. The scope and character of the evidence afforded by these sources deserve some detailed consideration.

European knowledge of Yorubaland was for a long time extremely limited geographically. Some first-hand accounts are available of the coastal states—of Ijębu from the early sixteenth century,[2] and of Lagos from the eighteenth century.[3] But Europeans did not penetrate into the interior and gain first-hand knowledge of the other Yoruba states until very late. Probably the first European to describe the interior from personal acquaintance was an unnamed Frenchman who visited Qyǫ during the eighteenth century, but his account survives only at second hand.[4] The earliest substantial first-hand account of the interior is that of Commander

---

[1] The description of Yoruba (i.e. Qyǫ) in the *Infaq al-maysur* of Sultan Bello of Sokoto consists mainly of traditions of the origin of the Yoruba.

[2] The earliest description of Ijębu is that of the Portuguese writer Duarte Pacheco Pereira, who wrote probably in *c.* 1505–8. It is quoted in Chapter II below.

[3] See Chapter II.

[4] See J. Adams, *Remarks on the Country Extending from Cape Palmas to the River Congo* (London, 1823), p. 93.

Clapperton, who visited Ọyọ only in 1826.[1] As the nineteenth century progressed, the amount of first-hand documentation steadily increased. Important in this process were the penetration of Christian missionaries into the interior, initiated by the visit of T. B. Freeman to Abẹokuta in 1842, and the establishment of an official British presence in Yorubaland, beginning with the placing of a resident Consul at Lagos in 1852. Before about 1840, however, there is an almost total lack of first-hand evidence for the greater part of the Yoruba country.

There is, none the less, a certain amount of written evidence in the records of European governments and the published accounts of individual European travellers. But it is for the most part hearsay evidence, picked up at the periphery of Yoruba country. Some material on Yorubaland was collected by Europeans at Benin.[2] Much more was gathered at the important slave port of Whydah, in the kingdom of Dahomey, and at other places in the same area.[3] But even this hearsay evidence is very limited in its geographical scope. The evidence from Whydah relates almost entirely to the kingdom of Ọyọ, and primarily to the relations of Ọyọ with Dahomey and other states in the area.

The conventional historical material available for Yorubaland before, and even during, the nineteenth century is thus limited in several respects. There is, in any case, very little of it. Much of what there is is not first hand, but hearsay. It throws light on only a limited area of Yorubaland. It is also often limited in scope by the particular interests of the European writers, being mainly restricted to trade and matters relevant to it. And many of the European sources, especially the earlier ones, suffer from a further defect, of which historians have sometimes been insufficiently aware. This is the common practice among writers of reproducing the statements of their predecessors and conflating them with the information they derived from new first-hand sources. Often it is necessary to make an exhaustive comparison of texts before it can be decided how much of any writer's testimony can be accepted as a true

[1] See H. Clapperton, *Journal of a Second Expedition into the Interior of Africa* (London, 1829), pp. 1–62.
[2] e.g., De Barros's description (apparently) of Ifẹ, quoted in Chapter II below.
[3] See the passages from W. Bosman, *A New and Accurate Description of the Coast of Guinea* (London, 1705), and A. Dalzel, *A History of Dahomey* (London, 1793), in Chapter II below.

reflection of contemporary conditions. One must concur with the plea put forward by A. W. Lawrence 'for subjecting the sources for African history to that kind of critical appraisal which has customarily been applied to Greek and Roman authors'.[1] Some of the problems involved in using the sort of written evidence available for early Yoruba history are examined in Chapter II of this book.

The deficiencies of the conventional (contemporary, written) sources compel the historian of the Yoruba to seek material from other sources. An obvious alternative is traditional history, accounts handed down orally from generation to generation. The distinction conventionally made between written and oral sources is in fact somewhat beside the point. The crucial distinction is between first-hand and hearsay evidence, and, as we have seen, most of the written evidence for Yoruba history is hearsay. There is no *a priori* reason why transmission of a story vertically, through time, should lead to greater distortion or inaccuracy than transmission horizontally, through space. A traditional account of, say, events in Qyǫ in the late eighteenth century recorded by Johnson (in the 1890s)[2] need not have passed through more hands than a contemporary account of the same events recorded by a European at Whydah. Traditional history no doubt suffers from such distorting influences as local patriotism, but in this it does not differ in principle (though perhaps it does in degree) from written history, and the same criteria of evaluation can be applied to both.

There are, however, several problems which arise particularly with respect to oral history, which require special attention. First, history is frequently used in Yorubaland to justify situations or claims in the present. This can easily lead to tendentious distortion or fabrication. This is especially true, of course, of those legends which purport specifically to explain the origins of existing institutions or conditions. It is therefore important in collecting oral traditions to ascertain whether particular stories have such a 'propaganda' function, so as to be aware of possible bias. Second, it is extremely relevant to the value of oral history to know by what process the material has been transmitted down to the current informant. In many Yoruba kingdoms there are specialist historians, often with official positions at court, such as the *arǫkin*

---

[1] A. W. Lawrence, 'Some Source Books for West African History', *J.A.H.*, ii, no. 2 (1961), p. 227.

[2] S. Johnson, *The History of the Yorubas* (Lagos, 1921), was completed in 1897.

at Ọyọ. It is to be presumed that, while their testimony may be subject to especial bias towards an 'official' view of history, transmission of stories by such groups of specialists involves less danger of alteration than is the case with traditions preserved by less formal processes.

A special problem arises over the use of published oral traditions. There exist for Yorubaland a great number of histories written by local historians from oral traditions, the earliest being Johnson's collection of Ọyọ tradition, *The History of the Yorubas* of 1897.[1] These are normally written in English or Yoruba, though at least one example is known in Arabic.[2] It is perhaps debatable whether such works form an acceptable source for the historian. In principle, no doubt, the historian should always seek access to the oral traditions directly, rather than accept them at second hand through the medium of local histories. But this is not always possible. In the first place, many of these historians, certainly the earliest such as Johnson, had access to traditions which are now no longer current. And in the second place, their works (and this again applies especially to Johnson), are increasingly becoming sources for 'oral tradition', so that work in the field may serve only to 'confirm' the already published account. The local histories have thus become primary sources in the sense that it is no longer possible to get beyond them to the evidence on which they are based. It is therefore difficult to avoid using the local histories. But the historian should do so with extreme caution. One problem is that many of them are not merely collections of local traditions. Many writers are acquainted with Johnson and other published traditional histories, and sometimes with the published accounts of European missionaries and explorers or even of modern scholars. Thus they often offer a synthesis of the traditions which they have themselves collected with the material published earlier. A detailed comparative study of texts is needed to establish the existence and extent of such literary contamination before the value of a writer's testimony can be assessed.

A major problem in the use of oral history is that of chronology.

---

[1] Johnson's work is based upon oral traditions only in its earlier sections. For the later nineteenth century he was an eyewitness.

[2] Viz. the *Ta'lif akhbar al-qurum min 'umara bilad Ilurun*, a history of Ilọrin, by Ibn Kukura, on which see B. G. Martin, 'A New Arabic History of Ilorin', *Research Bulletin* of the Centre of Arabic Documentation, University of Ibadan, i, no. 2 (1965).

While for those events referred to in contemporary written sources we possess more or less precise dates A.D., oral tradition provides no such absolute dates. In traditions events are usually dated only by attribution to the reigns of particular rulers. This gives a sequence of events for the particular kingdom involved, but if these events are to be brought into a true relationship with those recorded in the written sources, and with those recorded in the traditions of other kingdoms, some means has to be found to determine approximate A.D. dates for them.[1] In some instances, events are referred to in both written and oral sources, but the correlation of the two categories of evidence is often very speculative. Where traditions record precise lengths for the reigns of the successive rulers, it is in theory possible to calculate dates by reckoning backwards from the earliest known A.D. date (usually in the nineteenth century). It is presumably from such calculations that the precise dates frequently attributed to reigns in the local histories are derived. But it is rare for a complete series of regnal lengths to be recorded, and even where they are it is uncertain how far their accuracy can be trusted. Otherwise, it is necessary to proceed by establishing an average reign-length for the particular kingdom involved in recent times, and by extrapolating this backwards in time to determine approximate dates for individual reigns. The validity of this procedure depends upon the assumption that the factors affecting the average length of reign, such as the mode of succession, have remained constant. The question also arises of how accurately and completely the successive rulers are enumerated in the traditions. Despite these drawbacks, however, such calculations, employed with caution, can produce usable results. This enables us to see beyond the limits of the individual kingdoms and, by establishing a chronological framework in terms of A.D. dates, to have some insight into developments in the Yoruba country as a whole.

Some of the problems connected with the use of traditional history as a source are examined in greater detail, by reference to particular examples, in Chapter III.

Besides the overtly historical traditions there exist various forms of oral literature among the Yoruba which may contain material of historical value. In Chapters IV–VI detailed studies are offered of the literature of the cult of Ifa, the Yoruba god of divination (by

[1] On the problems involved, see E. J. Alagoa, 'Dating Oral Tradition', *African Notes*, iv, no. 1 (1966).

Dr. Abimbọla); of *oriki*, praise-songs in honour of individuals, families, and communities (by Chief Ayọrinde); and of proverbs and topical songs and chants (by Chief Delanọ). Such forms of oral literature are in one respect superior as sources to the narrative histories, namely that, having a formal structure, they are probably transmitted with less alteration from generation to generation. A rather different aspect of 'oral tradition', ceremonies, which in Yorubaland often claim to re-enact historical events, is dealt with in Chapter VII (by Dr. Ogunba). It would be wrong, of course, to regard these sources as completely distinct from the more normal oral history. The purveyors of traditional history are usually acquainted with the poems and ceremonies which throw light on history, so that these serve as mnemonics for, or even sources of, traditional history. Their separate treatment in this book is due to the fact that a considerable amount of specialized knowledge in the particular field is needed in order to assess their value for the historian.

The historian of the Yoruba also draws upon disciplines more remote from that of the conventional historian. Much evidence can be obtained from a study of the material remains of the past. The contribution of archaeology to Yoruba history will ultimately be immense, though at the moment there is relatively little material available, and there are special problems of relating the information it provides to that derived from written and traditional history. Archaeology is discussed in Chapter VIII (by Professor Willett). Surviving objects of Yoruba art, other than those recovered by excavation, can also be made to yield historical information, though their direct value is limited by the fact that among the Yoruba, unlike for example in the kingdom of Dahomey,[1] art was not commemorative of actual events. The contribution made by the study of Yoruba art objects is discussed in Chapters IX and X (by Mr. Williams and Father Carroll). In Chapter XI the contribution of linguistics is treated (by Dr. Adetugbo), and in Chapter XII that of social anthropology (by Dr. Lloyd). Finally, in Chapter XIII a military historian (Mr. Smith) attempts to reconstruct the conditions of Yoruba warfare and to show how these can throw light on the course of events in Yoruba history.

From all these different disciplines the historian of the Yoruba

[1] See, e.g., P. Verger, 'Notes on the bas-reliefs in the royal palaces of Abomey', *Odu*, no. 5 (n.d.).

draws his material. From a synthesis of the various categories of evidence a reliable history of the Yoruba can be reconstructed. The recoverability of Yoruba history varies, of course, from area to area, from period to period, and from subject to subject. More is known of Ọyọ than of Ekiti, more of the eighteenth century than of the sixteenth, more perhaps of political and military than of economic and social developments. But this is not a situation peculiar to Yoruba history, and it in no way jeopardizes the possibility of Yoruba history. Just as the sources and the methods differ, so will the results differ, from those of conventional history. The history of ancient Greece is a more illuminating parallel, both in terms of the character of the available sources and of the obtainable results, than that of modern Europe.

CHAPTER II
Contemporary Written Sources

R. C. C. LAW

THE purpose of this chapter is to illustrate, through the analysis of particular examples, some of the observations made in Chapter I on the character of the contemporary written sources available for the study of Yoruba history. Since it is felt that the period after *c.* 1840, for which there is an increasing amount of contemporary material from missionary and government records, presents few peculiar problems, attention is restricted in this chapter to the earlier periods for which contemporary documentation is sparse.

1. EUROPEAN TRADE WITH IJẸBU

Until the nineteenth century, European activities were restricted to the coast, and the only Yoruba states of which Europeans had any first-hand knowledge were Ijẹbu and, later, Lagos. Of the numerous accounts of Ijẹbu two are selected for examination here. The first is that of the Portuguese writer Duarte Pacheco Pereira:[1]

> The channel [of the *Rio de Laguo*, i.e. the Lagos channel] has two fathoms at high tide, but its entrance is very dangerous, with shallows of sand on which the sea breaks during the greater part of the year, so that the channel is scarcely seen; only small vessels of thirty to thirty-five tons can enter it. Once inside the mouth it broadens out into a great lake over two leagues wide and as many long. Twelve or thirteen leagues up this river is a large city called Geebu [Ijẹbu Ode], surrounded by a great moat. The river of this country in our time is called Agusale, and the trade is mainly in slaves (who are sold for twelve or fifteen brass bracelets each), but there is also some ivory.

Pereira, who wrote probably between 1505 and 1508, was personally acquainted with the coast, and his book was intended to be a practical guide for navigation. There is therefore no reason to

[1] Duarte Pacheco Pereira, *Esmeraldo de situ orbis*, trans. and ed. G. H. T. Kimble (London, 1937), p. 124.

doubt his testimony that Portuguese traders had established direct contact with the Ijẹbu, through the Lagos channel and the lagoon, or his evidence about the content of their trade. There is one minor problem connected with this passage, in the phrase, 'The river of this country in our time is called Agusale'. The text as published certainly reads *rio* (river), but it seems likely that it should rather be *rey* (king), and that Agusale represents Awujalẹ, the title of the Ọba of Ijẹbu Ode.

More problems arise in connection with the second account, that of the Dutch writer Olfert Dapper:[1]

Gaboe [Ijẹbu] lieth at the River *Benyn* [Benin], eight days Journey above the great City of the same Name.

The *Europeans* get in this Country much *Akori* ['aggrey' beads], which they carry to the Gold-Coast, and many Jasper-Stones: but most of the Trade is for Slaves. The People seem to be good natur'd, and their Custom little differing from those of *Benyn*.

Dapper, whose work was published in 1668, never visited West Africa himself, but compiled his account from earlier publications and from the evidence of some first-hand informants, notably a merchant called Samuel Blomart.[2] It is therefore difficult to know to what period his account of Ijẹbu is referable. Even apart from this problem, it is difficult to take his account at its face value. While it is true that Ijẹbu can be approached from the Benin River through the waterways connecting it with the Lagos lagoon, Ijẹbu is not situated eight days up-stream of Benin. Dapper's geographical inaccuracy is underlined by the fact that he speaks[3] of *two* states, Jaboe and Gaboe, both of which probably represent Ijẹbu, his confusion probably being due to his inability to harmonize data from different sources. In view of this confusion, it is difficult to accept that Dutch traders were, as Dapper states, actually trading direct with Ijẹbu, and Professor Ryder has concluded[4] that probably they merely traded with Ijẹbu merchants who had come from their homeland to the Benin River.

---

[1] O. Dapper, *Neukeurige Beschrijvinge der Afrikaensche Gewesten* (Amsterdam, 1668), p. 506. The translation quoted is that of J. Ogilby, *Africa* (London, 1670), p. 479, which, for this passage at least, is tolerably accurate.

[2] Blomart is also named as one of the sources used by Sanson d'Abbéville in his *L'Afrique en plusieurs cartes nouvelles et exactes* (Paris, 1656).

[3] Op. cit., p. 495.

[4] A. F. C. Ryder, 'Dutch Trade on the Nigerian Coast During the Seventeenth Century', *J.H.S.N.*, iii, no. 2 (1965), pp. 197–8.

More generally, it is an illustration of the restricted interests of European writers on Africa that neither of these passages conveys much information beyond the existence and the content of trade between the Europeans and the Ijẹbu. Some interesting information may be gleaned from incidental remarks, however. Thus it is of some interest that (if the textual emendation in Pereira is correct) the Ọba of Ijẹbu Ode in *c*. 1500 was already entitled Awujalẹ, while Pereira's reference to a 'great moat' may indicate that the great earthwork known as the *Eredo* was already built in his day.[1]

2. LAGOS

Although, as appears from the passage of Pereira cited above, the Portuguese had penetrated through the Lagos channel into the lagoon by the beginning of the sixteenth century, direct contact with the Yoruba kingdom on Lagos island was apparently not established until very late, during the eighteenth century. The following description of Lagos is taken from the account of the English trader John Adams:[2]

The town of Lagos is built on a bank or island. . . . An active traffic in slaves was carried on at this place, particularly after Ardrah [Allada, the modern Porto Novo] was deserted by the French traders [in consequence of the abolition of the slave-trade by France in 1794]. It has always been the policy of the Lagos people, like those of Bonny, to be themselves the traders and not brokers. They therefore go in their canoes to Ardrah and Badagry, and to the towns situated at the NE. extremity of Cradoo [Ikorodu] lake [i.e. Lagos lagoon], where they purchase slaves, Jaboo [Ijẹbu] cloth, and such articles as are required for domestic consumption. The necessaries of life are here extremely abundant and cheap, and are brought chiefly from the country or northern margin of Cradoo lake, which communicates with Jaboo. . . . The population of the town of Lagos may amount to 5,000; but there are two or three populous villages on the north side of Cradoo Lake, over which the caboceer chief of Lagos has jurisdiction. This chief's power is absolute and his disposition tyrannical to excess; his name is Cootry.

Adams made ten voyages to West Africa between 1786 and 1800, and apparently visited Lagos on two of these voyages, but the

---

[1] Pereira's reference is so interpreted by P. C. Lloyd, 'Sungbo's Eredo', *Odu*, no. 7 (1959), p. 18.

[2] J. Adams, *Remarks on the Country Extending from Cape Palmas to the River Congo* (London, 1823), pp. 96–100.

precise dates of these visits are not known.[1] Since Adams, being himself a slave trader, had every interest in obtaining accurate information about the commerce of Lagos, and every opportunity of doing so, he can be regarded as a good source in these matters. It may also be remarked that his testimony is invaluable in establishing a chronological framework for the traditional history of Lagos, since the name Cootry which he attributes to the Ọba of Lagos in his day can be equated with that of Ologun Kutere, traditionally enumerated as the sixth Ọba of Lagos.

3. CLAPPERTON AND THE LANDERS ON THE REVOLT OF ILỌRIN

The first European traveller to gain and record substantial first-hand information about the Yoruba interior was Clapperton, who travelled from Badagry on the coast through Ọyọ into Hausa-land in 1825–6. He passed through the Ọyọ kingdom during a time of turmoil, when the kingdom was collapsing through the revolt of its vassal towns, in particular of Ilọrin, and the inroads of the Fulani. The information he collected on the origins of this crisis is of great interest. At the (unidentified) town of 'Ensookosoo' between Badagry and Ọyọ, in January 1826, he recorded:[2]

. . . the belief of my going to make peace with the Hausa slaves and the king gains ground. They have been in rebellion these two years, and possess a large town only two days' journey from Katunga [Ọyọ], called Lori [Ilọrin]. The Youribanis [Yoruba, i.e. Ọyọ] are evidently afraid of them; they say they have a great number of horses, and have been joined by many Fellatahs [Fulani].

Richard Lander, who accompanied Clapperton on this journey, left a fuller account:[3]

Two years previously to our landing from the Brazen [at Badagry, in November, 1825], the Hausa slaves belonging to the Sultan of Yariba [Yoruba] had rebelled against their sovereign, and fleeing into the woods

---

[1] Adams is uninformative about the dates of his visits to West Africa. But an earlier, shorter version of his book (London, 1822) is entitled *Sketches Taken During Ten Voyages to Africa Between the Years 1786–1800*, and the ten voyages are enumerated (without dates) in *Remarks*, pp. 204–7.

[2] H. Clapperton, *Journal of Second Expedition into the Interior of Africa* (London, 1829), p. 28.

[3] R. Lander, *Records of Captain Clapperton's Last Expedition to Africa*, vol. i (London, 1830), pp. 96–7.

had built themselves a considerable town, no more than two days' journey from the capital, which they called Lori. In it they strongly entrenched themselves, and, by addition of numbers of their struggling countrymen, who willingly flocked to their standard, had become so formidable in a short time, that they had successfully resisted all attempts of his Yaribean majesty to re-enslave them, and maintained their independence against the forces of an Empire. About the time of our journeying into the interior, it was reported that the insurgents had recently been enforced by a large body of Falatah horsemen, which proved in fact to be the case, and the news had struck so great a panic into the minds of the people of Yariba, that those residing in the vicinity of the mutinous slaves had emigrated to more remote provinces. . . . The Hausas had already begun to act on the offensive, and had made frequent incursions, even to the dwellings of their former masters, sacking and setting fire to their towns, and laying their country waste.

In 1830 Richard Lander, accompanied by his brother John, again visited Ọyọ. On this occasion they left the following account:[1]

They [the Fulani] have entrenched themselves in strong walled towns; and have recently forced from Mansolah [the king of Ọyọ] a declaration of their independence, whilst this negligent and imbecile monarch beholds them gnawing away the very sinews of his strength, without making the slightest exertion to apply a remedy to the evil, or prevent their future aggrandizement. Besides Raka, which is peopled wholly by Falatahs, who have strengthened it amazingly, and rendered it exceedingly populous, another town of prodigious size has lately sprung into being, which already far surpasses Katunga in wealth, population, and extent. It was first resorted to by a party of Falatahs, who named it Alorie [Ilọrin], and encouraged all the slaves in the country to flee from the oppression of their masters, and join their standard. They reminded the slaves of the constraint under which they laboured, and tempted them by an offer of freedom and protection, and other promises of the most extravagant nature, to declare themselves independent of Yariba. Accordingly, the discontented many miles around eagerly flocked to Alorie in considerable numbers, where they were well received. This took place as far back as forty years, since which, other Falatahs have joined their countrymen from Soccatoo [Sokoto] and Rabba [Raba]; and notwithstanding the wars (if mutual kidnapping deserves the name) in which they have been engaged in the support and maintenance of their cause, Alorie is become by far the largest and most flourishing city in Yarriba, not even excepting the capital itself. It is said to be two

[1] R. and J. Lander, *Journal of an Expedition to Explore the Course and Termination of the Niger*, vol. i (London, 1832), pp. 189–90.

days' journey—that is, forty or fifty miles, in circumference, and to be fortified by a strong clay wall with moats. The inhabitants have now vast herds and flocks, and upwards of three thousand horses; which last will appear a very considerable number, when it is considered that Katunga does not contain more than as many hundreds.

These three passages, providing information which if not quite first hand is at least very nearly contemporary, might be supposed *a priori* to constitute our best sources for the revolt of Ilọrin from Ọyọ. An analysis of them is therefore all the more interesting. It will indicate, first, that contemporary written sources are not necessarily more reliable than traditional ones, and second, the difficulties involved in integrating contemporary with traditional sources. The three passages only really become intelligible and valuable when considered in the light of the traditional material.

First, there is an obvious difficulty about the dates given. One expects to derive from contemporary sources precise chronological data, but in this case there is a flagrant contradiction. The evidence from 1826 places the revolt of Ilọrin two years before, i.e. in *c.* 1824, while that from 1830 places it forty years before, i.e. in *c.* 1790. This contradiction can only be resolved with the aid of the traditional material.

Second, the accounts of Clapperton and the Landers can be shown to be incomplete and even incorrect. It is instructive to compare the account of the revolt of Ilọrin given by the traditions.[1] The city of Ilọrin was founded from Ọyọ by one Laderin. Its revolt from Ọyọ occurred under Laderin's great-grandson Afọnja, who held the title of Arẹ Ọna Kakamfo, or commander-in-chief of the Ọyọ army. Afọnja led a mutiny of the Ọyọ army which forced the suicide of Alafin Awọlẹ. Subsequently he made himself independent of Ọyọ, and to strengthen his position invited a group of Fulani led by Mallam Alimi to settle in Ilọrin and incited a revolt of the Hausa slaves in the Ọyọ kingdom. Afọnja was ultimately overthrown and killed by the Fulani and Hausa, and Alimi's family became the rulers of Ilọrin. Wars between Ilọrin and Ọyọ continued and ended (after 1830) in the complete defeat of Ọyọ.

The accounts of Clapperton and the Landers bear little resemblance to this. They conceive the revolt of Ilọrin purely as a revolt of Hausa slaves aided by the Fulani, and it is even asserted

[1] S. Johnson, *The History of the Yoruba* (Lagos, 1921), pp. 188–200.

that Iḷọrin was founded by the Hausa (Lander, 1826) or by the Fulani (Lander, 1830). No awareness is shown of the role of Afọnja, or of the fact that Iḷọrin was a Yoruba town. The only hint of this aspect of the affair appears in Clapperton's account of the complaints of the Alafin in 1826: besides the revolt of the Hausa slaves, he also referred to 'the civil war occasioned by his father's death'.[1] Presumably by his 'father' he meant Alafin Awọlẹ. In view of their ignorance of the circumstances of the revolt of Iḷọrin, it becomes problematical to what Clapperton and the Landers refer when they offer dates for the revolt. They might refer to the original mutiny against Awọlẹ, to Afọnja's subsequent revolt against Ọyọ and incitement of the slave revolt, or to the overthrow of Afọnja and the Hausa–Fulani takeover of Iḷọrin. The contradictory dates offered might be explained as referring in fact to different stages in the revolt of Iḷọrin.

A resolution of the difficulties along these lines is in fact possible. There is evidence indicating that the death of Awọlẹ occurred in c. 1796.[2] The date given to the Landers in 1830 (c. 1790) therefore probably refers, somewhat inaccurately, to the mutiny which overthrew Awọlẹ. The date given to Clapperton and Richard Lander in 1826 (c. 1824) should then refer either to Afọnja's break with Ọyọ and incitement of the Hausa revolt, or to the overthrow of Afọnja by the Hausa and Fulani. There is evidence indicating that the slave revolt began in 1817,[3] so that the latter interpretation appears to be the correct one.

4. IRVING ON THE DEVASTATION OF EGBALAND

While Christian missionaries and other literate travellers did not penetrate the Yoruba interior to any great extent before the 1840s, they were often able to collect useful information on earlier events by interviewing eyewitnesses of those events who still survived. As an example of this, we here quote the account of the devastation

---

[1] Clapperton, op. cit., p. 39.

[2] On this date, see I. A. Akinjogbin, *Dahomey and Its Neighbours, 1708–1818* (Cambridge, 1967), pp. 175–6: it is calculated from the date of the death of Awọlẹ's predecessor Abiọdun, recorded in European records as 1789, and the statement of the traditions that Awọlẹ reigned for seven years.

[3] Viz. the testimony of Ali Eisami, a native of Bornu, who was a slave at Ọyọ at the time of the revolt, and whose evidence was recorded by S. W. Koelle in Sierra Leone in c. 1850: see P. D. Curtin (ed.), *Africa Remembered* (Ibadan, 1967), p. 212.

of the Ẹgba country in the 1820s which Dr. Irving obtained in the 1850s:[1]

To the north-east of and near to Ibadan are the extensive ruins of Owu. . . . With this city originated the civil war which reduced to ruins so many towns once large and prosperous. For some five years did a powerful army of the people of Ifẹ, Ijẹbu, and Yoruba [i.e. Ọyọ], lay siege to this town. . . . From this town the conquerors passed to Ikija . . . which was accused of having assisted Owu with provisions during the siege. . . . For four months the city, unassisted by the other Ẹgba towns, was besieged and taken by the Ijẹbu and Ifẹ army. . . . From Mr. Barber, native catechist at Ibadan . . . we derived much information. A native of Ijemo, he was taken captive at the destruction of that place, and followed his new master into Ijẹbu country. He was with the army which besieged Ikreku [Ikereku Idan]. The town, he states, was destroyed in 1826, as it was the year previously to his being liberated at Sierra Leone, which he knows to have been 1827. . . . Owu was the first town destroyed. After this fell Ikija. . . . From thence the conquering army of Ifẹs, Ijẹbus, and Yorubas, proceeded against other towns of the Ẹgbas. Kesin and Emere soon fell. They then settled in the Ẹgba towns of Erunwon and Ijemo, and a part pitched on the road to Itoko. Here they found cause of quarrel with Ijemo, and destroyed it. Itoko next fell. Returning through the ruins of Ijemo they passed through Ọba and Itoku to Ijeun . . . where they settled. The Ijẹbus, wishing, on account of the slave-trade, to have the army nearer them, invited them to come to their country. A quarrel at the same time fell out between the two chief leaders of the army, Laboshinde and Maye. Hence a division took place in the army. Laboshinde . . . went with the Ijẹbus, and the king gave them the town of Ipara . . . to pitch in. Maye went and settled in Iporo. From these separate places the two divisions of the army went out daily, kidnapping and destroying the smaller towns, the Ijẹbu slave-dealers always offering a ready market for their captives. The Ẹgba towns of Igbore, Imo, Igbein &c, joined their strength together in the attempt to destroy the camp at Ipara . . . but the enemy defeated them with much slaughter; and, as a consequence, Igbore, Imo, Igbein &c, fell in turn. About a twelvemonth after this, more or less, a quarrel was sought with Ikreku. . . . Messengers were sent to Laboshinde, at Ipara, for aid. He besieged Ikreku from the south, Maye from the north, and both were defeated. A reconciliation now took place between the two chiefs. Maye left Iporo . . . and joined Laboshinde at Ipara. From this quarter—south—they besieged Ikreku

[1] E. C. Irving, 'The Ijẹbu Country', *Church Missionary Intelligencer*, vii (1856), 67–71.

the second time; and although the town was assisted by the Ẹgba towns of Itoku, Ọba, and Erunwon,—Ikreku, after a few months' siege, fell; and, as a matter of course, Itoku, Ọba, and Erunwon, shared its fate, the three latter being stormed and taken in one day. It was after this the army moved to Ibadan, destroying all the Bagura [Gbagura] towns . . . till not one remained.

It is noteworthy how much more coherent and detailed is Irving's account than those of Clapperton and the Landers of the revolt of Ilọrin discussed above. Irving made much more systematic inquiries and therefore had a much clearer conception of the events he was attempting to describe. It is reasonable to accept the sequence of events reconstructed by him as accurate, and Barber's evidence for dating the fall of Ikereku to 1826 seems secure. This is not, of course, to say that Irving's evidence is necessarily completely free from error or omission. He was, after all, attempting to reconstruct, some thirty years after the event, a very complicated and confused campaign. It is interesting to compare his account with that of Johnson, who, though writing much later, may also have talked to eyewitnesses.[1] Johnson gives a much more detailed account of the destruction of the Gbagura towns which Irving mentions at the end of the passage quoted. He is unaware of the division of the army into two sections based on Ipara and Iporo, and believes that the whole army encamped at Ipara. He also refers to the destruction by the forces at Ipara of a number of Ijẹbu Rẹmọ towns, of which Irving makes no mention. The differences between the two accounts are probably to be accounted for on the supposition that Johnson derives from informants who were with Labọṣinde at Ipara (and therefore knew of the Rẹmọ episode), while Irving got his information from (apart from Barber) members of Mayẹ's group. By comparing and combining the two accounts it is possible to construct an extremely detailed narrative of the campaign which can be accepted with some confidence as accurate.

5. A POSSIBLE ACCOUNT OF IFẸ FROM BENIN

The Edo kingdom of Benin was well known to the Europeans long before Yorubaland, and European visitors to Benin occasionally picked up scraps of information there about the Yoruba

[1] Johnson, op. cit., pp. 223–4.

interior. One apparent instance of this is the following passage
from the Portuguese writer De Barros:[1]

Among the many things which the King Don Joao [of Portugal] learnt
from the ambassador of the King of Beny [Benin], and also from Joao
Affonso d'Aveiro who visited Benin in 1486, of what they had been told
by the inhabitants of these regions, was that to the east of Beny at
twenty moons' journey . . . there lived the most powerful monarch of
these parts called Ogane. Among the pagan chiefs of the territories of
Beny he was held in as great veneration as is the Supreme Pontiff with
us. In accordance with a very ancient custom, the King of Beny, on
ascending the throne, sends ambassadors to him with rich gifts to
announce that by the decease of his predecessor he has succeeded to
the Kingdom of Beny, and to request confirmation. To signify his
assent, the Prince Ogane sends the King a staff and a headpiece of
shining brass, fashioned like a spanish helmet, in place of a crown and
sceptre. He also sends a cross, likewise of brass, to be worn around the
neck . . . without these emblems the people do not recognize him as
lawful ruler, nor can he truly call himself King. All the time the
ambassador is at the court of Ogane he never sees the prince, but only
the curtains of silk behind which he sits, for he is regarded as sacred.
When the ambassador is leaving, he is shown a foot below the curtains as
a sign that the prince is within and agrees to the matters he has raised;
this foot they reverence as though it were a sacred relic. As a kind of
reward for the hardships of such a journey the ambassador receives
a small cross, similar to that sent to the King, which is thrown round
his neck to signify that he is free and exempt from all servitudes, and
privileged in this native country. . . . I myself knew this, but in order to
be able to write it with authority (although the King Don Joao in his
time had enquired well into it), when in the year 1540 certain ambassadors of the King of Beny came to this Kingdom, among whom was a
man of about seventy years of age who was wearing one of these
crosses, I asked him the reason, and he gave an explanation similar to
the above.

It is hardly necessary to examine what evidence De Barros had
for his account, since his researches were evidently meticulous,
and there seems no reason to doubt that he accurately records
what he was told. The problem for the historian of the Yoruba
raised by this passage is rather whether it refers to Yorubaland or

---

[1] Joao De Barros, *Da Asia*, quoted in G. R. Crone, *The Voyages of Cadamosto
and Other Documents* (London, 1937), pp. 126–7.

not. Benin tradition[1] asserts that the royal dynasty of Benin originated from Ile Ifẹ, and that parts of the bodies of deceased ọbas of Benin were sent to Ile Ifẹ for burial. On the face of it, therefore, it would seem reasonable to refer De Barros' account to Ifẹ, especially as the name Ogane can be interpreted as a version of Oghene, which is the usual Bini name for the Ọwọni (Ọba) of Ifẹ. But there are objections to this. In the first place, Ile Ifẹ is not 'east', but north-west, of Benin. In the second place, and more serious, the cross which plays so important a role in the ceremonies described by De Barros, while it appears in the court art of Benin, is unknown at Ile Ifẹ. This has led some scholars to deny that De Barros refers to Ifẹ at all. Professor Ryder has suggested[2] that 'Ogane' was a rule in the Igala area (north-east of Benin) and that the connection of the Benin dynasty with Ifẹ was only established later. This is not the place to attempt a resolution of this dispute. But its existence serves as a warning of the problems involved in using the kind of hearsay information provided by early European writers on the Yoruba interior.

6. AN ỌYỌ INVASION OF ALLADA

In the early seventeenth century, European traders established contact with the kingdom of Allada.[3] Through Allada and its successor (after 1724) the kingdom of Dahomey, Europeans gained a considerable amount of information about Yorubaland. Most of this information related to Ọyọ, which during the eighteenth century both extended its political influence over Dahomey and engaged in substantial trade with the Europeans through the coastal ports of the area. An early reference to Ọyọ operations in the area is provided by the Dutch writer Bosman:[4]

Farther In-Land are yet more potent Kingdoms than this [Allada]; but I know nothing, or at most but very little of them; except that while I

[1] See J. U. Egharevba, *A Short History of Benin*, 3rd edn. (Ibadan, 1960), esp. pp. 6–9.
[2] A. F. C. Ryder, 'A Reconsideration of the Ifẹ-Benin Relationship', *J.A.H.*, vi, no. 1 (1965), pp. 25–37.
[3] This is the original Allada, not to be confused with its offshoot, also called Allada, the modern Porto Novo, mentioned in the passage of Adams quoted above.
[4] W. Bosman, *Nauwkeurige Beschryving van de Guinese Goud-Tand-en Slave Kust* (Utrecht, 1704). The quotation is from the English translation, *A New and Accurate Description of the Coast of Guinea* (London, 1705), pp. 396–8.

was here [at Whydah, in 1698] one of their Ambassadors came to the King of *Great Ardra* [Allada], to advertise him from his Master, *That several* Ardrasian Negroes *had been with, and made Complaints to him: And to advise him to take Care that his Viceroys treated these poor Men more gently; or else much against his Will, he should be obliged to come to their Assistance, and take them into his Protection.*

The King of *Great Ardra* instead of making a proper Use of this wholesome Advice, Laughed at it, and in further despight to that King, Murthered his Ambassador; upon which he was so violently as well as justly Enraged, that with the utmost Expedition he caused an Army (by the *Fidasians* [Whydah] augmented to the number of Ten Hundred Thousand Men) to fall into their Country; and these being all Horsed and a warlike Nation, in a short time Mastered half of the King of Ardra's Territories and made such a Slaughter amongst his Subjects that the Number of the Dead being innumerable, was commonly express'd by saying that they were like the Grains of Corn in the Field.

The *Fidasians* reported to me of the mentioned People, that it was customary in their Wars, to Cutt off all the Privities of slaughtered Enemies, and carry them off with them; as also, that none durst presume to take an Enemy prisoner, that was not furnished with One Hundred of these Trophies.

... the Slaughter was prodigious great; and ... the General of this great Army contenting himself therewith, returned home, expecting to be very well received by his Master, but found himself mistaken: For the King as a Reward of his Heroick Expedition, caused him to be Hanged on a Tree; because according to his Order he did not bring the Person of the King of *Great Ardra* along with him, on whom and not his Subjects he aimed his Revenge ... this Great Monarch did not account himself satisfied by the Death of so many Thousand Men for the Murder of his Ambassador, but would rid the World of the particular Occasion of it.

This Nation strikes such a Terror into all the circumjacent *Negroes*, that they can scarce hear them mentioned without Trembling. And they tell a Thousand strange things of them.

Bosman does not name the invaders of Allada, but his reference to their being 'All Horsed' makes it very probable that they were the Ǫyǫ, who were the only nation in the immediate hinterland of Allada to use cavalry in large numbers. The identification of the Ǫyǫ as the invaders was made by subsequent writers.[1] It may

---

[1] e.g. by J. Barbot, *A Description of the Coasts of North and South Guinea* (London, 1732), p. 352; T. Astley, *A New Collection of Voyages and Travels*, vol. iii (London, 1746), p. 87; A. Dalzel, *A History of Dahomy* (London, 1793), p. 13.

be noted that there is no recollection of this campaign in recorded Ọyọ traditions.

7. THE INTERNAL HISTORY OF ỌYỌ

Most of the information which Europeans gained of Ọyọ through Whydah, Allada, and Dahomey refers, like that of Bosman, to the external relations of Ọyọ, military, political, and economic, with the states of the area. But there are occasional references to other aspects of Ọyọ history, including its internal politics. An example is the following passage from the British writer Dalzel.[1]

The Eyeos [Ọyọ] are governed by a king, no less absolute than the King of Dahomy, yet subject to a regulation of state, at once humiliating and extraordinary. When the people have conceived an opinion of his ill government, which is sometimes insidiously infused into them, by the artifice of his discontented ministers, they send a deputation to him, with a present of parrots' eggs, as a mark of its authenticity, to represent to him that the burden of government must have so far fatigued him, that they consider it full time for him to repose from his cares, and indulge himself with a little sleep. He thanks his subjects for their attention to his ease; retires to his apartment, as if to sleep; and there gives directions to his women to strangle him. This is immediately executed; and his son quietly ascends the throne, upon the usual terms, of holding the reins of government no longer than whilst he merits the approbation of the people.

About the time of Adahoonzou's accession [as king of Dahomey, in May 1774], the ministers of the king of Eyeo, being tired of his government, had attempted, as had been their usual practice, to depose their monarch in the manner which has been mentioned. . . . But this Prince had the good sense to despise, and the fortitude to resist, such a ridiculous custom. He, therefore, peremptorily refused the parrot's eggs, which had been offered for his acceptance: telling his ministers that he had as yet no inclination to take a *nap*, but that he was resolved to *watch* for the benefit of his people.

The ministers were extremely disappointed and astonished at this unexpected contempt of a political custom, the abolition of which must destroy their power: they endeavoured, therefore, to effect by force, what they could not accomplish by this stale trick. *Ochenoo*, the prime minister, put himself at the head of the rebel party, which, though formidable, was soon defeated by the adherents of the Sovereign, with great slaughter. Ochenoo himself, with all his numerous family, were

[1] Dalzel, op. cit., pp. 12–13 and 156–7.

put to death by the victors; who did not even spare the pregnant women, but ripped open their bellies, and cut to pieces the immature fruit of their womb. Thus, by his spirited conduct, the King of Eyeo emancipated himself from the tyranny of his ministers, and established a remarkable precedent to direct his successors on similar occasions.

Dalzel cites as his source for the first passage, giving a general description of the Ọyọ kingship, the slave-trader Robert Norris, and it is, in fact, an elaboration of an account given in Norris's own book, which was written in 1773.[1] His source for the events of 1774 was Lionel Abson, who was at that time Governor of William's Fort, the British trading establishment at Whydah. The general accuracy of their information is confirmed by a comparison with Ọyọ tradition.[2] Ọyọ traditions recall that the Alafin could be rejected and forced to commit suicide by a council of seven chiefs called the Ọyọ Mesi, speaking through their leader, the Başọrun. A period of protracted political instability, with the rejection of several successive Alafins, culminated in the seizure of effective power by the Başọrun: Gaha was in turn overthrown by force and executed by Alafin Abiọdun. There can be little doubt that Dalzel is here referring to these disturbances, and that the civil war of 1774 was that in which Abiọdun overthrew Gaha. The 'ministers' are clearly the Ọyọ Mesi, and the 'prime minister' the Başọrun.

Dalzel's evidence serves the historian of Ọyọ to confirm the (far more detailed) traditions of its internal troubles and, by dating Abiọdun's *coup d'état* to 1774, to set them in some sort of chronological framework. His detailed accuracy should not, however, be taken for granted. To take one minor point, the parrots' eggs to which he refers were more probably receptacles for poison than 'a mark of authenticity'.[3] More serious is the fact that the details he gives of the *coup d'état* of Abiọdun are quite different from those recorded in Ọyọ tradition. Dalzel speaks of an abortive rising by the Başọrun after the Alafin had defied a demand for his suicide; the traditions record that Abiọdun secretly

---

[1] R. Norris, *Memoirs of the Reign of Bossa Ahadee, King of Dahomy* (London, 1789), pp. 11–12. Though not published until 1789, this section of Norris's book was written (according to the statement on p. 1) in 1773.

[2] Johnson, op. cit., pp. 168–86.

[3] Clapperton found parrots' eggs used as receptacles for poison at Ọyọ in 1826 (Clapperton, op. cit., p. 49).

arranged a rising by the provincial towns, whose forces marched on the capital. It is difficult to decide which of these versions to prefer (or whether they should be combined). There is no *a priori* justification for preferring Dalzel, as the contemporary source, since his information was only hearsay and could easily have passed through as many hands as the traditional account. It might be argued, however, that the particular detail of Abiọdun having rejected a formal demand for his suicide is quite likely to have been suppressed in the Ọyọ tradition, which represents an 'official' version very favourable to Abiọdun.

8. ỌYỌ–BORGU RELATIONS

The Europeans at Whydah also heard and occasionally recorded news of Ọyọ operations in more remote areas, especially when these had some direct relevance to their own interests, the state of commerce. For example, Lionel Abson made the following report to his superiors in explanation of high slave prices at Why-dah:[1]

To this pitch is Whydah already arrived and the reason is simple, the Ihos [Ọyọ], the nation the king of Dahomey pays tribute to, have received 2 months ago a total overthrow from a country by name Barrabbas, having lost in the battle 11 umbrellas and the generals under them. These were the people by whose excursions [*sic*] used to give life and commerce to Porto Novo and Badagree [Badagry], now they have 8 ships at the latter and by letters received 3 days agoe from thence no-body had purchased a single slave for better than 2 months, Porto Novo has 6 ships and none of them have purchased a slave in 3 months.

In this account, Barrabbas probably represents Bariba, the Yoruba name for the Borgu, their neighbours to the north. The war of 1783 can, in fact, be plausibly equated with an incident recorded in Borgu (but not in Ọyọ) tradition when the Ọyọ made an unsuccessful attack on the Borgu town of Kaiama.[2]

---

[1] L. Abson to R. Miles, 26 September 1783, Public Record Office, London, T.70/1545.
[2] For the Borgu traditions, see E. C. Duff, *Gazetteer of Kontagora Province* (London, 1920), p. 28; H. B. Hermon-Hodge, *Gazetteer of Ilorin Province* (London, 1929), p. 144.

9. A DESCRIPTION OF QYQ

The final passage selected for quotation is taken from the French writer Pierre Labarthe:[1]

... les Ayaux [Qyǫ]. Ces derniers forment un peuple brave, nombreux et fort étendu, les Dahomets leur doivent tribut, leurs possessions s'étendent à 20 lieues à l'est-nord-est du Glegoi [Grehue, i.e. Whydah] leur pays est gras et fertile, les moutons qui en viennent sont un tiers plus haut et plus gras que ceux de France, ils ont d'excellents chevaux, des vivres en abondance. Les signes d'échange paraissent rares chez eux; car, pour un cauris, qui vaut à Juda [Whydah] la cinquième partie d'un liard, on peut faire un repas : ce sont eux qui fournissent la maijeure partie des ésclaves à cette côte, ils se sont jetés de préférence vers Badagrys Epée [Ekpe] et Porte-Nove [Porto Novo], parce qu'on leur Permet de venir traiter sur les bords de la mer.

Labarthe's account was published in 1803, but it is based on evidence from an earlier period, in the case of this passage information derived from a voyage by Denys-Bonnaventure in 1788. It is included here not because it is of especial value for the historian but rather, on the contrary, to serve as an example of the many European descriptions of Yorubaland during the earlier periods which, however interesting as illustrating the extent of European knowledge of Yorubaland, provide little or no hard information of value to the historian. It should not be forgotten that a great deal of the written evidence available before the nineteenth century falls into this category.

[1] P. Labarthe, *Voyage à la côte de Guirée* (Paris, 1803), pp. 104-5.

CHAPTER III
Traditional History

R. C. C. LAW

THIS chapter has the same form as the preceding. It is intended to illustrate, by the analysis of particular examples, the observations contained in Chapter I on the use of oral traditions as a source for Yoruba history. While it is hoped that the commentaries offered below on the various texts will prove of use in resolving the historical questions involved in the examples, the main concern is not to suggest answers to those questions, but to indicate the sort of difficulties involved in the use of oral traditions as historical sources, and the procedures of evaluation applicable to them.

1. THE ORIGIN LEGEND OF THE ỌYỌ YORUBA

The classic version of the legends of the Ọyọ Yoruba about the origins of the Yoruba in general and of the Ọyọ in particular is that recorded by the Rev. Samuel Johnson:[1]

The Yorubas are said to have sprung from Lamurudu one of the kings of Mecca whose offspring were:- Oduduwa, the ancestor of the Yorubas, the Kings of Gogobiri [Gobir, in Hausaland] and of the Kukawa [Bornu]. . . .

The Crown Prince Oduduwa relapsed into idolatry during his father's reign, and as he was possessed of great influence, he drew many after him. His purpose was to transform the state religion into paganism, and hence he converted the great mosque of the city into an idol temple, and this Asara, his priest, who was himself an image maker, studded with idols.

Asara had a son called Braima who was brought up a Mohammedan. During his minority he was a seller of his father's idols, an occupation which he thoroughly abhorred, but which he was obliged to engage in. . . .

By the influence of the Crown Prince a royal mandate was issued ordering all the men to go out hunting for three days before the annual celebration of the festivals held in honour of these gods.

[1] S. Johnson, *The History of the Yorubas* (Lagos, 1921), pp. 2–12.

When Braima was old enough he seized the opportunity of one of such absences from the town of those who might have opposed him to destroy the gods whose presence had caused the sacred mosque to become desecrated. The axe with which the idols were hewed in pieces was left hanging on the neck of the chief idol. . . . Enquiry being made, it was soon discovered who the iconoclast was. . . . He was immediately ordered to be burnt alive for this act of gross impiety. A thousand loads of wood were collected for a stake, and several pots of oil were brought for the purpose of firing the pile. This was the signal for a civil war. Each of the two parties had powerful followers, but the Mohammedan party which was hitherto suppressed had the upper hand, and vanquished their opponents. Lamurudu the King was slain, and all his children with those who sympathised with them were expelled from the town. The Princes who became Kings of Gogobiri and of the Kukawa went westwards and Oduduwa eastwards. The latter travelled 90 days from Mecca, and after wandering about finally settled down at Ile Ifẹ where he met with Agbọ-niregun (or Ṣetilu) the founder of Ifa worship.[1]

. . . Oduduwa and his sons swore a mortal hatred of the Moslems of their country, and were determined to avenge themselves of them; but the former died at Ile Ifẹ before he was powerful enough to march against them. His eldest son Ọkanbi . . . also died there, leaving behind him seven princes and princesses who afterwards became renowned. From them sprang the various tribes of the Yoruba nation. His first-born was a princess who was married to a priest, and became the mother of the famous Olowu, the ancestor of the Owus. The second child was also a princess who became the mother of the Alaketu, the progenitor of the Ketu people. The third, a prince, became King of the Benin people. The fourth, the Ọrangun, became king of Ila; the fifth, the Onişabẹ or king of the Ṣabẹs; the sixth, Olupopo, or king of the Popos;[2] the seventh and last born, Ọranyan, who was the progenitor of the Yorubas proper, or as they are better distinguished Ọyọs.

All these princes became kings who wore crowns as distinguished from those who were vassals who did not dare to wear crowns, but coronets called *akoro*. . . .

. . . Ọranyan was the youngest of Oduduwa's children, but eventually he became the richest and most renowned of them all. How this came about is thus told by tradition:-

On the death of the King, their grandfather, his property was un-equally divided among his children as follows:-

The King of Benin inherited his money (consisting of cowry shells),

---

[1] On Ṣetilu and his alleged introduction of the cult of Ifa, cf. Johnson, op. cit., pp. 32–4.

[2] *Popo* is the Yoruba name for the Egun people, who inhabit Badagry, Porto Novo, and other places in the same area.

the Qrangun of Ila his wives, the King of Sabẹ his cattle, the Olupopo the beads, the Olowu the garments, and the Alaketu the crowns, and nothing was left for Qranyan but the land. Some assert that he was absent on a warlike expedition when the partition was made, and so he was shut out of all movable properties. Qranyan was, however, satisfied with his portion, which he proceeded forthwith to turn to good account with the utmost skill. He held his brothers as tenants living on the land which was his; for rents he received money, women, cattle, beads, garments, and crowns, which were his brothers' portions, as all these were more or less dependent on the soil, and were deriving sustenance from it. And he was the one chosen to succeed the father as King in the direct line of succession. To his brothers were assigned the various provinces over which they ruled more or less independently, Qranyan himself being placed on the throne as Alafin or Lord of the Royal Palace at Ile Ifẹ.

According to another account, Qranyan had only a bit of rag left him, containing earth, 21 pieces of iron, and a cock. The whole surface of the earth was then covered with water. Qranyan laid his portion on the surface of the water, and placed on it the cock, which scattered the earth with his feet; the wide expanse of water became filled up, and the dry land appeared everywhere. His brothers preferring to live on dry land rather than on the surface of the water were permitted to do so on their paying an annual tribute for sharing with their younger brother his own portion.

It will be noticed that both traditions attribute the land to Qranyan; hence the common saying "Alafin l'ọni ilẹ" (the Alafin is the lord of the land). . . .

When Qranyan was sufficiently strong, he set off for an expedition against Mecca to which he summoned his brothers, to avenge the death of their great-grandfather, and the expulsion of his party from that city. He left Adimu one of his father's trusty servants in charge of the royal treasures and the charms, with the strict injunction to observe the customary worship of the national gods. . . .

It is said that the route by which they came from Mecca and which occupied 90 days, was by this time impassable owing to an army of ants blocking up the path, and hence, Qranyan was obliged to take another route which led through the Nupe or Tapa country. All his brothers but the eldest joined him, but at Igangan they quarrelled over a pot of beer and dispersed refusing to follow his lead. The eldest brother calculating the distance through the Tapa country lost courage and went eastward promising to make his attack from that quarter should his brother Qranyan be successful in the west. Qranyan pushed on until he found himself on the banks of the River Niger.

The Tapas are said to have opposed his crossing the river, and as he could not force his way through, he was obliged to remain for a while near the banks, and afterwards resolved to retrace his steps. To return, however, to Ile Ifẹ was too humiliating to be thought of, and hence he consulted the King of Ibariba [Borgu] near whose territory he was then encamping as to where he should make his residence. Tradition has it that the King of Ibariba made a charm and fixed it on a boa constrictor and advised Ọranyan to follow the track of the boa and wherever it remained for 7 days and then disappeared, there he was to build a town. Ọranyan and his army followed his directions and went after the boa up to the foot of a hill called Ajaka where the reptile remained 7 days, and then disappeared. According to instructions Ọranyan halted there, and built a town called Ọyọ Ajaka. This was the ancient city of Ọyọ. . . .

Ọranyan remained and prospered in the new home, his descendants spread East, West, and South-West; they had free communication with Ile Ifẹ, and the King often sent to Adimu for whatever was required by him out of the royal treasures for the new city.

In the process of time Adimu made himself great because he was not only worshipper of the national deities, but also custodian and dispenser of the King's treasures. . . . But this Adimu who became of so much consequence from his performing the royal functions was originally the son of a woman condemned to death, but being found at the time of execution to be in the way of becoming a mother she was temporarily reprieved, until the child was born. The child at its birth was dedicated to the perpetual service of the gods, especially the god Ọbatala, to which his mother was to have been sacrificed. . . .

When Adimu was announced to the Kings and Princes all around as the person appointed by the King to take charge of the treasures, and to worship the national deities during his absence, it was generally asked "and who is this Adimu?" The answer comes "Ọmọ Oluwọ ni", the son of a sacrificial victim: this is contracted to Ọwọni the title of the Ọba of Ifẹ. . . .

According to another account, after the death of Ọkanbi, Ọranyan having succeeded and assumed the command emigrated to Oko where he died, and the seat of government was removed thence in the reign of Ṣango[1] to Ọyọkoro, i.e. the aforesaid ancient City of Ọyọ.

Ọranyan may have actually died at Oko, but his grave with an obelisk over it is certainly shown at Ile Ifẹ to this day[2]. . . .

Johnson cites as his informants for this account the *arọkin*, the hereditary bards and historians of the Ọyọ court[3]. But since he

---

[1] Ṣango was a son of Ọranyan and his second successor as *Alafin*.

[2] i.e. the *Ọpa Ọranyan*, or Staff of Ọranyan.

[3] Johnson, op. cit., pp. vii–viii, 3: and on the *Arọkin*, cf. ibid., pp. 58, 125–6.

frequently cites variants, it is possible that he had additional sources which he does not specify.

Johnson's story purports to explain why things are as they are. It explains not only how the Yoruba came to live where they do, and how Ọyọ was founded, but also the origins of such political arrangements as the right of certain ọbas to full crowns (ade) and the paramountcy of Ọyọ, and the etymologies of titles such as onilẹ and Ọwọni. It is clear that legends specifically concerned with the origins are especially liable to distortion, or even to pure fabrication. While they may preserve a genuine tradition of how the present state of affairs arose, they may equally be merely ingenious speculations or rationalizations. Moreover, origin myths are frequently tendentious, and suffer distortion for ulterior purposes, seeking to validate claims to superiority or suzerainty, or to friendship or community. But to say this is not to deny that material of historical value may not be derived from such myths, providing rational principles of evaluation are employed.

Purely internal analysis does not take us very far. One cannot, for example, refute a traditional account because it is inconsistent, as it may incorporate without harmonizing authentic and valuable material from different sources. Nor can a story be discounted because, being miraculous in nature, it cannot be literally true, for authentic material may be reproduced metamorphosed into or embellished with miraculous elements. For example, one does not need to believe the story of the boa constrictor to hold that it is evidence for the early connection of Ọyọ with Borgu.[1]

The evaluation of such material depends on external evidence. Occasionally this may be evidence of a different sort. For example, it is possible to refute Johnson's assertion that the Ọpa Ọranyan at Ile Ifẹ marks the site of Ọranyan's grave, because the site has been excavated and no grave was found.[2] The story of Ọranyan's burial there is thus exposed as speculation, an attempt to explain why the obelisk was called by his name. It is also demonstrable that the claim to a common origin with 'Kukawa' cannot, *in its present form*, represent a genuine tradition, since Kuka was only founded as the capital of Bornu in c. 1813. (It could still, however,

[1] Cf. the opinion of H. U. Beier, 'Before Oduduwa', *Odu*, no. 3 (n.d.), p. 28: 'The important historical fact that emerges is that Old Ọyọ seems to have been founded on land belonging to the King of Ibariba or Borgu.'
[2] F. Willett, 'Ife and its Archaeology', *J.A.H.*, i, no. 2 (1960), p. 242.

be a later modification of an authentic tradition of a connection with Bornu.) But usually we depend upon collecting more evidence of the same sort—traditional accounts—and upon a comparative analysis of all the variants. A few examples of this approach will be given.

First, there exist among the Yoruba numerous origin legends which, while agreeing in tracing descent from Oduduwa and Ile Ifẹ, do not refer to a migration from elsewhere. These myths assert, usually, that Oduduwa was the son of Olúdùmarè, the supreme god of the Yoruba, who let him down from héaven on a chain to create earth where there was previously only water in the manner attributed to Ọranyan in one of Johnson's variants (see above). The spot where he first landed was Ile Ifẹ. This, for example, is the usual version given at Ile Ifẹ itself.[1] It is not clear what significance should be attached to the coexistence of migration and creation legends. Possibly the creation legend is no more than a mystification of the special position of Ile Ifẹ. But it is possible to interpret it as a claim to autochthonous status. The different myths could be explained as originally referring to different elements in the population, the Ifẹ legend to an autochthonous element, the Ọyọ legend to later immigrants, who perhaps conflated the histori- cal tradition of their own migration with the indigenous myth of origin from Oduduwa and Ile Ifẹ. At any rate, the various accounts of Oduduwa's parentage and origins must raise doubts about his historical status: other legends even make him a female deity, the wife of Ọbatala, who is said to have created mankind out of clay.[2]

Second, even the migration legend itself exists in numerous variants. Apart from less important differences of detail, one major point should be made. Ulli Beier has pointed out that several variants make no claim to origin from Mecca, but speak merely of a migration from beyond a great river (the Niger). Beier argues that this makes it likely that the claim to origin from Mecca is not an original element of the tradition, but a later elaboration, intended to link the Yoruba to the prestigious civilizations of the east, added after Mecca became known through Ọyọ's contacts with the Muslim north.[3]

[1] Johnson, op. cit., p. 143.
[2] See the versions cited by J. O. Lucas, *The Religion of the Yorubas* (Lagos, 1948), pp. 93–5.
[3] H. U. Beier, 'The historical and psychological significance of Yoruba myths', *Odu*, no. 1 (n.d.), pp. 19–20.

In this connection, it is noteworthy that very similar claims to origin from the east occur in the origin legends of neighbouring peoples. The Borgu claim descent from one Kisra (of whom Oduduwa is said to be the nephew), who was driven out of Mecca (like Oduduwa himself) for opposing Islam.[1] The Hausa claim to derive from the migration of one Bayajidda from Baghdad: the Yoruba are said to have descended from one of his illegitimate sons.[2] When such similarities occur, the question arises whether they are to be accounted for in terms of a common origin for the peoples concerned or (as seems to the present writer more likely) in terms of a later contamination of the traditions with each other. On Beier's view, the Yoruba would presumably be the borrowers of this theme in their traditions.

It should also be stressed that a myth of migration, even if accepted as fundamentally historical, cannot be assumed to refer to the whole people. It is unlikely that, as the legends often seem to imply, the Yoruba migrated *en masse*, as an already distinct and recognizable people. Numerous myths refer to the existence of previous occupants when Oduduwa arrived,[3] and it is likely that some of these would be assimilated rather than exterminated or expelled. This hypothesis raises a series of problems about which elements in Yoruba culture—language, political and social institutions, religion, art—are to be attributed to the hypothetical immigrants and which to the indigenes. Such questions are unlikely to be settled by a study of the legends themselves, though we may note Johnson's assertion that Oduduwa found the Ifa cult already established at Ile Ifẹ on his arrival. Solutions are to be sought rather in the fields of archaeology, linguistic analysis, and the study of Yoruba political and social structure and material culture.

Finally, an obvious complex of distortions can be detected of the tendentious type referred to earlier. This is an Ọyọ legend, and it seeks to 'explain' why all the other Yoruba ọbas owe tribute to the *Alafin* of Ọyọ. One of Johnson's explanations of how Ọranyan came to own the land, as we have seen, retails a story normally told of Oduduwa himself. There can be little doubt that the achievement of creating the earth belongs rightly to Oduduwa, and that its

[1] H. B. Hermon-Hodge, *Gazetteer of Ilọrin Province* (London, 1929), pp. 115–117.

[2] J. Hogben and A. H. M. Kirk-Greene, *The Emirates of Northern Nigeria* (Oxford, 1966), pp. 145–9.

[3] See H. U. Beier, 'Before Oduduwa', loc. cit.

attribution to Ọranyan is a later rationalization of the Ọyọ claim to hegemony among the Yoruba. The same is probably true of the claim that with Ọranyan the royal line moved from Ile Ifẹ to Ọyọ, the *Ọwọni* of Ifẹ being descended from a mere caretaker left in charge of the palace. Ifẹ tradition derives the *Ọwọni* from Oduduwa.[1] It is of course possible that there was a transfer of power from Ile Ifẹ to Ọyọ in the time of Ọranyan. But it is much more likely that the legend was altered to justify claims put forward by Ọyọ much later when it became militarily dominant.

2. THE ORIGIN OF THE OGOGA AT IKẸRẸ

At Ikẹrẹ, a town of the Ekiti Yoruba, the original *Ọba*, the *Olukẹrẹ*, has been overshadowed and reduced to purely religious functions, and effective political power now rests with the *Ogoga*. Several different accounts have been recorded of the circumstances under which the first *Ogoga* was established at Ikẹrẹ.

Father Oguntuyi, a local historian, recorded two accounts at Ikẹrẹ while working for the Yoruba Historical Research Scheme:[2]

According to the *Ogoga* and his chiefs, the *Ogoga* was the son of the Ọba of Benin; a dispute about the succession led to his leaving Benin for Agamo forest. He settled there, and hunted and killed an elephant. . . . Being a Benin prince he had great influence over the aborigines and so settled down, was feared and respected, and hence acknowledged as head . . . and has since been recognized as the Ọba of Ikẹrẹ.

According to the *Olukẹrẹ*, the *Ogoga* . . . was a Benin hunter who first stayed at Iṣarun under Akurẹ. He shot an elephant which he chased to Ikẹrẹ. The elephant was found and killed at Uro. Afterwards the *Ogoga* was lodged by the *Olukẹrẹ*. He came in the company of his wife and a dog.

In his published history of Ado Ekiti (a town neighbouring Ikẹrẹ), Father Oguntuyi gives a quite different account,[3] which presumably represents the Ado traditions on the subject. He refers to a war between Ado and Ikẹrẹ in the region of *Ewi* Ata of Ado, which he dates to 1444–71:

[1] See Aderẹmi, the Ọni of Ifẹ, 'Notes on the City of Ifẹ', *Nigeria Magazine*, no. 19 (1937).

[2] A. Oguntuyi, 'History of Ikẹrẹ' (n.d.), Report for the Yoruba Historical Research Scheme, in files of Y.H.R.S., School of African and Asian Studies, University of Lagos.

[3] A. Oguntuyi, *A Short History of Ado-Ekiti* (Akurẹ, n.d.), pp. 17–18.

When the Olukẹrẹ could no longer bear the ill-treatment, he appealed
to *Ogoga*, a very skilful elephant hunter, a Benin who had long lived at
Agamo near Igbara Odo and hunted in the forest between Ikẹrẹ and
Igbara. *Ogoga* sent word to Ọba Ẹwuare of Benin who came to the aid of
the Ikẹrẹs. He conquered Ado. . . . As a result of this war *Ogoga* became
the Ọba of Ikẹrẹ, most probably appointed as such by the Benins themselves.

Here it is an illustration of one drawback in using oral evidence at
second hand, through local historians such as Father Oguntuyi,
that it is quite uncertain whether the words 'most probably'
indicate a choice by Oguntuyi between conflicting accounts or an
inference of his own without direct support in any tradition known
to him.

In an article on Ikẹrẹ, Ulli Beier has recorded two further
variants:[1]

One story is that the *Ogoga* is a brother of the Deji of Akurẹ. . . . When
he lost the contest for the throne of Akurẹ to the Deji, the *Ogoga* felt
annoyed and went to settle in Agamo. Being a mightly elephant hunter
he paid frequent visits to the forest near Ikerre, where the people elected
him their *ọba* because he showed greater prowess than the Olukere, the
then ruler of the town.

The most widely believed story about the coming of the *Ogogas* says
that the *Ogoga* was the eldest son of the Ọba of Benin, and according to
Benin tradition should have succeeded his father. However, he was born
at evening time, and the messenger whom his mother sent to the *ọba*
to announce the birth of her son believed he could wait until morning
time to deliver the message. In the meantime another wife gave birth
to a child in the middle of the night and her message was immediately
delivered to the Ọba. On the following morning therefore a dispute arose
between the mothers as to who was the senior child and therefore the
heir to the throne. Both children were sent to Uselu, the place where the
crown prince is supposed to remain until his installation. When the
ọba died however, the people of Benin installed the *Ogoga*'s rival and
Ogoga left angrily and came to live in Agamo. Hunting in Ikerre one
day, he killed a mighty elephant and he sent the tusks as a present to
the Ọba of Benin. The Ọba of Benin was so pleased that he sent the
Ogoga a crown, asking him to wear it where he had slain the elephant.

Unfortunately Beier does not specify informants for these two
versions, but it appears that both were recorded at Ikẹrẹ. The

[1] H. U. Beier, 'The palace of the *Ogogas* of Ikerre', *Nigeria Magazine*, no. 44
(1954).

second is, of course, in part an elaboration of the *Ogoga's* account recorded by Oguntuyi, but it adds the assertion that the *Ogoga* was appointed *Ọba* by the *Ọba* of Benin.

It will be noted that the only version to place the arrival of the *Ogoga* at Ikẹrẹ in a datable historical context is that in Oguntuyi's history of Ado, which is self-consciously concerned to produce an ordered narrative. But while we do not know in detail what evidence Oguntuyi had for his date,[1] it can at least be said that it is quite plausible. Published Bini traditions confirm that *Ọba* Ẹwuare campaigned in Ekiti, though without specifying Ado or Ikẹrẹ.[2] Chief Egharevba, the local historian of Benin, dates Ẹwuare's reign to *c.* 1440–73. This date, which is probably approximately correct,[3] is consistent with Oguntuyi's dating of the reign of *Ewi* Ata, but this concurrence cannot be safely regarded as confirmatory, since Oguntuyi probably wrote with Egharevba's work before him.

The disagreements in detail between the five accounts cited above are not fortuitous, but follow a pattern, and illustrate the sort of tendentious distortions to which 'origin' legends are especially subject. The uncertainty over whether the *Ogoga* was of royal birth, and whether he was appointed by the *Ọba* of Benin or elected by the people of Ikẹrẹ, is obviously a reflection of the *Ogoga's* position in Ikẹrẹ as the usurper of a primacy which once belonged to the *Olukẹrẹ*. It is no surprise that the *Ogoga* regards his line as of royal origin, while the *Olukẹrẹ* apparently does not, or that the *Ogoga* prefers to believe that his ancestor became *ọba* through the choice of the people of Ikẹrẹ. The humiliating circumstance of Bini military protection appears only in the account of Ikẹrẹ's neighbours and enemies, the Ado.

On the other hand, a comparison of the variants also reveals points of agreement which can be taken as historical fact. The first is the Bini origin of the *Ogoga*. The only version which does not affirm this derives the *Ogoga* instead from Akurẹ, a town which was itself subject to Benin.[4] There can be little doubt that the establish-

---

[1] Probably Oguntuyi calculated his dates by working backwards from recent times through a series of traditionally remembered regnal lengths.

[2] J. U. Egharevba, *A Short History of Benin*, 3rd edn. (Ibadan, 1960), pp. 14–16. This passage is discussed below.

[3] See R. E. Bradbury, 'Chronological problems in the study of Benin history', *J.H.S.N.* i, no. 4 (1959).

[4] Egharevba, op. cit., p. 82.

ment of the *Ogoga* at Ikẹrẹ was connected with the extension of Bini influence into Ekiti which, to judge from Bini traditions,[1] began under *Ọba* Ẹwuare. It cannot, however, be ruled out that the *Ogoga* came immediately from Akurẹ, since the Akurẹ connection also appears in the *Olukẹrẹ's* account, according to which the *Ogoga* settled first at Iṣarun 'under Akurẹ'.

The second common element, present in *all* versions, is the theme of elephant-hunting. It seems certain that the first *Ogoga* was an elephant hunter. This might be an interesting detail of no great historical importance. But it is possible to argue that this element in the traditional accounts alludes to an economic aspect of the Bini expansion into Ekiti. One account represents the installation of the *Ogoga* as *Ọba* of Ikẹrẹ as a direct consequence of his supplying ivory to the *Ọba* of Benin. Perhaps one of Benin's interests in Ekiti, an effect if not a motive of the intervention at Ikẹrẹ, was to secure supplies of ivory. It is suggestive that Bini traditions record that ivory-carving flourished at Benin under *Ọba* Ẹwuare,[2] whom Oguntuyi identifies as the *ọba* who installed the *Ogoga* at Ikẹrẹ.

3. BINI TRADITIONS: ỌBA ẸWUARE AND THE YORUBA

Information on the history of the Yoruba is to be found not only in the traditions of the Yoruba themselves, but also in those of neighbouring people who maintained contact with them. The published traditions of Benin, in particular, make several references to Bini relations with the eastern Yoruba. The example here cited describes events in the reign of *Ọba* Ẹwuare of Benin, traditionally dated to *c.* 1440–73:[3]

When the Ọwọ people rebelled, Ikẹn [a war-chief of Benin] was despatched with a large army against them. . . . Ikẹn marched quickly against the Ọwọs and after a short but severe fight they surrendered.

After the conquest, Ikẹn despatched his soldiers with the captives and spoils in advance, a day before he had planned to leave Ọwọ himself. The enemy again attacked Ikẹn who was left without bodyguard. He died bravely, fighting instead of taking flight. When the tidings of Ikẹn's death reached Benin City everyone was very sorry. There is now a proverb, "Ikẹn knows how to make war but does not know how to escape".

---

[1] Cf. no. 20.
[2] Egharevba, op. cit., p. 18.   [3] Egharevba, op. cit., pp. 15–16.

About the same time that Ikẹn was sent to Ọwọ, Ọrọnmuza, the Ono-
gie of Umẹlu, was sent with many troops to bring the rebellious people
of Akurẹ to their minds. At first he was worried by the problem of how
to attack Akurẹ but he ultimately concluded that it would be best to enter
the town from various directions. This he did successfully and put the
whole town in a state of consternation and perplexity. The troops which
went by Ikperha and Okelisa road overcame the defences and surrounded
the court of the Alakurẹ. He surrendered and they took him into captivity. Three quarters of the town, Tsikan, Ọdọkpetu and Usọlọ,
offered resistance but they were finally crushed.

The Alakurẹ, whose name was Orito, was a very old, bald-headed man.
He pleaded for mercy before Ọrọnmuza saying that he was too old to go
to Benin, and asking to be allowed to remain at Akurẹ. . . . He said he
would carry out whatever orders the Ọba of Benin gave to him.

After considering the matter for a week Ọrọnmuza agreed that the
Alakurẹ should remain at Akurẹ but he appointed a political Resident or
Ọdiọnwere to be in charge of the town. Ọrọnmuza returned to Benin
after eighteen days' absence.

Besides illustrating the wealth of detailed material relevant to
Yoruba history which can be recovered from the traditions of
Benin, these stories serve also to illustrate certain typical mechan-
isms of distortion in traditional history. The most remarkable fact
is that the recorded traditions of Ọwọ and Akurẹ[1] do not even
mention these campaigns. At Akurẹ no king called Orito is remembered. It is of course logically possible that the Bini traditions are
pure fabrications, but it is much more likely that Ọwọ and Akurẹ
were conquered by Benin, and that their traditions have been
subjected to a form of patriotic censorship which suppresses
ignominious defeats and subjections to alien rule.

This is not to say that the Bini traditions are necessarily a
complete and accurate record of the events concerned. One
notable feature is that both campaigns are described as suppressions
of 'rebellions', though there is no recorded tradition of any *ọba*
earlier than Ẹwuare having conquered either town, or even having
campaigned in Yorubaland. This is probably an instance of the
common tendency to justify a state of affairs by projecting it
backwards in time. We have met a more thoroughgoing and

---

[1] For the traditions of Ọwọ, see M. B. Ashara, *History of Ọwọ* (Ọwọ, 1951);
for those of Akurẹ, see S. O. Arifalo, 'An Analysis and Comparison of the legends
of Origin of Akurẹ', University of Ifẹ, Original Essay, B. A. Special Hons. in
History, 1966.

consistently worked out example of this in the Ọyọ origin myth. Probably Ẹwuare was the first ọba to conquer in Yorubaland, but in traditional memory his conquests were legitimized by the assumption that the conquered territories had really been subject to Benin even before.

Finally, it may be noted, as an exercise in 'reading between the lines' of a patriotically coloured tradition, that while the account of the Akurẹ campaign is perhaps circumstantial enough to carry conviction that it did end in victory, the Ọwọ story, though presented as a victory, does not conceal the fact that the campaign ended in the defeat and death of the Bini commander.

4. DEFEAT OF ỌYỌ BY IDANRE

The story quoted here is from the traditions of the kingdom of Idanre, recording an unsuccessful attack by the Ọyọ. It was recorded for the Yoruba Historical Research Scheme by I. A. Akinjogbin, whose chief informants at Idanre were the *Olori*, the court singers:[1]

In the time of Beyọja the 3rd Ọwa of Idanre: The Eyo War was fought. It is believed that the invaders came from Northern Yoruba country— around Ọyọ. Perhaps the purpose was to recover the original Oduduwa crown. Chief Odunwo was one of the outstanding warriors in that battle. The invaders came on horses. They were however conquered by strategy. There is a song commemorating that. All the palm wine kegs in the vicinity were poisoned. Egbedi prepared the poison. The invading armies having drunk the palm wine, died before day-break the following morning. Their leader, the Eleyo, was taken and beheaded. The name of the Balogun was Aloro.

It is not proposed to examine whether the war referred to in this story actually took place, or had the result described, the defeat of the Ọyọ, but to draw attention to one difficulty which stands in the way of accepting the details of the story as an accurate record of the course of the campaign. The pattern, of the attackers engaging in looting and rendering themselves incapable and then being ambushed, occurs several times in campaigns of the Ọyọ. The first instance is in a contemporary (but hearsay) account of the Ọyọ invasion of Dahomey in 1729, recorded by William Snelgrave at Jakin,[2] according to which the Dahomians defeated the invaders

---

[1] I. A. Akinjogbin, Report on Idanre History for Yoruba Historical Research Schemes, Y.H.R.S. files, University of Lagos.

[2] W. Snelgrave, *A New Account of Some Parts of Guinea* (London, 1734), p. 59.

by withdrawing and allowing them to loot and consume great quantities of French brandy and then attacking them while they were inebriated. A rather similar account occurs in a Dahomian tradition describing the defeat of a later Qyǫ invasion, of *c*. 1820,[1] when the invaders were ambushed while looting quantities of red silk cloth which had been left purposely in order to distract them. Ęgba traditions of the successful revolt of the Ęgba against Qyǫ rule[2] also allege that the Ęgba allowed the Qyǫ to occupy the town of Igbein and then ambushed them while they were dispersed through the town engaged in looting. Now, it may be that the Qyǫ did suffer defeats of this sort on more than one occasion, perhaps even that for some reason they were particularly liable to this sort of error, but the recurrence of this stereotyped pattern of events must throw doubt on whether these stories can be taken seriously. The incorporation of such stock themes is a common source of distortion in oral tradition.

5. THE POTSHERD PAVEMENTS OF ILE IFĘ

Pavements made of potsherds have been discovered at many sites in the town of Ile Ifę. Tradition in Ifę gives what purports to be an account of their origin:[3]

. . . a tyrannical female Oni Oluwo, who did not like her clothes to be splashed with mud during the rains, set the people to work paving all the streets of the town with potsherds, until, in their exasperation, they ousted her . . . it was such hard work that the Ilefians decided never again to have a female Oni.

This tradition can be dismissed with confidence as a pure fabrication. In the first place, it is clear that the 'potsherd pavements' were not street pavements but compound floors. The story is thus an aetiological legend based upon an erroneous idea of what it was whose origin needed to be explained. In the second place, the story of a female *ǫba* whose demands on her subjects are so unreasonable that they resolve never again to have a female ruler is a stock theme of the type referred to in connection with the previous example. For instance, at Ileṣa the story is told of a female Qwa who

---

[1] A. Le Herisse, *L'ancien royaume de Dahomey* (Paris, 1911), p. 320.

[2] J. B. O. Loṣi, *History of Abęokuta* (Abeokuta, 1923), pp. 4–9.

[3] W. Fagg and F. Willett, 'Ancient Ifę, An Ethnographic Survey', *Odu*, no. 8 (1960), 23; F. Willett, 'The Discovery of new brass Figures at Ifę', *Odu*, no. 6 (1958), 33.

expressed dissatisfaction with the rich spoils gained from a victory over invaders from Nupe.[1] The tradition therefore is compounded of a speculative explanation of the use of the pavements and a stereotyped tale about the excesses of female rulers, which no doubt itself was devised to explain why, despite traditions of female ǫbas in earlier times, women were not longer eligible for succession to the throne. Its historical content is *nil*.

6. THE CORRELATION OF LAGOS AND BENIN TRADITION

The present dynasty of ǫbas of Lagos, it is agreed by both Lagos and Benin traditions, originated from Benin. There is, however, considerable disagreement between the two sets of traditions over the detailed circumstances under which the Bini dynasty was installed in Lagos. Here will be considered one of these disagreements, that over the chronology implied by the different accounts. The traditions of Benin are explicit in attributing the Bini conquest of Lagos to a specific ǫba's reign: that of Ǫrhǫgbua.[2]

Some of the towns and villages failed to pay their yearly tribute to him, so he marched against them, soon after his accession, with a large army. He made his camp (*eko*) on Lagos island, and from there attacked his enemies for many years. . . . Soon after his arrival home Ǫrhǫgbua sent one of his grandsons, Ẹsikpa by name, to be Eleko of Eko instead of recalling the army home. . . . When Ẹsikpa died his remains were brought to Benin City for interment. . . . He was succeeded by his two sons Ẹdo and Guǫbaro in succession.

Chief Egharevba, from whom this account is taken, dates the reign of Ǫrhǫgbua to *c*. 1550–78, and Bradbury's study of Benin chronology[3] shows that this is not far wrong. Lagos traditions[4] agree in naming the first three ǫbas of Lagos as Aṣipa, Ado, and Gabaro, but do not name the Ọba of Benin involved in the conquest. Moreover, they appear to imply a chronology inconsistent with the date of Ǫrhǫgbua's reign. Lagos tradition enumerates only twelve ǫbas down to the British conquest of Lagos in 1851, and the sixth ǫba, Ologun Kutere, can be shown to have been

---

[1] J. Abiọla and others, *Itan Ijẹṣa* (Ileṣa, 1932), pp. 47–8.
[2] Egharevba, op. cit., pp. 30–1.
[3] Cf. p. 34 n. 3.
[4] See esp. J. B. Wood, *Historical notices of Lagos, West Africa* (Lagos, 1878); J. B. O. Loṣi, *History of Lagos* (Lagos, 1914).

reigning in the 1780s.[1] It is difficult to accept that the five rulers (representing only three generations) before Ologun Kutere can have covered over two hundred years, as is implied by Ọrhọgbua's date of c. 1550. The Lagos evidence would suggest rather c. 1650, at earliest, for the beginning of the dynasty. There are several possible solutions to this contradiction, the most simple being perhaps to suppose that some names have been forgotten in the traditional king-list of Lagos. But this case, in which two sets of traditions refer to the same events, but attribute to them quite contradictory dates, serves as an illustration of the dangers involved in using lists of rulers, without any external control, as the basis for reconstructing chronology.

[1] For further details, see R. C. C. Law, 'The dynastic chronology of Lagos', *Lagos Notes and Records*, ii, no. 2, 1968, pp. 46–54.

CHAPTER IV
The Literature of the Ifa Cult

WÁNDÉ ABÍMBÓLÁ

THE IFÁ CULT

IFA, otherwise known as Ọ̀rúnmìlà, is the Yoruba god of wisdom. He is one of the principal deities of the Yoruba people. He is believed to be one of the great ministers of Olódùmarè (the Almighty God) sent from heaven to earth to perform specific functions.

There are many myths about the coming of Ọ̀rúnmìlà to the earth, his life here on earth, and his deeds and exploits both on earth and in heaven. The most common myths say that Ọ̀rúnmìlà came to the earth in the company of the other major Yoruba deities, e.g. Òòṣàálá, Ṣànpọ̀nná, Èṣù, Ògún, etc. Each of these deities was charged with certain specific functions. For example, Ògún was charged with supervising matters dealing with war or other exploits demanding the use of iron. Ọ̀rúnmìlà was charged with the function of using his profound wisdom, knowledge, and understanding to put the earth in order.

One of the praise-names of Ọ̀rúnmìlà is *akéré-finúṣọgbọ́n* (the small one with a mind full of wisdom). Ọ̀rúnmìlà is therefore believed to have complete knowledge and understanding about all matters both on earth and in heaven. His knowledge covers the whole range of time and space. He is completely informed about the past, the present, and the future.

Ọ̀rúnmìlà's knowledge covers everything pertaining to man and the other things created by God Almighty. But he also knows about the other gods—their histories, their wishes and desires, the things they love and hate. 'We have evidence in the oral traditions that he (Ọ̀rúnmìlà) was one of the earliest products of Olódùmarè and that it was his special privilege to know about the beginnings of most things, including the origins of most of the divinities.'[1]

[1] E. Bọ́lájí Ìdòwú, *Olódùmarè, God in Yoruba Belief* (London, 1962), p. 76.

All the principal deities, according to the myths mentioned above, first arrived at Ifẹ̀ (the mythical ancestral home of the Yoruba) from where many of them went to other parts of Yorubaland. Ọ̀rúnmìlà stayed in a quarter known as Òkè-Ìgẹ̀tí while he was at Ifẹ̀. That is why he is known as *Ọkùnrin kúkúrú òkè Ìgẹ̀tí* (the short man of òkè Ìgẹ̀tí).[1]

Ọ̀rúnmìlà lived for a long time at Ifẹ̀ until he, like some of the other principal gods, left Ifẹ̀ for other parts of Yorubaland. There is evidence in other myths that he lived in many different parts of Yorubaland, but it was at Adó that Ọ̀rúnmìlà spent the greater part of his later life. But we do not know for certain to which of the three or four Adó in Yorubaland the myths refer, although we might guess, from other myths, that the Adó referred to is Adó Èkìtì. Due to the long period of time that Ọ̀rúnmìlà spent at Adó, we have the saying *Adó nílé Ifá* (Adó is the home of Ifá).

One of the most famous myths about the later life of Ọ̀rúnmìlà on earth can be found in Ìwòrì Méjì (the third *Odù*).[2] This myth tells how Ọ̀rúnmìlà first lacked children but later had eight male children. All the eight children bear names similar to the titles of some kings of Èkìtì and Ọ̀wọ̀ areas, e.g. Alárá, Ajerò, Ọlọ́yẹ́moyin. It was an insult from one of these eight children, according to this myth, which finally led to the return of Ọ̀rúnmìlà to heaven.

At that time, according to Yoruba mythology, any person could travel from heaven to earth and vice versa. The only physical separation between heaven and earth was a small gate manned by a miserable and mysterious gate-keeper. All the principal deities including Ọ̀rúnmìlà went to and from heaven just at will or whenever God Almighty summoned them to do so.

When Ọ̀rúnmìlà finally returned to heaven, the earth was turned into great confusion, want, misery, and anxiety. Rain refused to fall. Pregnant women could no longer bear their children alive, the childless remained childless. Small rivers dried up. Corn, beans, and other farm products could not develop and bear fruit.

The people of the earth therefore persuaded the children of Ọ̀rúnmìlà to go to heaven and beg their father to return to earth. When the eight children of Ọ̀rúnmìlà reached heaven, they found their father at the foot of *ọ̀pẹ̀ àgùnká, èyí tó yà sí ya búkà mẹ́ríndínlógún* (the much-climbed palm-tree which had sixteen separate

[1] W. Abimbọ́lá, *Ìjìnlẹ̀ Ohùn Ẹnu Ifá*, Apá Kìíní (Glasgow, 1968), p. 30.
[2] W. Abimbọ́lá, *Ìjìnlẹ̀ Ohùn Ẹnu Ifá*, pp. 26–31.

hut-like groves on its top). They then started to beg Ọrúnmìlà to return to earth. But Ọrúnmìlà refused. Instead of returning, he gave his children sixteen palmnuts which are today the famous *ikin* or sixteen sacred palmnuts of divination by Ifá. With these palmnuts and other sacred instruments, priests of Ifá believe that they can find out the will of Ọrúnmìlà from time to time. Other instruments used, apart from the palmnuts, are *ọ̀pẹ̀lẹ̀* (the sacred chain of divination) and *ìyẹ̀rósùn* (the sacred powder of divination). Another prominent instrument in the paraphernalia is *ìbò* (cowry shell and bone for casting lots in order to find the appropriate Odù).

Divination by Ifá is not the only form of divination among the Yoruba. There are other gods connected with divination but none of these other systems and cults of divination is as important as the cult of Ifá divination. The Ifá cult is semi-secret. The literary corpus used for divination is regarded and held up as a great secret which the uninitiated should not know about. Priests of Ifá themselves are called *babaláwo* (fathers of the secrets). It requires quite a rigorous and long training to be initiated as a priest of Ifá.

Most Yoruba towns have quite a substantial number of Ifá priests. But apart from these priests and their trainees, there are very few other adherents of Ọrúnmìlà since the cult is not open to the uninitiated. The Ifá cult is, therefore, quite unique since most of the cults of the other gods have adherents from outside the circle of their active priests and priestesses.

Nevertheless, the cult of Ifá divination is a very popular one. Most Yoruba men and women at one time or another in their lives have visited Ifá priests for purposes of divination especially when they have problems. There are also public and semi-public divination ceremonies in most towns in connection with public ceremonies and rituals. In this way, many Yoruba men and women get to know a good many of the 'secrets' of Ifá divination, so that these secrets are, in fact, no more than open secrets.

Most Ifá priests would say that Ọrúnmìlà is the principal deity of the Yoruba people. Judging from the wisdom and understanding pertaining to him, one would readily admit that Ọrúnmìlà is the principal deity of the Yoruba people. 'There is no doubt that Ọrúnmìlà is universally worshipped in Yorubaland. His cult is found everywhere. Therefore his priests would claim that he is a universal king. The substance of this claim is that the Yoruba have implicit faith in Ọrúnmìlà as the oracle of divinity.'[1] However, if one considers other matters, one would agree with those people who claim that Òòṣàálá (and not Ọrúnmìlà) is the most prominent deity of the Yoruba people.

Nevertheless, the worship of Ifá certainly occupies a central place in Yoruba religious and mythical beliefs. The Yoruba believe in Ifá divination for both divine guidance and general advice about their lives. They rely on Ifá to tell them how to solve many of their day-to-day problems. In traditional Yoruba society, before any man does any important thing, he will consult Ifá. Such matters include inquiries about the course of life of a new child; inquiries about other important matters like marriage, going on journeys, building new houses, and installation of chiefs.

There is, indeed, hardly any problem about which the Yoruba will not consult Ifá. This is the meaning of the Ifá poem quoted below:

> Ifá ló lòní;
> Ifá ló lòla;
> Ifá ló lòtunla pèlú è;
> Ọrúnmìlà ló nijó mérèèrin Òòṣá dááyé![2]

> Ifá is the master of today;
> Ifá is the master of tomorrow;
> Ifá is the master of the day after tomorrow;
> To Ifá belong all the four days[3]
> Created by Òòṣà on earth

IFÁ LITERARY AND DIVINATORY CORPUS

Every priest of Ifá is expected to learn by heart a good deal of material with which he determines the problems of his clients. This profound body of material is known as the Ifá literary and divinatory corpus.

The corpus falls into two broad divisions. The first part is the *Odù*. The *Odù* are 256 in number and they are believed to be deities in their own right. They are said to have 'descended' down from heaven to earth. But the relationship between the *Odù* and Ọrúnmìlà himself is not quite clear. The myths about Ọrúnmìlà and the *Odù* do not seem to define clearly whether the *Odù* came

---

[1] Ìdòwú, op. cit., p. 26.
[2] Abimbólá, *Ìjìnlè Ohùn Ẹnu Ifá*, p. 99.
[3] Traditional Yoruba society had a four-day week.

with Ọ̀rúnmìlà to the earth or whether they came during the time of
Ọ̀rúnmìlà's stay on earth or after. Most of the myths about the
relationship of the *Odù* to Ọ̀rúnmìlà are very conflicting and
disorganized.

The *Odù* themselves fall into two parts. The first part comprises
sixteen of the *Odù*, known as the principal sixteen *Odù*. They contain the best-known and the best-remembered parts of the literary
corpus.

The other part comprises the remaining 240 *Odù*. They are
known as the *Ọmọ-Odù* or junior *Odù*. They are also called
Àmúlù-Odù because they bear two names combined into one. The
junior *Odù* contain the rare parts of the literary corpus.

From a literary point of view, the *Odù* can be said to be the
'books' of Ifá divinatory literature. Each *Odù* has its own character
which, to some extent, agrees with the substance of the poems
contained in it.

The other part of the Ifá literary and divinatory corpus is the
ẹsẹ. These are the literary materials in prose and poetry which have
been handed over from Ọ̀rúnmìlà to his children and disciples
while he was on earth and which priests of Ifá have been handing
down to one another from one generation to the other for many
hundreds of years.

Each *Odù* of Ifá contains an unlimited number of *ẹsẹ* of which
every Ifá priest learns a good number. Despite the frequent loss of
ẹsẹ Ifá due to the death of Ifá priests from time to time, it is still
possible nowadays to collect more than six hundred *ẹsẹ* in each
Odù.

The greater part of *ẹsẹ Ifá* is rendered in poetic form. There are
also certain portions which may be rendered in prose form but
even this type of prose has a form which closely approaches poetry.
One may therefore be fairly accurate to speak of *ẹsẹ Ifá* as 'poems'.
These poems are of varying lengths. There are very long poems and
there are extremely short poems as well. Some poems are so long
that they can be chanted for several hours while some are so short
that they can be dismissed in one minute or two.

The subject-matter of *ẹsẹ Ifá* is the whole range of Yoruba
thought and belief. There is no subject that cannot feature in
ẹsẹ Ifá. Prominent among the subject matters usually found in
ẹsẹ Ifá are the myths and histories of Yorubaland. *Ẹsẹ Ifá* also
embrace subjects like medicine, magic, observations about various

aspects of nature, e.g. plants and animals, rivers, seas, and lagoons. Ẹsẹ Ifá also discuss abstract subjects which are highly speculative and philosophical. As mentioned above, therefore, ẹsẹ Ifá embraces the whole range of the Yoruba world-view from the earliest times until the present day.

Every ẹsẹ Ifá is, however, presented as a historical poem. Each ẹsẹ is believed to be an accurate account of what once happened or what has once been observed in the past. Furthermore, the past event is presented as an accurate record of a past divination involving a past priest of Ifá and his clients. Each ẹsẹ, therefore, contains the names of the people involved in the past divination in question, the occasion of the divination, and its result. In this way, every Ifá priest makes his client see what happened or was observed in the past so that his client may learn from the experiences of the past. 'History is the language of Ifá divination, and "histories make men wise".'[1]

TRANSMISSION OF ẸSẸ IFÁ

As mentioned above, the ẹsẹ Ifá are believed to have been handed down by Ọ̀rúnmìlà to his children and disciples when he was on earth. After his final return to heaven, his children, as mentioned above, went to seek their father in order to beg him to return to earth. Ọ̀rúnmìlà refused but gave them the sixteen sacred palmnuts of Ifá divination with which Ifá priests today find the appropriate Odù and ẹsẹ relevant to each man who comes to them for divination. These sixteen sacred palmnuts are also the authority or sanction from Ọ̀rúnmìlà to his children to enable them to practise the art of divination.

Other Ifá myths show how ẹsẹ Ifá was passed on from the children and disciples of Ọ̀rúnmìlà to other people. This was how the Ifá literary and divinatory corpus was generally disseminated among the Yoruba people.

The process of transmission of ẹsẹ Ifá begins with the rigorous training which every would-be priest is expected to undertake for a number of years before he is initiated. Most people start the training around the age of ten and continue the formal part of the

---

[1] W. Abimbọ́lá, 'The Place of Ifá in Yoruba Traditional Religion', *African Notes*, ii, no. 2 (Jan. 1965), 4.

training for some ten or fifteen years depending on their abilities and other circumstances.

During this long period of time, the prospective priest is completely apprenticed to a master-priest with whom he lives and spends most of his time. He does many household jobs for his master. The master sends him on errands. He assists his master in the daily consultations which his master receives from the public. He helps his master in making sacrifices and in preparing charms and medicines.

For the first few years, the training is informal. The would-be priest just obeys his master, watches him very closely, and sits by him during every course of divination. In this way, he comes into contact with all the paraphernalia of the divinatory system so that he can recognize them and know their names and the purposes for which they are used. He also comes into contact with the *Odù* and the *ẹsẹ* informally.

The formal part of the training starts two or three years after the prospective priest has started living with his master. The first part of the training consists in making him familiar with the process of finding the right *Odù* by using *ikin* (the sacred palmnuts) and *ọpẹlẹ* (the sacred chain). The next part of the training consists in making the apprentice know how to use *ikin*, *ọpẹlẹ*, and *ibọ* (the sacred cowry-shell and bone) to find the appropriate *ẹsẹ*.

Once the would-be priest has mastered the use of the three instruments of divination mentioned above, his master starts to make him learn the *ẹsẹ* by heart parrot-fashion and by imitation of the master-priest whenever the latter chants or recites the *ẹsẹ*. Several formal lessons of this kind are held each week until he knows a good deal of the *ẹsẹ* in each *Odù*.

Another important part of the training lies in learning the processes of making different kinds of sacrifices. A good deal of this part of the training is, however, informal. The would-be priest learns the making of sacrifices more by experience than by formal teaching although he is quite free to ask any questions of his master.

When the master-priest is satisfied that the most important and useful parts of the divination system have been learnt by the would-be priest, he gives the latter the opportunity to be initiated. The Ifá initiation ceremony is one of the most thorough ceremonies among the Yoruba people. Hundreds of items of food products, herbs, roots, animals, and other materials are assembled for the ceremony. Guests are invited from distant places and the ceremony takes many days to complete.

Part of the ceremony is the sojourn of the would-be priest and other important priests of Ifá in the forest for a few days. During this period, he is thoroughly examined on all aspects of the divinatory system. He is also cautioned and admonished on how to use the knowledge he has acquired to his own advantage and to the advantage of humanity.

For Ifá priests, however, the end of the initiation ceremony is not the end of the process of learning. It would be more appropriate to say that it is the beginning. It is only after initiation that the priest of Ifá begins to specialize in a particular field. There are many areas in which an ambitious priest may specialize. These include medicine, magic, rare poems, and the chanting of ẹsẹ Ifá known as iyèrè.

Most Ifá priests prefer to leave their normal abodes in order to specialize in a particular field. The choice of a place of specialization is however determined by the abode of the priest-specialist under whom the new priest wants to learn. Specialization does not take the form of apprenticeship. The new priest and the priest-specialist live together almost as equals and it is hardly apparent to those who know them that one is a teacher and the other a pupil.

Nevertheless, specialization is a most necessary part of the training of Ifá priests. It is specialization that sustains the divinatory system and prevents it from being destroyed, despite all the shattering outside-influences under which Yoruba society has been for the last century.

Specialization is, however, just one necessary step in the life-long learning process of Ifá priests. The diligent priest of Ifá learns every day by experience. He is forced by circumstances to consult better-informed colleagues on various subjects beyond his knowledge. This happens day by day as the priest of Ifá finds himself faced with new problems which he cannot solve and which his clients keep bringing to him.

The priest of Ifá also learns more by attending the weekly, monthly, and yearly meetings of Ifá priests in his area. During these meetings, competitions in chanting ẹsẹ Ifá are held. Whenever a priest of Ifá chants a complete sentence from an ẹsẹ Ifá, his colleagues are supposed to answer him with the word han-in, and if he misses another sentence, his colleagues will protest that he is perverting the divinatory system. The protest may take the form of grumblings in the first instance to warn him that he is making a mistake. But if the priest persists in his mistake, more violent means including shouting him down or sending him out of the assembly may result.

THE PROBLEM OF CHANGE IN ẸSẸ IFÁ

It is interesting to note that, despite this rigorous training designed to keep the corpus intact and free from adulteration, the literary corpus continues to grow. How does growth or change come about despite all the forces that the system has built up against such a thing?

First of all, change comes into the corpus due to the fact that the corpus is handed down orally from generation to generation. It is impossible not to have some kind of change over a long period of time in the process of oral dissemination of so profound a system.

Environmental conditions also lead to change. For example, every priest of Ifá chants and recites the corpus in his own local dialect. The content of the corpus collected in each area deals more with matters affecting that particular area.

What has been said above will prove that although there is change in ẹsẹ Ifá, the change is not due to any deliberate effort on the part of Ifá priests. No Ifá priest sits down to compose or modify any ẹsẹ Ifá. Any change is, therefore, to be regarded as unintentional.

But what has been said so far will not explain growth in the corpus—the type of growth that makes one find fairly recent matters in the content of ẹsẹ Ifá. If, however, one asks Ifá priests about this, they will merely dismiss it as one of the matters relating to the divinatory powers of Ọrúnmìlà. Ọrúnmìlà knows the future in its entirety just as his knowledge comprehends the past and the present. The knowledge of Ifá comprehends all time. It would not be surprising, therefore, if Ifá had known several centuries ago that the world would one day have trains and aeroplanes. If we believe this, we should no longer be astonished to find new subjects cropping up from time to time in the corpus.

One cannot, however, leave such matters at the level of belief. Could there be a possibility that Ifá priests, unintentionally at least, compose new ẹsẹ or modify the existing ones? I will readily admit that such a possibility is highly feasible. Ifá priests themselves say that there are certain spirit-messengers of Ifá who come from heaven at night to teach Ifá priests new ẹsẹ and to remind them of old ones in their dreams.

Could it be that it is during such occasions that Ifá priests unintentionally compose new ẹsẹ and modify old ones? However, one cannot ask such a question which is outside the realms of speculation. One most probably needs to be an Ifá priest in order to experience this dream-teaching device.

What has emerged so far is that there is quite a lot of change especially by way of growth in the Ifá literary and divinatory corpus. It is interesting to note, however, that such changes do not affect the system drastically. The corpus remains the most reliable body of oral literature among the Yoruba, and the rigorous training of Ifá priests continues to make the corpus as reliable as it has always been, despite all the devastating influences that have come upon Yoruba society for many years.

HISTORICAL EVIDENCE FROM THE IFÁ CORPUS

Evidence From Personal Names

As mentioned above, each ẹsẹ Ifá is presented to the client as an accurate record of a past divination. Most ẹsẹ Ifá start with a list of the names of the priests of Ifá involved in the past divination in question.

Names of Ifá priests are actually cognomens. Among the Yoruba, hunters and priests of Ifá are very fond of bearing cognomens. Such cognomens may be derived from certain heroic qualities of the bearer or his personal weaknesses. Among hunters, cognomens usually refer to the former.

A close examination of names of Ifá priests reveals an interesting point. This is the fact that important objects of everyday life are usually prominent in the names of Ifá priests. Since the greater part of ẹsẹ Ifá contains literary materials many hundreds of years old, one can look at names for ancient tools and implements of the Yoruba people which are either no longer in use nowadays or which have a restricted application. A list of such implements and tools can serve to give valuable hints about Yoruba history.

In the poem below, lines one, two, and four are names of Ifá priests involved in the previous divination referred to by the poem.

Line four mentions the *àkàtànpó* or cross-bow as part of the name of an Ifá priest.

Example I

Pá-bí-ǫsán-já;
Ǫsán-já,
Awo wǫn lóde Ìtóri;
Àkàtànpó-jákùn-ó-dòbììrì-kálè;
A díá fún Ọ̀rúnmìlà,
Ifá ńlèé táyé Olúufè orò sǫ
Bí ęni tí ńsǫgbá.
Ta ní ó wàá bá ni táyée wa wǫnyí sǫ?
Ewé ǫ̀pèpè tilè sǫ.[1]

Sudden-as-the-snapping-of-leather-string;
Leather-string-snaps,
The Ifá priest for them in the city of Ìtóri;
Cross-bow-loses-its-string-it-dances-all-over-the-ground;
Cast Ifá for Ọ̀rúnmìlà,
When Ifá was going to mend the life of the king of Ifè
As one mends broken calabash.
Who, then, will help us mend these our lives?
Palm-tree grows its leaves right from the ground.
It is Ọ̀rúnmìlà who will help us mend these our lives.
Palm-tree grows its leaves right from the ground.

The cross-bow mentioned in the poem above was a common implement for hunting and fighting in medieval Europe. Some cultures of West Africa are known to possess this implement but one does not know for certain when, how, and from where this implement entered West Africa. The Yoruba cross-bow is made of wood and it has a tough string attached firmly to it. The poem above hints that the Yoruba cross-bow has a leather string called *ǫsán*.[2]

The hint contained in the poem above is, therefore, of some significance. It points to the possibility that the cross-bow was once a widely used implement among the Yoruba.[3]

Another important implement for fighting and hunting among

---

[1] W. Abimbǫlá, *Ìjìnlè Ohùn Ęnu Ifá*, p. 33.

[2] All Yoruba leather strings are called *ǫsán*. *Ǫsán* is used also in beating certain drums, *bàtá* and *gúdúgúdú*.

[3] For further discussion on the cross-bow see R. S. Smith, 'Yoruba Armament', *J.A.H.* viii, no. 1 (1967), 97.

the Yoruba is *èṣín*. This implement was very prominent until fire-arms became widely used among the Yoruba in the early part of the last century. *Èṣín* is actually a throwing spear. The poem below refers to the throwing spear. The part of the poem that refers to the throwing spear is again a part of the name of a priest of Ifá.

Example II

Ká-múrin-pọ́nná,
Ká-fi-yan-ọmọlójú;
Ká-fẹ̀ṣín-yan-ọmọlẹ́kà-ọrùn;
Bàbáa wọ́n kú,
Wọn ò jogún *ẹrú*;
Ìyáa wọ́n kú,
Wọn ò jin *àmù ìlẹ̀kẹ̀*,
Bẹ́è ni wọn ò *jogún àkísà* jííní;
A díá fún Ọ̀rúnmìlà,
Wọ́n ńfi joojúmọ́ọ́ fi babaá ṣépẹ̀.[1]

Take-a-hot-piece-of-iron-
And-use-it-to-remove-the-pupil-of-the-eyes;
Take-a-throwing-spear-
And-use-it-to-remove-the-nerves-of-the-neck;
Their-father-died-
They-did-not-*inherit-slaves*;
Their-mother-died-
They-did-not-share-a-*pot-load-of-beads*-
And-they-did-not-inherit-the-smallest-*piece-of-cloth*;
These were the priests
Who cast Ifá for Ọ̀rúnmìlà
When they were cursing the father[2] everyday.

Evidence From Place Names

Like personal names, place names are very common in *ẹsẹ Ifá*. They are usually mentioned as part of the previous divination referred to by almost every *ẹsẹ Ifá*. Such place names could be very good sources of information about the geographical and demographic past of an area. This is especially the case with an area which has been associated with constant shift of population or which has once been shattered by war or any other catastrophe. The task of recording place names for such an area becomes even

[1] W. Abimbọ́lá, *Ìjìnlẹ̀ Ohùn Ẹnu Ifá*, p. 149.
[2] 'Father' here refers to Ọ̀rúnmìlà.

more compelling in the case of a society where literacy is just taking root. Very soon, if such place names are not recorded and investigations made about their locations, they will be unknown to future generations. If the oral literature where the place names are preserved is sufficiently rooted in the community, the place names concerned remain in the memories of those who take the trouble to learn such oral literature, but the places to which such names refer are no longer identifiable. This is the case with many Yoruba place names in ẹsẹ Ifá, whose origin the present writer has been unable to trace.

Place names in Ifá may be names of famous towns, villages, markets, and compounds or quarters within a very big town. Among the Yoruba, names and locations of markets change frequently. Towns, villages, and compounds can also change their names. This possible frequent change in name and sometimes in location presents the historian and the archaeologist with a great difficulty in pinning down any particular place name mentioned in a body of oral literature to any definite location.

Nevertheless, place names mentioned in a body of oral literature can be used to advantage in locating ruins and in giving other relevant information about such ruins that can be of significance. It is the constant reference to place names in ẹsẹ Ifá that first made the present writer aware that there are so many ruins dating from the last century in Ọ̀yọ́ divisions.[1]

One of the ruins of Ọ̀yọ́ division constantly mentioned in Ifá verse is Ìká. (Not to be confused with Ìká Méjì which is an Odù of Ifá.) The ruins of Ìká or Ahoro Ìká now stand some forty miles north-west of present Ọ̀yọ́. The poem below is a small part of a long epic on Ìká.

Example III
Àró Ìká kìí jajá;
Ọ̀dọ̀fin Ìká kìí jàgbò;
Ẹjẹmu Ìká kìí jòrúkọ;
Olórí Ìká ò gbọdọ̀ jorí ajá.
. . . .
Nígbà èèkíní
Mo wọlé Oníkàámògún,
Èmi ò bá Oníkàámògún ńlé.
. . . .

<hr>

[1] W. Abimbọ́lá, 'Ọ̀yọ́ Ruins', *African Notes*, ii, no. 1 (Oct. 1964), 16–19.

Ó wáá kù dèdè kí nwọ káà kẹrìndínlógún,
Mo wáá bá Oníkàámògún,
Ó káwọ́ Ifá,
Ó fi lérí;
O faṣọ àká bora.
Pààká mẹ́ta ló jókòó ti Oníkàámògún,
Oníkàámògún mọ àká mẹ́ta sáàrin ìta,
Ó so ìbaaka mẹ́ta mọ́ ìdí àká.[1]
. . . .
The Àró of Ìká does not eat dogs;
The Ọ̀dọ̀fin of Ìká does not eat rams;
The Ẹ̀jẹmu of Ìká does not eat he-goats;
The head-chief of Ìká does not eat the head of dogs.
. . . .
On the first occasion,
I entered the palace of the king of Ìká,
I did not meet the king of Ìká at home.
. . . .
But as I was about to enter the sixteenth palace building,
I met the king of Ìká;
He placed his hands which were full of Ifá instruments
On his own head;
He was dressed in the costly robes called àká.
Three small masquers sat by the side of the king of Ìká.
The king of Ìká built three storage barns in his open courtyard.
He tied three mules to the poles supporting the storage barns.

The poem above depicts the city of Ìká probably at the time of its glory. The King of Ìká had four subsidiary chiefs. He had a very big palace which contained sixteen separate buildings. He had storage barns in his courtyard. He had three mules at his disposal. All of these items tend to show that Ìká was probably a big town with four separate quarters administered by four subsidiary chiefs. The King of Ìká was also probably a rich and powerful king at the time this poem was 'composed'. It would require excavations by archaeologists on the ruins of Ìká to prove or disprove the hints contained in the poem above.

Similar hints to the ones given above can be mentioned about Ifè. 'Because we have an Ilé-Ifè in Western Nigeria today, it is quite understandable that people naturally think that this is the

[1] W. Abimbọ́lá, *Àwọn Ojú Odù Mẹrẹ̀ẹ̀rìndínlógún* (Ibadan, in press).

Ilé-Ifẹ̀ which figures in the oral traditions concerning Yorubaland. . . . Opinion is still divided on the location of Ifẹ̀ but one is at
least certain now that it is more than likely that the Ilé-Ifẹ̀ of
tradition was anywhere else but where the present one is.[1]
Ifá verse refers to seven different Ifẹ̀. The first, and possibly the
original one, is *Ifẹ̀ Oòdáyé*. Others are *Ifẹ̀ Ńlẹẹrẹ, Ifẹ̀ Oòrè, Ifẹ̀
Oòyèlagbòmoró, Ifẹ̀ Wàrà, Òtù Ifẹ̀*, and the present Ifẹ̀ referred to as
Ilé-Ifẹ̀. Further investigation into other bodies of Yoruba literature needs to be made before one can substantiate these hints about
Ifẹ̀.

*Poems Telling Histories of The Foundation of Particular Yoruba
Towns.*

There is a large body of *ẹsẹ Ifá* referred to as *Odù tó tẹ ìlú* (the
Odù cast on the occasion of the foundation of towns). The poems
in this collection are of two kinds. The first class is that relating to
the foundation of particular towns and settlements, foretelling
future happenings in the towns concerned. The second class is that
relating to the early years of particular towns and settlements.
Poems in the second class usually have more historical information
than the poems in the first class. One can examine the second class
for information about the difficulties of early settlers in some Yoruba towns. The poem below tells the history of the difficulties of the
early settlers at Ìbàdàn.

Example IV
Òpó-ilé-níí-fibi-ṣóńṣó-ṣorí;
Ó-fibi-èyí-sìmìnì-wọlẹ̀;
Ló díá fún wọn lóde Ìbàdàn
Níjọ́ tí wọn ò mesì
Tí ńpa wọn lọ́mọ́ọ́ jẹ.
Lóròòru lesì ńpọmọ àwọn ará Ìbàdàn.
Ni wọ́n bá méèjì kẹ́ẹ̀ta,
Wọ́n looko aláwo.
Wọ́n ní kí wọn ó rú iṣu ewùrà,
Kí wọn ó rú ẹtù àti lẹ́hù ọpẹ.
Ìgbà tí wọ́n rúbọ tán,
Wọ́n ṣe Ifá fún wọn.
Wọ́n wọ iṣu ewùrà náà nínú.
Wọ́n da lẹ́hù ọpẹ sí i nínú pẹ̀lú ẹtù.

[1] Fẹla Ṣówándé *Ifá* (Yaba, Forward Press, 1964), pp. 45–6.

Wón wáá dé e lójú padà.
Wón fi ògúnná lé e lórí.
Wón gbé e sí èhìn odi.
Bí esì ti dé ibè lóru,
Tí ó gbé işu náà há ęnu,
Tí ó fi ehín tè é,
Ni ògúnná bá ré bó lu ètù àti léhù;
Ló bà gbiná mó esì lénu,
Ni esì bá kú. [1]

It-is-the-house-pillar-which-has-a-pointed-head;
It-enters-the-ground-with-the-very-pointed-part;
This was the priest of Ifá who cast Ifá for them at Ìbàdàn.
At the time when they knew not the bush-pig
Which was killing their children for food.
Every night, the bush-pig killed the children of the people of Ìbàdàn.
They had to add two cowry-shells to three
And go for divination from a priest of Ifá.
They were asked to make sacrifice with one water-yam;
They were asked to make sacrifice with gunpowder and the woollen
    fibre of palm-tree,
After completing the sacrifice,
They made the medicine of Ifá for them.
They bore hole into the water-yam
And they put the woollen fibre of palm-tree and the gunpowder into the
    hole.
Then they covered up the hole.
They then put a burning charcoal over the hole.
They put everything outside the city limits.
As soon as the bush-pig got there at night,
It put the yam into its mouth,
And pressed its teeth on it,
The burning charcoal dropped into the combination of wool and gun-
    powder;
The whole thing then exploded in the mouth of the bush-pig,
And the bush-pig died.

The poem above is taken from *Òsé Méjì* which is the *Odù*
believed to have been cast on the occasion of the foundation of
Ìbàdàn. While the details of the story told by the poem are not to be
taken at their face value, there are some important hints contained
in them which are of historical significance.

[1] This poem was collected from Mr. Fágére, a native of Ibadan now living at
No. 56, Ibadan Street, Èbúté Méta, Lagos.

First, the central point of the whole poem—the question of the man-eating bush-pig and how to destroy it. This part of the poem is very credible. Ìbàdàn was founded on the edge of the forest and the savannah—a usual hideout of bush-pigs. The many hills and valleys in and around Ìbàdàn can also serve as hide-outs for bush-pigs.

Secondly, the poem mentions gunpowder as one of the instruments used in the stratagem that finally killed the bush-pig. This shows that gunpowder was known to the inhabitants of Ìbàdàn at this time (Ìbàdàn was founded in 1829). Recorded history supports the point that gunpowder was known to the people of Ìbàdàn in or after 1829 since we have it on record that guns were first used in the 1820s by the Yoruba during their prolonged years of war in that century.[1]

EVIDENCE RELATING TO THE INTRODUCTION OF ISLAM INTO YORUBALAND

One central theme of many Ifá poems, especially the epic poems, is conflict—conflict between Ọ̀rúnmìlà and his children; conflict between priests of Ifá; conflict between supernatural powers and the powers of men; conflict between Yoruba traditional religion and either Islam or Christianity. For historical purposes, the most relevant in this tradition of conflict are the poems contained in Òtúá Méjì dealing with the inevitable conflict between Yoruba traditional religion and Islam. This must have occurred at the time of the latter's propagation in Yorubaland.

Some of the poems relating to the conflict between Islam and Yoruba traditional religion depict Islam as a faith embraced by former slaves of Ifá who were brought up by Ifá but who later deserted him. Such people are regarded as bearing an irrevocable curse upon their own heads and are therefore doomed to a lifetime of trouble. Some poems in this class depict Muslims as thieves who enter the city gates at night and steal the people's foodstuffs. Other poems in this class depict Muslims as a leisurely sect who wear grand clothes every day and look everywhere for free gifts.

The poem below depicts the violence with which Islam possibly entered Yorubaland. It tells of the exploits of one Àlùkáádí (Arabic Al-Kādi) who was so wicked that he reduced the town in which he was living to ruins and destroyed himself in the process.

[1] See J. F. A. Ajayi and R. S. Smith, *Yoruba Warfare in the Nineteenth Century* (Cambridge, 1964), pp. 17–21.

58   THE LITERATURE OF THE IFA CULT

Example V

Ìgbúnwọ́-méjéèjì-ò-ṣeé-gbẹ̀rù-sájà;
A díá fún Àlùkáádí,
Ọmọ Aálà.
Ní ojoojúmọ́ tí Àlùkáádí bá jí,
Á sọ wí pé òun ó pa igba èèyàn.
Àfi bó bá sì pa igba náà kó tóó dáwọ́ dúró.
Bó bá pa wọ́n tán,
Yóó sì gbá ogún ilée wọn.
Á á ní 'igba péré ni ng ó pa,
Àlùkáádí;
Igba péré ni ng ó pa,
Àlùkáádí.
Díẹ̀díẹ̀ ìlú ńdẹyọ.
Ni àwọn tó kù ní ìlú bá mééjì kẹ́ẹ̀ta,
Wọ́n looko aláwo.
Àwọ́n lè ṣẹ́gun Àlùkáádí báyìí?
Ni wọ́n dá Ifá sí.
Wọ́n ní ẹbọ ni kí wọn ó wáà rú,
Wọ́n sì rú u.
Èṣú ló di àgbó,
Mo ló di àfàkàn.
Ó ní ta ló rú?
Ta ni ò rú?
Wọ́n ní gbogbo ará ìlú ló rú
Àfi Àlùkáádí nìkan ni ò rú.
Ni Èṣú bá di atẹ̀gùn,
Ó tẹ̀ lé Àlùkáádí;
Ló bá gba orí lọ́wọ́ọ rẹ̀.[1]

The-two-elbows-cannot-lift-up-a-load-to-the-ceiling;
Cast Ifá for Àlùkáádí,
The son of Allah.
Every day whenever Àlùkáádí woke up,
He would promise to kill two hundred people.
And until he finished killing the two hundred,
He would not rest,
After killing them,
He would carry their belongings away.
His usual song was:
'I will kill only two hundred,
Àlùkáádí.
I will kill only two hundred,

[1] This poem was collected from Mr. Adéjare of Ilé Bẹẹ̀ṣin, Ọ̀yọ́.

Àlùkáádí.'
Little by little the town was becoming desolate.
Then, the remaining inhabitants of the town
Added two cowry-shells to three,
And went to a priest of Ifá for divination.
Could they possibly conquer Àlùkáádí?
That was what they cast Ifá upon.
They were asked to make sacrifice,
And they made it.
Then Èṣú said:
It is time, let us go.
I said, it remains for us to mention to whom we are going.
Èṣú asked who made sacrifice and who did not?
They said all the inhabitants of the town made sacrifice except Àlùkáádí
    who did not.
Then Èṣú turned himself into wind,
And pursued Àlùkáádí,
And relieved him of his head.

EVIDENCE ON ANCIENT YORUBA PRACTICES AND TRADITION ON VARIOUS SUBJECTS

One can also examine ẹsẹ Ifá to find out ancient Yoruba practices on various matters which have now been abandoned or discarded. I will take only one example for consideration on this subject.

Take the institution of slavery for example. It is a well-known fact that the institution of slavery existed in many African communities prior to the era of international slave-trade. The thing African historians have always emphasized is that the institution of slavery in Africa was different from the institutions of slavery elsewhere which arose out of the slave-trade era.

Example II (line five) above shows one of the features of Yoruba slavery. Slaves among the Yoruba could be inherited just like beads and clothes mentioned in the same poem. This, however, does not mean that Yoruba slaves were inhumanly treated at that time. One interesting feature of Yoruba slavery, for example, is that a slave could buy himself off from his master if he saved sufficient money to repay the original sum his master used to buy him. Slave owners in traditional Yoruba society usually allowed their slaves to take off some time each week to do some useful and gainful things on their own. In this way, a slave could actually save enough money to pay for his own ransom. If a slave failed to ransom himself before his master died, he was inherited, along with the other belongings of his master, by his master's survivors.

Many other examples could be given of the useful information which ẹsẹ Ifá give on many aspects of Yoruba history. As I have mentioned before, most of information supplied by ẹsẹ Ifá on Yoruba history is in the nature of hints which would have to await corroboration from other sources for them to be established as concrete facts of history. Nevertheless, some of these hints are very important and of very high stand in terms of reliability. The problems involved in the use of ẹsẹ Ifá as sources for historical evidence and the reliability that one can put on such evidence is fully discussed below.

THE RELIABILITY OF THE IFÁ CORPUS AS A HISTORICAL SOURCE

There can be no doubt that there are problems involved in the use of Ifá divination-poems as sources for historical evidence. Indeed, to use any poem at all as a source for historical evidence is fraught with difficulties. As Vansina says: 'In assessing the value of poetry as a historical source, it must be remembered that its psychological function and its aesthetic qualities distort the facts described. Furthermore, the kind of historical information transmitted by poetry is usually of a rather vague, generalised nature, and it is often impossible to attribute it to any definite period of the past. But poetry can be used as a historical source mainly because it gives indications of the psychological attitude adopted by certain people towards certain historical events.'[1]

The aesthetic aspect of poetry mentioned above makes poetry lend itself easily to the use of myths and symbolism in the expression of historical events. The great problem with the use of Ifá as sources for historical evidence is the difficulty of separating myths from actual facts. Myth is here defined as 'what one wants to believe about the past and is based on belief and emotion'.[2]

Dating is another problem. Dating of facts is a useful exercise, sometimes overdone by historians. Facts are facts whether one can ascribe dates to them or not. But dating sometimes helps in establishing the facts, and it is here that Ifá divination-poems are weak-

---

[1] J. Vansina, *Oral Tradition* (London, 1965), p. 150.
[2] G. I. Jones, 'Oral Tradition and History', *African Notes*, ii, no. 2 (Jan. 1965).

est. One can hardly find any direct information from Ifá divination-poems that can help in dating any historical events they may refer to. One has to rely on other sources in order to be able to date the historical facts mentioned in Ifá.

However, the problems mentioned above do not preclude the historian from using Ifá divination-poems as sources for historical information. It only means that one has to take the historical evidence revealed by Ifá verse first as hints—hints that one may have to discard completely or take seriously subject to further revelation from other sources. By other sources, I do not mean only written sources. Other bodies of oral literature may be used to check or validate historical information revealed by Ifá verse. Examples of such bodies of oral literature are *Ìjálá*, *Oríkì*, and *Rárà*. It is the view of the present writer that where three or four different bodies of oral literature present a certain fact in the same light, that fact should be allowed to stand as a historical fact even without the corroboration of written evidence. Whether historical evidence is written or oral the most important thing needed to establish it as a fact is corroboration.

One great advantage that Ifá divination-poems have over some other bodies of oral literature concerning their utilization for historical purposes is the fact that Ifá poems are handed down from one generation to another with the utmost care. The rigorous training of Ifá priests analysed above makes the transmission of *ęsę Ifá* almost completely free from the type of adulteration that will disrupt the system and make the whole corpus unreliable. Discipline is the corner-stone of reliability and worth in the transmission and dissemination of all bodies of knowledge. The system of the Ifá literary and divinatory corpus thrives on discipline to the extent that the violent changes of modern times have not been able to disrupt the system.

The Ifá literary and divinatory corpus is not alone in its strict enforcement of discipline. This is a general characteristic of all bodies of literature used for religious purposes. 'The characteristic feature of this type of poetry is the care which is taken to ensure that it is transmitted accurately. . . . Like other traditions connected with religion, those belonging to this category are transmitted with care, transmission being in the hands of specialists.'[1]

---

[1] Vansina, op. cit., p. 150.

CONCLUSION

Ifá divination-poems contain a number of important hints which, if critically examined and cross-checked from other sources, could stand as important facts of history. The poems contain hints from cognomens of Ifá priests which refer to ancient and important implements and tools of the Yoruba people which are either no longer in use or which have a restricted application. There are also hints from the numerous place names in ẹsẹ Ifá which throw light on lost Yoruba towns and villages and also reveal information about the early years of some thriving Yoruba towns. The thirteenth Odù, Òtúá Méjì, contains a large body of literature depicting conflict between Yoruba traditional religion and Islam at the time of the latter's introduction into Yorubaland. There are also poems which yield evidence on certain ancient traditional practices which today are no longer found in Yoruba society.

There are, however, several problems involved in the use of Ifá verse as a source for historical evidence. One such problem is the mixing of important facts of history with myths and legends. These problems are, however, not insoluble provided the historian fore-warns himself of possible dangers and takes pains to cross-check from all other available sources whether oral or written. So the problems involved in the use of Ifá verse as a source of evidence for Yoruba history are not of the nature that adversely affects the reliability of the corpus as a source for historical information.

Finally, it is worth noting that much work is yet to be done to collect the remaining thousands (or possibly millions) of ẹsẹ Ifá still lying in the memories of our priests of Ifá. Although we can now claim that a reasonable cross-section of these poems is now in our hands, many more years of hard work still remain before us before we can actually have all the details. When a good many more of these poems are collected, a clearer picture is likely to emerge concerning the use of these poems as sources of information for historical evidence.

CHAPTER V
Oriki

CHIEF J. A. AYQRINDE

THROUGHOUT Yorubaland, no child is given a name without also being given an *oriki*, which is an important adjunct to any name. *Oriki* could be described as a praise-name, cognomen, or nickname. It describes the child's character, or the circumstances of its birth, or what he or she is hoped to become. It may be given either at the time of the naming ceremony of the child, or later as a result of the child's subsequent development. The word *oriki* is derived from *ori* (head, or origin) and *ki* (to cite), and so means, 'to cite one's origin'.

All chiefs and prominent personalities have *oriki* describing their character and achievements, which serve, as it were, as their 'signature tunes', to announce their approach or presence. These may be very long. It is this class of *oriki*, recording the exploits of prominent individuals, which is of most value to the historian. In addition, lineages (*idile*) have their own peculiar *oriki*—called *oriki orilę*. Towns may also have *oriki*.

Oriki are recited by several categories of performers. Among the styles in which *oriki* are performed are: *ijala-ǫdę*—the style of the hunters' guild; *ewi*—a style peculiar to the Ęgbado Yoruba; *ęṣa*—the style of the Egungun of the *labala* group; *ege*—a style originally peculiar to the Owu, who now live in Ibadan and Abęokuta, but assimilated by the Ęgba, sung by both men and women; *rara*—a style practised by the Ibadan and Qyǫ, sung by both men and women, but especially by women during festivals, funerals, marriages, and chieftaincy installation celebrations; *ęfę*—practised by the Ęgbado and the neighbouring people of Ijio in Qyǫ Division of Qyǫ Province. Singers of *ijala*, *ege*, *rara*, and *ęfę* may be accompanied by talking drums, which can themselves be used for performing *oriki*. *Oriki* can also be performed with the *Qmǫ-Oluwo-Alagbędę*, the traditional blacksmith's hammer.

On ceremonial occasions, *oriki* may be performed by professional

drummers and *akigbe* (criers), who recite for money the *oriki* of
prominent individuals (or of their families or ancestors) whom they
encounter. The *kakaki* and *ekutu* flautists and buglers may
operate in the same way. In Ibadan, Ọyọ, Ẹdẹ, and Ondo, the
kakaki and *ekutu* players and the *akigbe* have always formed part
of the staff of the palace of the *ọba* or *balẹ*. They serve as reception-
ists and are usually quartered in vantage points in the forecourt of
the *Afin* (palace), where no visitor can pass without being seen by
them. By this arrangement, they are the first to see any visitor to
the palace, and they announce his approach to the *ọba* or *balẹ* by
reciting his *oriki*. This is age-old custom, and it serves to prepare
the *ọba* against the arrival of any visiting personality.

    Oriki, of course, must be used by historians with great caution.
Though they set out to record the events of a man's life, they seek
to present these in the most favourable and glorious light, as their
principal function is to exalt and glorify him. The character of the
historical material provided by *oriki* is best illustrated by the
quotation of some examples.

ORIKI OF PROMINENT INDIVIDUALS
1. Oluyọle, Baṣọrun of Ibadan (died 1847).

> Oluyọwọn, Baṣọrun!
> A r'ítẹ̀lẹ̀ ọ̀kọ̀ fulú ará;
> Onlogbo! Iba, a-ṣe-buruku-ṣe-rere
> Olobele! Igbo! Atabatibi
>
> A ri tọkọsi f'agan l'ẹnu
> A f'adamọ t'oro l'aiya;
> A le tẹmbẹlẹkun jina
> Bi ẹni pe k'o lọ ku si igbo baba Oridagogo.
> A r'ododo p'ogo l'ori ẹṣin.
> Ọlọkọjọbi! Irin wọwọ wi,
> Ondẹsẹ! Iba! a f'ọkọ la'ja.
> Egungun kan ko de 'Jẹbu ri,
> Iba l'o m'egun wọ'gbo Rẹmọ;
> Egun f'aṣọ, Iyanda si f'aṣọ,
> Ẹbẹ l'a nbẹ Iyanda k'o to f'agọ 'lẹ.
> Nko tete mọ b'ẹsẹ nku bii ojo;
> Odo kan gẹrẹ to nwọn npe l'Ogunpa,
> Ogede ẹru Onyọwọn l'o f'ẹsẹ mu'do na gbẹ.
>
> Ẹni a ni k'o ma wọ 'Badan mọ
> T'o ba t'Elekurọ wọ'lu;

O de'le tan, Iba ni nwọn fi ọ jẹ.
Olobele! Iba! a f'ọkọ la'ja.
Iba! ti i bo ile, ti i bo oko!

Iba! Ọwara-ojo
Al'apo-ayan
Onlogbo! Iba! a ṣe buruku ṣe rere

Oluyọwọn, Baṣọrun!

Always in his best on visitations to relations.
Owner of Ilogbo! Iba! The wicked as he is equally kindly.
Olobele: the proverbial Igbo bird that often feeds on the eggs of
other birds—a fulsome person.

A man who used tọkọsi gun to break Afgan's mouth,
And used adamọ drums to cause boredom to Oro.
He sent the intriguer away to a far-off land
As if to wish him to commit suicide in the field of Oridagogo's
father.

A man who used the scarlet to outshine the erstwhile well-dressed
man on horseback.
The descendant of blacksmiths and possessor of an abundance of
wrought iron.
Ondẹsẹ! Iba—settler of quarrels with a spear.
Egungun was never known in Ijẹbuland before,
It was Iba who introduced egungun into Rẹmọland.
Egungun pulled at the cloth, Iyanda too pulled more tightly;
Much persuasion was needed before Iyanda would let go of the dress.
I hardly knew that the marching sound of men could be as that of the
thundering rain;
A river down the slope known as Gẹgẹ
Was waded dry by the march of the multitude of Onyọwọn's slaves.
A man who was dared to come to Ibadan
But entered the city through Elekurọ;
Was installed as Iba on arrival.
Olobele! Iba! Settler of quarrels with a spear.
Iba! who covers the home and the country.

Iba! The proverbial heavy rain.
Owner of a quiver that is full of instantaneous and efficacious
preparations.
Onlogbo! Iba! The cruel and the gracious alike.

2. Ibikunle, Balogun of Ibadan (died 1864).

Ibikunle Oloke!
Agbagba-Àasè!
Balogun, a tẹ'ni bi aje,
Jagun! a to bii aila.
A ṣe 'yiowu bii Olodumare
A r'owo lo gẹrẹgẹrẹ n'ile ol'omi;
A tó ó f'iṣẹ ogun ran,

O ta gbogbo ọkunrin kààkàà l'aiya.
O l'oko l'Ogbere,
Ibikunle l'oko l'Odo-Ọna;
A b'oju oko gbẹrẹngẹdẹ
T'o fi d'odi Adeṣẹgun.

Alagbala j'aiya-j'aiya, baba 'Kuẹjọ,
Agbala 'Bikunle j'oko ẹlomiran lọ;
Ab'agbala to koriko sare tan
Agbala nla baba Ojo-Gan.

O l'ara, Ara lọ l'Ọ́hán,
Ó l'Ọ́hàn lù 'Kọgùsì
Daranija baba Ogunmọla,
Gba'gun l'oju baba Aṣipa.
L'ọta-l'ẹtu baba Osi'Badan.
A-pe-wa p'olori ija nla
Baba Orowusi t'o j'Ẹkẹrin

A f'olugbongbo ti dọ bii Olodumare,

O jagun Alake, o p'ọmọ Alake,
O jagun 'Gbein, Ibikunle d'oro ni'gbekun
O na Ṣomuyi, O n'Apati,
O yọ 'gi gbongbo o nl'Alọla kiri;

O f'airo, o jare Ẹgba,
O p'Alọla, t'o ran wọn wa 'gun,
O f'ọran gbogbo jare-jare.
Obiriti! a-ji-p'ọjọ-ku-da.

O r'ori Ẹgba ṣ'aba l'Oloriṣa-oko,
O si tun f'ori ṣ'aba l'Oke-kere
O tun f'ori ṣ'aba l'Alabata
Obiriti! ya'gbo, ya'ju bii Ọṣun Apara.

Bii yio ba wọn ja, t'oju t'imu nii fii pọn ṣẹṣẹṣẹ
A pọn l'oju'ja ṣẹri-ṣẹri!

Ǫkunrin kiribiti-pi!
O ki l'ǫwǫ ki l'ẹsẹ bii Ogidan.
O f'ǫwǫ gun 'mu'Jẹbu apa Ǫtun,
Adeyǫwǫn ǫba wǫn tii j'Awujalẹ!
O f'ǫwǫ gun 'mu 'Jẹbu apa Osi
A f'aimǫ ko to ma f'ǫwǫ gun 'mu Jimba n'Ile 'Lǫrin
A b'imu tayǫ ẹnu.

O pa 'Jẹbu, o ri 'Jẹbu,
O ri 'Jẹbu bii ẹni ri 'po;
O ri 'Jẹbu tan, o ko'ju rẹ s'ode
Nibi awǫn gbe nta yangan.

Ani k'o ma do n'igbo,
Balogun do n'igbo, o ba 'gbo jẹ;
Ani k'o ma do l'ǫdan,
Balogun do l'ǫdan,
O f'ǫdan ya pẹrẹngẹdẹ bii aṣǫ.

Ẹni a ni ko ma d'Awẹrẹ,
T'oko Ǫlá ló ba lǫ l'Ẹ́dẹ,
Ǫlà kò gbǫdǫ̀ r'oko,
Tìmì kò gbǫdǫ̀ r'odò.

O lǫ fun wǫn d'aro l'Agbale,
Nwǫn ni Ibikunle lo sǫ mi da bayi o!
Ò lǫ kí Baálè mi hìnìn!
O ni'Hìn-hìn'! Ibikunle lǫ l'ónǐ!
Ò lǫ kí Tìmì b'omi s'ára
O ni 'Ng o tilẹ wẹ l'oni! Ibikunle lǫ!

A gb'órí 'gbẹ dì'gbẹ́,
A gb'órí ogun ṣí'gun;
Ogun 'Jẹ̀ṣà l'a dì
Ẹ̀fǫ̀n ní k'ó má r'ǫ́nà lǫ

Balogun ṣán'gbó, ó wa 'di k'ára
Ibikunle f'olóìbó Ẹ̀fǫ̀n j'iyán tán;
A ndá apépe wǫn, a nda alǫlǫ wǫn
A-wa-ja l'Oloke nw'eebu Ariwo.
Ó ya'ra tú abà erě,
Ó t'iná b'oro wǫn l'oko
Ó b'aṣǫ sílẹ̀ b'Élérìwò kó sílé,
Ǫ̀ta Kóngò, Baba Kẹrẹ̀ẹ́

Ó jà ní pópó 'Lǫla b'erin ti i w'óko
Erin kò w'óko n'Ilǫlà

N'Ílaṣè ni baba Kúẹ̀jọ gbe w'óko.
Jagun! A l'ọgbọn n'íkùn bii Oibo.

Nwọn ndágba ní'lé Olúfọ́n,
Balogun ni nwon fi nda'rúkọ;
Nwon nlù'lù l'Ejìgbò-Òkòró,
Balogun ni nwon fi nda'rúkọ;
Nwọn nlù kìnjin n'ilé 'Lọrin
Balogun ni nwọn fi nsọ'rúkọ.

Ọ̀kanṣoṣo Àjànàkú mì'gbó kìji-kìji,
Ibikunle ní oun kò mì Igbo mọ́,
Ó ní Oun! ọ̀kanṣoṣo àjànàkú
Tii 'mì gbogbo aiye kìjikìji.

Ẹni Ọlọrun rán n'iṣẹ pe k'ó wa jẹ,
Iṣẹ t'Ọlọrun ran 'Bikunle, ó sì jẹ k'ó tó lọ.
Ẹ̀wọ̀n t'ó t'ọpẹ kò t'erin dá dúro,
Ìtàkùn t'o pe k'erin má da'nà

T'oun t'erin ní nlọ.
Balogun! tó! tó! tó! tó! fǔn!!!
Nkò jẹ bú ọ l'eke lai lai!
Alárá l'ó bu ọ l'eke!

Òbìrìtí! ǒ sọ 'lú rẹ̀ da'horo!
Ikọ̀gùsì l'ó bú baba mi l'eke!
Onílél'ọlá! ǒ sọ 'lú rẹ̀ d'ahoro!
Ajerò Àjàká l'ò bú ọ l'eke!
Arówólò! ǒ sọ 'lú rẹ̀ d'ahoro.

Balogun! Olúgbaiya! mo bẹ̀ ọ!
Àgbàká l'ěfín ngbà 'gbó!
Balogun mo bẹ̀ ọ! Olúgbaiya!
Àgbàká n'igbà ngb'ọ̀pẹ!
Àgbàká l'ẹsẹ̀ ngb'ọ̀nà!
Àgbàká l'odi ngbà 'lú!
Olúgbaiya! mo bẹ̀ ọ!
Àgbàká l'abiyamọ ngba'ja m'ọmọ rẹ̀!

Arówólò!
O gb'aiya won n'ilé!
Ró-gi-ró-'gbẹ!
O gb'aiya wọn l'ogun.
Arówólò!
Ọkọ wọn n'ile,
Ro'gi-ro'gbẹ!
Ọkọ wọn l'ogun!

Òrìṣà tí yio ṣe bí i ògun kò si mọ̀,
Ojú l'asan l'orí inú wọn nyá kiri;
Bí kò ba yún, nwọn kò le yún,
Bí kò ba rìn, nwon kò le rìn;
B'Ibikunle-Olǒkè kò ba sí
Nwọn kò lè dá jà Akátá l'ogun.

Oibo! ẹ má gún mọ́!
Ijẹbu! ẹ má wa mọ́!
B'Oibo kò gún, b'Ijẹbu kò wa,
Ẹ̀tù 'Bikunle-Olǒkè tó wǎ lò lailai.

Ẹni dúro dè erin dúro dè'kú,
Ẹni dúro d'ẹfọ̀n, dúro dè'jà:
Ẹni dúro dè ěgún alágàngán
L'ọrun ni o nfẹ lọ.

Ibikunle l'ẹ kò l'ọnà ni ẹ kò yà!
Àfi ẹnití kò ní Ondùgboyè ba l'ọrun
Ọgbàràgàdà! Ọkunrin tǒtọ!
A wọ́n Kurunmi l'aṣẹ 'jà sọnù.

Ṣàngba fọ́! Ọlọràn kùn lọ bíi oyin!
Ibikunle yè̀'rí bẹ̀sẹ́, ó s'ẹrù kalẹ̀;
Orukọ l'ó mú lọ, kò m'oyè lọ,
Ó m'oṣùka rẹ̀ l'ọwọ baba Kuẹjọ.

Ibikunle! the Lord of his Quarters,
The proverbial magnificent door.
The Captain that disgraces men as would the dearth of money,
The Warrior! As regular as the Moslem afternoon prayers.

A strongly witted man with incomprehension comparable to that of
Olúdùmarè.
The affluent with enough to spend and to spare at the brewery.
A reliable military errant,
A challenger of all men.
Owner of farm land at Ogbere,
Ibikunle also has farm at Odo-Ọna;
A wide expanse of farm land,
Extensive as far as the city [fortification] wall at Adesegun.

Father of Kuẹjọ, owner of dreadfully fearsome backyard.
Ibikunle's backyard is even bigger than other people's farms;
His backyard is wide enough a track for hyenas' full-length race,
Proverbial big backyard, father of Ojo-Gan.

He drove the sojourners of Ara to Ohan
Drove Ọhan people against 'Kọgusi
Admirable at expeditions, father of Ogunmọla,
Fierce-striker at war, father of Aṣipa;

A stockist of bullet and gunpowder, father of Osi of Ibadan.
Usually commissioned to subdue the Head of any rebellion,
Father of Orowusi the Ẹkẹrin
Keeper of inseparable cudgel like Olúdùmarè.

He fought against Alake's Army and killed his son;
Ibikunle fought against Igbein, and became a terror in captivity.
He struck at Ṣomuyi, struck at Apati,
Uses a short cudgel to drive Alọla about.

Without stating his case, he had the judgement against the Ẹgba.
Killed Alola that ordered them to the expedition.
Ever winning in any case,
Obiriti, a changer of one's fateful day.

He had Ẹgba heads for erecting a hut at Olorịṣa-Oko.
He also used them for hut-making at Oke-kere
And as well for a hut at Alabata.
Obiriti—overflowing in this direction and that like the [River]
      Ọṣun Apara.
When in a fighting mood, both eyes and nose were usually blood red,
Always in a bloody mood at the theatres of war.
A really hefty personality,
With strong plump hands and the feet of a gorilla.

Despiteful of the Ijẹbu on his left,
Adejọwọn the Awujalẹ;
Also spiteful of the Ijẹbu on his left,
It is unlikely he will not mete out the same treatment to Jimba in
      Ilọrin,
The man with a nose disproportionately long for his mouth.

He killed Ijẹbu and planted Ijẹbu,
Planted Ijẹbu as one would plant a post;
Planted Ijẹbu face outwards—
Opposite the corn market.

He was dared to camp in the forest,
The Balogun camped in the forest and despoiled it.
He was dared to pitch his tent in the field,
The Balogun pitched his tent in the field,
He ravaged and rent the whole field as one would a cloth.

A man who was fore-warned not to call at Awẹrẹ,
He marched through the farms at Ọla at Ẹdẹ.
Ọla dared not move anywhere,
Timi must stay put in his palace.

His departure made them heave a sigh of relief at Agbale,
They all in chorus sighed, 'Ibikunle has been responsible for our
  impoverished state'.
He departed and the Balẹ breathed a sigh of relief;
He said, 'Thank God, Ibikunle has at last left today'.
His departure made Timi have a good bath,
Saying, 'I will have my bath today, Ibikunle is gone!'

He plans another expedition while still executing the first,
He barely quells a rebellion before he opens fire on another front,
He planned the Ijẹṣa war;
Ẹfọn was pitching a blockade.
The Balogun cleared the forest and dug trenches,
Ibikunle pounded and ate away the yams of aristocratic Ẹfọn in an
  unminding manner;
Pillaged their *apepe* yams, pillaged their *alọlọ* yams,
Even the sprouting yam-sets of Ariwo completely went in for it too.

He empties the granaries in a jiffy.
And sets fire to all the poisons in the village.
He nakedly entered the house with Eleriwo,
An enemy of Kongo, father of Kẹrẹ.

He fought like lightning in the Lọla's open field, like an elephant,
The elephant fiercely ravaged Ilọla field,
Kuẹjọ's father, he really plundered the field at Ilaṣẹ.
The warrior! witty as a European.

When *agba* drums are sounded in Olufọn's house,
It was always in praise of the Balogun.
When they beat the drums in Ejigbo-Okoro,
It was also in praise of the Balogun.
When *kinjin* drums are sounded in Ilọrin,
It was in praise of no one else but the Balogun.

A lone elephant that rocks the jungle,
Ibikunle has given up the idea of just rocking the jungle,
He always says he is a lone elephant
That rocks the whole world to its foundations.
A God-sent fulfilment of a mission.
The mission that God gave to Ibikunle, he executed before his death.

A chain with thickness of a palm-tree is incapable of stopping an
    elephant.
Any creeper that aims to obstruct the elephant from crossing the
    road
Will surely follow the elephant in its trail.
Balogun! My unending respects for you!
I will never charge you as a liar for ever.
It was Alara who took you for a liar.

Obiriti! The result was the subsequent despoliation of his town.
Ikọgusi that took my father's words for falsehood,
Onilel'ọla! his town was thus in utter ruins.
Ajero-Ajaka that took your words for lies,
Arowolo! his town became a completely deserted place.

Balogun! Olugbaiya, I implore you,
The smoke screen has often spread round the jungle.
Balogun! I beseech you, Olugbaiya,
The climbing-rope has often retrieved the palm-tree.

The sole of the feet has always led the path,
The city has always been surrounded by the wall.
Olugbaiya! I entreat you!
The nursing mother usually ties the shawl for carrying the baby
    securely round her.

Arowolo!
You outwit them all in town.
Ro'gi-ro'gbẹ (charger of the trees and of the fields),
A champion in the battlefield.

Arowolo!
Master in town,

Rogi-ro'gbẹ!
Terror in the battlefield.

There is no deity that can excel Ogun;
Others are just full of mere affront.
Without his leadership, they cannot move an inch.
Without his company, they cannot march confidently on.
If Ibikunle, Lord of his quarters, is no more,
They cannot even challenge the jackal to a duel.

Europeans may stop sailing and disembarking;
Ijẹbu may even boycott coming with their wares.
If the European stops sailing and the Ijẹbu ceases to come,

Ibikunle's inexhaustible stock of gunpowder,
Lord of his quarters, is there for our everlasting use.
Whoever dares the elephant dares death.
Whoever dares the buffalo dares its charge.
Whoever dares the matchet-carrying masquerade,
Desires a free invitation to go to heaven.

If Ibikunle is coming from the opposite direction and one fails to
  clear the way,
Perhaps the man desires to join Ondugboye in heaven.
Ọgbaragada, the man,
Who broke Kurunmi's gate asunder in an instant.

What a lamentable thing! All sighed for sympathy with the echoes
  of the honey-bee.
Ibikunle has let down the cargo—he is no more!
He is gone with his name and left his title.
The father of Kuẹjọ has left with his head pad.

ORIKI OF TOWNS

1. Akurẹ

Akurẹ Oyemẹkun!
Ọmọ a-bọ 'da silẹ f'ogun enu pa ni (a-ro-ka)
Ọmọ a f'ojo gb'ewura k'ẹru ọba ma yin (wa) esẹ
Ọmọ 'lọja mẹfa a n'na lorijọ (l'ojumọ)
A-koko na Oritagun;
A tun na Igbein.
A na Idi-agba;
A na Ọja Oṣodi-Anaye.
A na Mọṣalasi,
A tun na 'ja Mopọn.

Akurẹ!
O l'omi meji, o pe ejeji l'ala.
Ala ile tabi t'oko?
Ala na ni o wa d'omi, ẹbọ!
Ala ti a ti nperi,
Ala na ni o ma tun wa d'omi ọmọ.
Oṣi 'i t'Akurẹ do (k'o) ma n'ala kan;
Ala t'emi i (wa) ninu okẹ.
Ọmọ ọl'ọja Oṣodi-Anaye.
Ọmọ ọl'ọja gba l'ori ogiri.
Ọl'ọja kan ka nt'ẹru'mọde,
Ka ntagbalagba gija-gijo;

Ibẹ n'a ti t'agba koro-koro mẹfa.
Ọja Oṣodi ka a ti nri ohun ẹwa a ra!
Akurẹ! o mo ra de mi o!
Akurẹ! nlẹo!
Ọmọ a-ṣ'oro ni'gba ekuyẹ (ebolo) nja;
Ọmọ a ṣ'oro ni'gba ebirẹ (ebolo) ngbọn-'wu l'oko.
Igbi ebirẹ ngbọn-'wu lẹlẹ l'ori igi
Ni ko bere mi si l'ona Oye.

Akurẹ of Oyemekun!
Where the sword is renounced and tell-tale is substituted as a
    means of causing one's death-knell.
A planter of water-yam in the rains to prevent the Ọba's slaves from
    digging for the yam-stub in the soil.
Owner of six markets that are open daily for business.
You first transact business at Oritagun,
Then Igbein,
And also Idi-agba.
You market at Oṣodi-Anaye,
Then at Mọṣalasi,
And also at Mopọn.
Akurẹ!
That had two streams and named them Ala,
The urban or rural Ala?
The Ala has become the sacrificial water.
The Ala being mentioned
Has now become the water for the children.
No Akurẹ can be so poor as not to have an ala (white cloth).
My own white cloth is in the bag.
The child of the owner of Oṣodi market where prosperous business
    is done.
The child of the owner of the market where goods are smuggled over
    the walls.
The owner of the market where the child slave is sold,
Where adults are sold into slavery;
It was at the same market that six stalwarts were sold into slavery.
Oṣodi market where things of beauty are also available for purchase.
Akurẹ! Please buy mine for me too.
Hey! Akurẹ!

The child of him who celebrates festivals during the season of the
    ebolo vegetable.
The child of him who celebrates festivals when *ebolo* vegetables are
    in flower.

You ask me the way to Oye when the *ebire* vegetable puts out its
flowers.

2. Ileṣa (Ijẹṣa)

> Ijẹṣa ko ṣe-ori, oni'lẹ-obi.
> Ọwa! ọmọ Oluyeye.
> Ijẹṣa ko ri idi iṣana
> Ile ni ẹru Ọwa to nmu'na re oko.
> Ẹni Ijẹṣa ko ki,
> Ẹ ma rahun;
> Kiki, ẹru-Ọwa,
> Kan-kan-kan l'on'ni ni l'ara.
> Ijẹṣa ko se-ori,
> Mo tẹ atin-n f'Ọwa;
> Ọwa! ọmọ a-b'okun-l'ẹri (Obokun)
> Ijẹṣa! ọmọ odo a-pa'na da.
> Ọwa ni ki nwa jẹ,
> Nko jẹ;
> Ijẹṣa Abẹni ni ki nwa wẹ
> Nko wẹ.
> Igbati Ọwa ni ki nwa jẹ ti nko jẹ,
> Ti Ọwa ni ki nwa wẹ ti nko wẹ;
> Ni nwọn ba ni ẹ ma jẹ ki oni-ifọn wẹ mọ
> Ẹ jẹ ki Mo-r'ọla-hun fi ọwọ ọpọ yi mi l'ara.
> Nko kan bẹrẹ,
> Nko kan ile-ọba;
> Nko ti i kan ile-Ijẹṣa.
>
> Ijẹṣa te bii ẹni le lali.
> Ijẹṣa-Abẹni san'ṣọ si 'baradi,
> Ọwa ni o nsan'ṣọ si gbọgbọlọ itan.
> Ọwa! ọmọ a-b'okun l'ẹri,
> Ijẹṣa, ọmọ odo a-pa'na da.
> Ote ni mi,
> Atinn ni ẹru-Ọwa.

Ijẹṣa are never the produce of shea-butter but of kola.
Ọwa, child of Oluyeye!
Ijẹṣa had no idea of matches,
The children of Ọwa have always taken the torch from home to the
    farm.
If Ijẹṣa do not greet you,
Do not allow that to bother you,

The greeting of the children of Qwa
Has never been mellow, but harsh.
Ijẹṣa was never wont to produce shea-butter,
An *Atinn* mat is usually spread for the Qwa to sit upon.
Qwa! owner of a big pond akin to the sea,
Ijẹṣa who had a stream that diverted the road.
Qwa invited me to dine with him,
I declined the hospitality.
Ijẹṣa-Abini invited me to bathe,
I refused that invitation also.
When Qwa invited me to dine with him and I declined,
When he invited me to bathe and I refused,
They said the man with craw-craw should no more be disturbed from
    taking a bath,
He should be left to Morọlahun to caress him
Without a grass-thatched roof,
I do not feel the presence of the *Qba*'s palace,
Without seeing *gbodogi* leaves,
I do not have a feeling of being on Ijẹṣa soil.
Ijẹṣa, prominent as the colouring made with ground *lali* leaves.
Ijẹṣa–Abini often girdled his loins at the waist
While Qwa girdled his at the thighs.
Ijẹṣa! Owner of a big pond that can be likened to the sea;
I am Ote,
While the children of Qwa are as flexible as *Atinn* mats.

NOTE
The texts of several *oriki orilẹ* can be found in S. A. Babalọla, *Awon Oriki Orilẹ*
(Glasgow, 1967).   For a study of *ijala*, see the same author's *The Content and
Form of Yoruba Ìjálá* (Oxford, 1966).

CHAPTER VI
Proverbs, Songs, and Poems

CHIEF I. O. DELANỌ

IN this chapter, we shall examine the possibility of using as sources of historical information the various categories of Yoruba oral literature. The literary forms considered in detail are as follows:

1. *Owe*—Proverbs.
2. *Orin*—Songs.
3. *Àròfọ*—Poems.

1. *OWE:* YORUBA PROVERBS

Yoruba proverbs are self-evident truths which give the gist of what one wants to say in a brief and unmistakable form. A proverb can drive home a point or describe a situation in a few striking words: hence the Yoruba proverb, 'Owe lẹṣin ọrọ, bi ọrọ ba nu, owe ni a fi nwa a', meaning, 'A proverb is a horse which can carry one swiftly to the idea sought.' Proverbs may have the form either of a plain statement of fact or of a warning. Their most important characteristic is that they bring out more sharply and clearly than ordinary speech the point one desires to make.

In fulfilling their primary function of presenting ideas or describing situations in a picturesque or challenging way, some proverbs recall particular events in the life of the community which created them and in which they are used. Such events are wars, battles, famines, or pestilences, as well as particular social experiences which are characteristic of the community. Since proverbs are handed down from one generation to another as truthful sayings tested by usage, information obtained from them may be more reliable than that which may be gathered from the other forms of oral literature considered in this chapter. Yet one must be careful in accepting proverbial lore as a basis for historical conclusions. One weakness of proverbs as a source for history is that, occasionally, they may be overtaken by events. Proverbs which correctly described conditions in one generation may cease to do so in the following generation. For example, 'Ogun ọmọde ki iṣere gba ogun ọdun', meaning, 'Twenty children will not play together for twenty years', was a self-evident truth one hundred years ago, when it described conditions in the days of slave-raiding and rampant disease, when life was very uncertain in Yorubaland. The situation has changed, and the proverb is now used to mean that, however friendly two or more people may be, they will have to separate one day. The fact that proverbs may in this way be applied to quite different sets of circumstances in succeeding generations detracts from their historical value as guides to past conditions.

Some examples of proverbs which do provide information of real historical value are:

(a) Bi o l'aiya ki o ṣe ika,
     bi o ranti iku Gaa ki o ṣe otitọ[1]

meaning, 'If you are bold enough, continue to do evil, but when you remember how Gaa died, change to speaking the truth and start doing good', a proverb used as a warning to those who persist in doing evil. The historical value of this proverb is that it confirms the story of Gaa (or Gaha) in Ọyọ history. This proverb inspired Samuel Johnson to find out about Gaa, who was a wicked *Baṣọrun* of Ọyọ. Johnson writes:[2] 'Gaha had great influence with the people and many followers. He lived to a good old age, and wielded his power mercilessly. He was noted for having raised five kings to the throne of whom he murdered four, and was himself murdered by the fifth.' Another account adds that Gaha was killed and his corpse cut up into small pieces.[3]

(b) The Owu War which began about 1821 led to the disintegration of the Yoruba country. The Owu and Ẹgba homesteads were destroyed, and the Ẹgba, after many difficulties and trials, settled in Abẹokuta (1830).[4] For many years after they had settled in Abẹokuta, the Ẹgbas fought wars of survival against their neighbours, especially Ibadan. There was a long period of enmity between the Ẹgba and Ibadan, and their armies clashed on several

---

[1] Chief S. Ojo, *Iwe Itan Ọyọ* (Ọyọ, n.d.), p. 67.
[2] S. Johnson, *The History of the Yorubas* (Lagos, 1921), p. 178.
[3] Chief S. Ojo, op. cit., p. 67.
[4] S. O. Biobaku, *The Ẹgba and their Neighbours, 1842–1872* (Oxford, 1957), p. 15.

occasions, for example in the 1870s. There was great suspicion between the Ẹgba and Ibadan: an Ẹgba found in Ibadan or an Ibadan found in Abẹokuta had to be killed.

> Abuni njẹ abuni, afinihan njẹ afinihan,
> Ewo ni 'Ẹ pẹlẹ mbẹ' ara Ibadan l'ojude Ṣodẹkẹ

> If you abuse me, it will be understood;
> if you point me out to my enemy,
> that also will be understood;
> but what if you hail me, 'How are you?',
> me, who am an Ibadan man, in front of Ṣodẹkẹ's house?

(Ṣodẹkẹ was the leader who led the Ẹgba to Abẹokuta.) This proverb is used to state that 'it is better to bring a direct charge against one in public than to foment intrigues against him in secret'. It serves the historian to confirm the existence of the enmity between the Ẹgba and Ibadan described above. A similar reflection of the hatred which is the aftermath of a prolonged war of aggression can be seen in the Ekiti proverb!

> 'Titan ọtẹ Ibadan bi jagun, nitootọ ṣugbọn a ku bi iwoo[1]
> taba s'ọkan ọmọ ẹni',

meaning, 'It is true that the war with Ibadan has ended, but its aftermath—hatred— remains like the seed of tobacco in the hearts of men.'

2. *ORIN:* YORUBA SONGS

In songs we find more passages of historical value than in proverbs. The reason for this is not far to seek: songs are frequently composed (orally) in order to praise or abuse individuals, to express love or hatred, or to propagate partisan accounts of events. Hence the Yoruba saying, 'Orin ni i ṣiwaju ọtẹ̀', meaning, 'Songs precede a war'. In such topical songs important information of historical value may be found.

Yoruba singers are aware of their responsibility to be accurate Hence we find the following in an *ègè*:[2]

---

[1] Ekiti dialect for *ehóró*.
[2] Recorded from Solomon Akinlọtan of Ifọ Station, Ẹgba Division.

Mo mọ̀ ọ́ jẹ,
Mo mọ̀ ọ́ mì,
Mo mọgbọn ka mi i tan,
Ko ma pa ni l'ara;
Mo mọjo agesẹ,
Mo mọrin ayẹku,
Mo mọ owẹnẹwẹnẹ ere 'yi a mba obirin ṣe l'oju
ọkọ rẹ̀ ko ma dija;
Nitori meji kọ, nitori awa ọ̀kọrin ni:
Ọrọ ẹnu wa o, k'Ọlọrun ma jẹ ko pani.

I like eating it,
I like swallowing it,
I know what to do after it has been swallowed,
So that it does not injure one;
I know when one whose two legs have been cut off is dancing;
I know when a cripple is walking;
I know how far one can flirt with a woman in the presence of her
husband without causing a fight;
All this knowledge is for only one thing;
It is because of us who are singers;
The words of our mouths,
May God save us so that they do not destroy us!

But there is a serious possibility of inaccuracy in songs, because
they are mostly transmitted from mouth to mouth, and in this
process many inaccuracies occur. The singers themselves appreciate this fact, because they were taught by different masters. When
they meet in public, therefore, and one of them sings songs
containing inaccurate details, he is immediately called to order by
his competitors interrupting his singing. This is a common practice
among Yoruba singers, whether singers of *ègè*, *ewì*, *igbàlá*, *ẹ̀sà*, or
ìjálá. Singers do not tolerate inaccuracies in the singing of others.
In illustration of this, I cannot help but quote in full the example
of the singers of *Ìjálá* (who are hunters) as recorded by Dr.
Babalọla:[1]
"When there are several *ijala* artists present at a social gathering,
the performance of each chanter is keenly listened to by all the
others, and if any of them thinks that the performer has committed
a grave textual error at a particular point, the critic cuts in, in

---

[1] S. A. Babalọla, *The Content and Form of Yoruba Ìjálá* (Oxford, 1966),
pp. 61–2.

ìjálá-chanting voice, and makes his criticism, beginning with a cliché such as the following:

Irọ́ l'opa, irọ l'o ṣù tà,
Alabàrí[1] l'o ri l'o pe l'elegbo.[2]

You have told a lie, you are hawking loaves of lies.
You have mistaken a seller of *àbàrí* for a seller of *ègbo*

Maa gbọ́ o
Bẹẹ kọ́ o
'Tori ọjọ mii, ọjọ ire

Listen to the correct version now.
Your version is wrong.
For the sake of the future, that it may be good.

In self-defence, an *ìjálá*-chanter, if criticized, would brazenly say:

Oju iru ẹni wọnyi naa ni
O ṣoju emi paa kete, agba ni ng o yà dà;
Mo kuro l'ọmọde agbekọrunroko

It all happened in the presence of people of my age.
I was an eye-witness of the incident;
Although I was not an elder then,
I was past the age of childhood.

Alternatively, the chanter may reply by pleading that the other should respect his integrity, and mind his own business.

K'a kata o ma tọ 'pó ọ̀yà,
K'ọya o ma si tọ 'pó akata
K'onikaluku o maa ba poro òpó ẹ lọ.

Let not the civet-cat trespass on the cane-rat's track
Let the cane-rat avoid trespassing on the civet-cat's track."

This indicates three things: (a) that Yoruba singers are aware of the importance of reporting facts accurately in their songs; (b) that inaccuracies still may occur; and (c) that singers will use

[1] Seller of *àbàrí*, a sort of pudding made from maize, plantain-flour and beans.
[2] Seller of *ègbo*, mashed boiled maize grains.

shameless lies, claiming that what in fact happened before they were born took place in their presence, to save their face and honour. During the excitement of festivals, when singers sing the praises of their ancestors, many inaccuracies may occur. The following are examples of topical songs of some historical value:

(a) After the British Government had put an end to the inter-tribal wars, the Ibadan soldiers became pests to the civilians. The contempt which the soldiers had for the civilians is shown in the following song sung by the soldiers:

> Agbẹ[1] jawusa[2] ṣẹnu yánkan yànkan;[3]
> Jagunjagun ni ijobi
>
> The farmers eat *awusa* nut and stain their mouths;
> Only the soldiers are entitled to eat kola-nuts[4].

(b) The *Arẹmọ* (eldest son) of the *Alafin* (king) of Ọyọ was not normally allowed to succeed his father on the throne, but compelled in early times to commit suicide and in later days to go into exile on his father's death. Prince Ọladigbolu therefore came to Ibadan and lived at Oke-Arẹmọ, near Yemẹtu. When the Ọyọ throne became vacant in 1911, Ọladigbolu who was living at Ibadan had a strong rival in another prince who had gone to live at Ila-Ọrangun: both of them hoped to be the next *Alafin*. The prince at Ila-Ọrangun was more popular than Ọladigbolu, but in those days there were no transport facilities between Ọyọ and Ila-Ọrangun, which made it possible for Ọladigbolu to reach Ọyọ before his rival, and he was recognized by the kingmakers before his rival reached Ọyọ. Hence his supporters sang this song:

> Apaaro fo piiri lati inu igbẹ wa,
> yio gboye lọwọ Akukọ[5]

---

[1] Lit. 'farmer', frequently used to refer to an ordinary citizen.

[2] *Awusa* is a local nut like cashew.

[3] A term of abuse: only children are excused if they stain their mouths with what they eat.

[4] Kola is the 'premier' nut used for divination, sacrifices, and as part of the dowry for a bride.

[5] Recorded from Mr. Samuel Popoọla Taiwo, aged 64, of E6/8 Alafara St., Ibadan.

The partridge flew straight from the bush,
And demanded to be selected as chief in place of the cock.

3. ÀRÒFÒ: YORUBA POEMS

There is little difference between singing and the tone in which
an àròfò is rendered; the meaning of the word àròfò, however,
justifies our classifying it as recital: a—noun prefix, rò—to think,
fò—to say. But it consists in speaking as if singing. Frequently
there is a chorus which, invariably, is a repetition of the original
line, repeated by the apprentice reciter. Àròfò is also called rárà;
an àròfò reciter is called asunrárà or onirárà, or sometimes akigbe
(crier) or alagbe (beggar). The professional àròfò reciter, in return
for 'alms', recites poems of praise, criticism, or abuse, turned in
whichever direction will satisfy his employer.

These poems are composed orally, and should be treated with
the caution necessary in considering any oral information. One
method of checking the accuracy of the accounts they give of
events is to collect several poems referring to the same events from
independent sources, and compare them. For this purpose I
recorded two versions of recitals describing the Adubi rising of
fifty years ago, popularly called the Adubi War, given by two oral
Wonwè reciters. These reciters 'hawk' history in the moonlight for
gifts of between a penny and threepence, according to the generosity of those whom they visit. Both recitals agreed in the major
details although the reciters were taught by different masters.
An account substantially the same was also recorded[1] eleven years
after the rising in a poem by the Ẹgba poet Ṣobọ Aro-bi-odu:[2]

Ẹni ba r'iku Ẹfuji[3] ko ma ṣẹṣin l'ooore,
Ẹni ọtẹ Adubi de l'oju rẹ ko ma f'owo Ọba tàràkà;
Ọtẹ nẹ[4] re gbe Lumloye[5] gberemi lọ,

Ko si nin'ẹgbẹ ọlọṣa, o njẹun l'ọgba ẹwọn,
Awọn ṣọja Oyinbo dana sunle rẹ,
Nwọn f'aṣọ rẹ ṣofu.

---

[1] viz. Lasisi Ọdẹyẹmi of Ifọ Nla, mud-wall builder, aged 61, and Solomon
Akinlọtan of Ifọ Station, aged 49.
[2] Arofọ Ṣobọ-aro-bi-odu (1929), p. 5.
[3] Efuji was a wealthy Ẹgba woman who was disembowelled by her horse
when it became uncontrollable and threw her.
[4] Ẹgba dialect.
[5] Lumloye: an Ẹgba chief arrested for allegedly helping the rebels.

One who witnessed Ẹfuji's death should not treat any horse kindly;
One who witnessed the Adubi rising will not be careless about what
   money [as tax] is due to the Government;
It is the rising which forced Lumloye to leave the town for overseas;
He was not among the burglars,
yet he was imprisoned;
The British soldiers burnt his house,
and destroyed all his clothes.

But even where there is such agreement between several different
versions over the details of events, one has to be cautious in
accepting their evidences for historical purposes.

A frequent limitation in the value of poems for historians is that
it may be unknown to what events they refer. For example:[1]

Ija kan, ija kàn ti nwọn ja l'Ọfa nkọ—
Oju tal'o to diẹ mbẹ?
Gbogbo igi t'o ṣ'oju ẹ l'o wọ'we
Gbogbo ikan t'o ṣ'oju ẹ l'o w'ẹwu ẹjẹ,
Ọgọọrọ agbọnrin t'o ṣ'oju ẹ l'o hu'wo l'oju ọdẹ;
Ṣugbọn o' ṣ'oju mi pa kete n'ile wa nibi nwọn bi mi l'ọmọ
Agba ni ng o ti i da, mo kuro lọmọde agbekọrun r'oko

What about a great fight that was fought at Ọfa—
Is there anyone who witnessed a bit of it?
Although the trees that saw it here all shed their leaves,
And the shrubs that saw it were all steeped in blood,
And the very stag that saw it grew fresh horns while the hunters
   looked on,
Yet I saw every bit of it, for it was fought where I was born.
I do not claim to be old, but I'm no more a child that must be carried
   to the farm.

All this poem records is that there was a bitter and fierce battle at
Ọfa. Further research may discover something about this battle,
but nothing more than the mere fact of the battle can be derived
from the poem. The poem in itself, therefore, while it contains
great literary beauty and merit, is of little historical value.

Finally, here are two examples of poems commenting on
contemporary events which are of real value for the historian:
(a) In 1908, during the reign of Baalẹ Layọde, there was a great

   [1] E. L. Lasebikan, 'Tone in Yoruba Poetry', *Odu*, no. 2 (n. d.).

chieftaincy dispute at Ogbomǫṣǫ. Akande, the professional crier for Laoye, the *Baalẹ* before Layǫde, followed the chiefs who were going to the *Baalẹ*'s house to take a decision on the matter, shouting:[1]

Ẹ pé biri, ẹ pé kóto,
Ẹ rò o 're, ẹ mà jẹ kó ni kókó;
Bi kò bá ti i hó, ẹ mà f'ogùn si i,
Bi ẹ bá f'ogùn si i, titiri ni i tiri;
À-rò-ṣòfò l'ǫkà yó dà;
Igbá kòtò ti Ìmǫràn dé mǫ́lẹ̀,
Ẹ maṣe jẹ́ ki o ṣí sílẹ̀;
Kòkòrò Àkerekère mbẹ níbẹ̀ tó lè ta ni;
Oyin mbẹ níbẹ̀ tó lè ta ni;
Paramǫ́lẹ̀ mbẹ níbẹ̀ tó lè bù ni jẹ;
Ǫká mbẹ níbẹ̀ tó lè bù ni jẹ;
Ǫmǫ olóoore ni kẹ́ ṣe lóoore,
Ǫmǫ ika ni kẹ́ ṣe níkà
Ẹ má fi Ǫ̀bàrà mógbètua,
Ẹ jẹ ká tìdí múgi gùn,
Kó ba lè yẹ ni!'
(Kó lè baa yẹ ni!)

You hold meetings, you appoint committees,
Stir it well so that there are no lumps in the starchy food [that you
    are cooking];
If the [water] has not boiled, do not put in the stirring stick;
If you start stirring it [before it has boiled] the starch will not cook
    properly;
Then the starchy food you are cooking becomes useless and a waste;
The little calabash which 'advice' kept closed, for goodness' sake, do
    not let it open;
There are scorpions in it which can sting;
There are bees in it which can sting;
There are night-adders in it which can bite:
There are vipers in it which can bite;
Be kind today to the child of a kind man;
Be cruel today to the child of a cruel man;
Do not say that what is bad is good,
Let us start climbing the tree from its trunk;
So that we may be blessed.

[1] N. D. Oyerinde, *Iwe Itan Ogbomǫṣǫ* (Jos, 1934), p. 136.

(b) In 1926 Aléṣinlọyẹ, who later became Baalẹ Okunọla Abaasi Aléṣinlọyẹ. was installed as the *Balogun* of Ibadan in *Baalẹ* Fọkọ's house. After the ceremony people were dancing on their way back to Aléṣinlọyẹ's house. Janta, one of the messengers of the *Alafin* of Ọyọ, who represented the *Alafin* at the ceremony, had a crier shouting the praises of the *Alafin* and abusing the Ibadan people and their newly installed chief:[1]

Oye kékèké ni nmu ni ṣabamọ,
Ẹru Alafin, Ọtakun gbọọrọ mu ara oko,
Kekere ọla ni i faara oko l'ẹnu ya,
Ẹ o wa ri bi o ti nfa Abaasi l'ẹnu ya bayi!

It is the small chieftaincy-posts that usually make one regret;[2]
The *Alafin*'s slave[3] who stretched a long rope to entrap the bush-man;[4]
It is the small honour which makes the bushman lose his head;
Do you not see how it is making Abaasi lose his head now?

This abuse of Janta inspired Daniel Tayọ Akinbiyi (now *Ẹkẹrin Olubadan*)[5] to bring an end to the *Alafin's* ill-treatment of Ibadan, and in 1930 he formed his friends into the Ibadan Progressive Union, which achieved the virtual separation of Ibadan from Ọyọ.

Here concludes our brief endeavour to find history in Yoruba oral literature. One great difficulty, it must be stressed, in this endeavour is that oral literature is embellished with fresh details from time to time as it is transmitted from one generation to another. It also contains a mass of detail that needs to be carefully sifted. One must watch for exaggerations, distortions, and shameless untruths, before one reaches the little gem beneath the heap of rubbish.

---

[1] Recorded from Chief D. T. Akinbiyi, *Ẹkẹrin Olubadan* of Ibadan.
[2] Frequently people regret being made chiefs, especially in small posts which attract no remuneration, because of the expenses connected with the office and the standard of life expected of a chief.
[3] i.e. Janta himself.
[4] This is a term of abuse.
[5] i.e. fourth chief in rank after the Olubadan.

CHAPTER VII
Ceremonies

OYIN OGUNBA

THE Yoruba love of ceremonies, like that of many African peoples, is a compound of both a comic and a serious mental disposition. Life, for the Yoruba, has endless resources of joy and can provide pleasure comparable to that of Elysium. But it is also potentially tragic, for the gods, in nervous control of the universe, demand from man a steady, periodic sacrifice as a demonstration of his continued loyalty and submission. No major achievement in the life of an individual, a group, or a community is considered possible without the active support of the supernatural. Ritual in such a community becomes a constant factor of life as may be shown in Yoruba child-naming, marriage, installation, initiation, and burial rites and also in the annual festivals of the various communities.

All these ceremonies, properly investigated, are capable of yielding valuable source-material for Yoruba history. Some burial rites, for instance, have certain remarkable features from cult to cult or place to place in the land and must hide some historical material in them. When, for example, *Okooro* of the Ekine cult in the waterside areas of Yorubaland dies, *Jigbo*,[1] another important character in the Ekine system, goes immediately to the house of the deceased and tries to resurrect him by performing a certain set of symbolic actions. He carries two special whips, one in each hand, goes alone into the room where the body lies in state, flogs it, and then goes out. Some minutes later he enters again and repeats the same set of actions, and also does this a third time. On coming out after the third attempt he bursts into bitter wailing, lamenting his failure to wake up the dead. Only after this rite can the body be given physical burial.

Different from the Ekine one is the burial rite of the *Alagẹmọ*

[1] *Okooro* is a kind of universal young man, carefree and nonconformist. *Jigbo* was once Ekine's bondman but he later persevered to freedom. In a way they are both kindred spirits.

in the Agẹmọ cult.[1] In this, the body is dressed up with long
raffia threads, the same costume as the deceased person has used
in his annual dances. The ẹru (luggage of charms) of the deceased
is put on his head and the body is then buried in an erect posture
still carrying the luggage. In this way he is dressed up perpetually
for his god and carries his ẹru eternally.

It is a common feature of human society the world over for rites
to have their genesis in some definite historical events. Ulli Beier
making a similar point has observed: 'Religious rites . . . frequently
commemorate historical events, and they are often continued long
after their original significance has been forgotten'.[2] Thus observances like those mentioned above can be a valuable pointer to the
past of the Yoruba. In this case the question will be to determine
whether such burial rites arose independently out of this soil and,
if so, the circumstances of the evolution, or whether they are a
result of some culture-contact, presumably through migrant
culture-carriers.

In the same way, all the other Yoruba ceremonies can yield
some source-material on Yoruba history. But by far the richest of
these are the installation rites and the annual festivals of the
communities and it is with those two that we shall be more
concerned. Installation rites, mostly those of the ọba, are important
because the Yoruba have for long operated a monarchical system
of government. The king, in this system, far from being a mere
primus inter pares, is in fact the magnificent living symbol of the
community. He is more of an idea than a person, being the pivot
of the life and history of his people. As he is divine, he is also the
main instrument for the achievement of supernatural purpose in
man. Festival rites are important for several reasons: first, they are
the chief media of the religious expression of the people; secondly,
the institution of the festival is in itself a giant cultural establishment which can accommodate virtually every experience of the
community and mould it into its own special idiom. In practice,
therefore, the festival often achieves more than mere religious
expression and has material that can be an important source for
the reconstruction of Yoruba history once the idiom is understood.

In using Yoruba ceremonies as a source for Yoruba history, an

[1] See also Oyin Ogunba, 'The Agemo Cult in Ijebuland', *Nigeria Magazine*,
no. 86 (Sept. 1965), 176–86.
[2] Ulli Beier, 'Oloku festival', *Nigeria Magazine*, no. 49 (1956), 168–83.

elementary, though important, distinction has to be made between the stories told about these ceremonies and the ceremonies themselves. Often, it will be found that the stories told by the traditional historians, though helpful, are only half-truths and that it is the ceremonies themselves that can yield relatively reliable historical material. The traditional historian's philosophy of history is certainly different from that of the 'responsible' literate historian of today. While the latter is concerned with events in relation to the hard facts of human nature and earthly experience, the former sees events as divinely inspired and shaped towards the fulfilment of the purpose of the gods. He makes an effort to regard the world as a colony of heaven. The result of this is that the historian keeps emphasizing the divine purpose even in the most mundane matters to the point at which the really valuable facts are clouded and confounded by the divine superimposition. The moral of a story becomes its flower and the concern for drawing a good one sometimes leads to the reshuffling of facts to achieve the desired permutation.

Another aspect of this philosophy can be seen at work in the ceremonies themselves. The details of things are not important *per se* but only in so far as they help to give meaning to a prevailing idea. Thus since the prevailing idea about these ceremonies is the sense of continuity, the details are sometimes left to be worked out by the individual performer or participant. As long as an appearance of sameness and continuity is kept the community hardly bothers itself about whatever little changes occur.

But however minute and imperceptible regular change is, its accumulation from year to year becomes significant when viewed in retrospect over centuries. It even gets to the point of altering the face and structure of the ceremonies, and it is this margin of change that allows the ceremonies to have a history as well as be a repository of the history of the community. It is also the relentless operation of this philosophy which, ironically, creates the difference between the traditional historian's stories and the history as can be deduced from the ceremonies themselves.

In effect, according to the traditional historian's imagination there is no history at all. Certain events take place at a particular cosmic time and remain so afterwards. The same events repeat themselves and are usually re-enacted annually. The whole of the community's history is thus circumscribed by the annual events and can be experienced during that period. But on the contrary relentless change is also of the essence of nature with things drifting towards growth or decay since nature cannot remain static. And so, in spite of the wishfulness of the traditional historian, Yoruba ceremonies have grown and decayed over the centuries and have thus, almost imperceptibly, accommodated a good deal of the change and history of the people. Since this history had to grow in defiance of the wish of the traditional historian, it had also to assume a special idiom sufficiently disguised to deceive the adversary.

The Range of Material

Some writers on Yoruba ethnology have emphasized the religious fact in all divisions of Yoruba life. They are of the opinion that religion is basic to all that the Yoruba think of and that the ghost of religion is present in every mundane activity. Thus E. Bọlaji Idowu writes of the Yoruba: 'The keystone of their life is their religion. In all things they are religious. Religion forms the foundation and all-governing principle of life for them. As far as they are concerned, the full responsibility of all the affairs of life belongs to the Deity. . . .'[1] One can express doubt about this statement and ask whether there is any community in the world that can have so much religion, as distinct from ritual, in its blood. One can also wonder whether the intense materialism evident in Yoruba ritual practice is not such as to limit seriously Yoruba religious pretensions.

But above all, one must reject this statement if it is meant to lead one to expect, for example, a thorough-going history of religion from a historical study of Yoruba ceremonies. The Yoruba are hardly pietistic in their religious practice and their awe before the supernatural is more cosmic fear than love. They are neither bedevilled with 'a darkness of the soul' nor liberal enough to construct a 'comrade God'. In the Yoruba system, ritual tends to accommodate everything from devotion to extreme profanity.[2]

Yoruba ceremonies, then, as a source for Yoruba history can yield such material other than the simply religious. From them one can reconstruct, at least in the barest outline, something of Yoruba political and cultural history, as well as the history of ideas.

[1] E. Bọlaji Idowu, *Olodumare, God in Yoruba Belief* (London, 1962), p. 5.
[2] This point has been further developed in my thesis: *Ritual Drama of the Ijẹbu People.*

The material is, in fact, likely to be thin on religious history as compared with the others.

POLITICAL HISTORY

Here we define political history as the history of migrations, conquests, settlements, and significant episodes in the life of communities. So defined, Yoruba ceremonies yield material in all these elements on the fortunes of the people over the ages.

Human beings, the world over, tend to be perennially restive and the Yoruba seem to have had their own full share of this human trait. Perhaps it is even true to say that this restiveness has been more intense in earlier centuries than it is now. War, famine, and pestilence, with their consequent mass suffering, and with their causes and significance only half understood, have usually led people to seek new abodes and new opportunites away from the burning centres of life. And so in the case of the Yoruba, even if one cannot credit the widespread story of an Egyptian ancestry, it will certainly be a stretch of the imagination to think that they have always occupied their present land. Conditions prevalent all over Africa before and since the Christian era are not likely to have encouraged such a stability.[1]

It is also becoming rather widely known that in spite of the apparent cultural uniformity among the various sub-groups which make up the Yoruba people today, these people are (or were) in fact heterogeneous. Certain Yoruba ceremonies can help to establish the fact that the people were initially diverse as well as indicate the process which has led to the present high level of cultural uniformity.

Let us amplify this important point with one example of a Yoruba ceremony—the installation rite of a paramount Yoruba ọba, the Awujalẹ of Ijẹbu-Ode.[2] The installation ceremony lasts for three lunar months. The ọba-elect leaves the town and stays in a tent about two miles outside town during the whole period, except the last two days. During the period he is dressed in black apparel, the symbol of poverty and mourning. During the last two days of his 'exile' he goes on foot through a part of the Ijẹbu kingdom in the company of many people. On the first day he goes through

[1] See for example J. D. Fage, An Introduction to the History of West Africa, 3rd edn. (Cambridge, 1962), for some of the major political upheavals in West Africa in the past thousand years.
[2] P. C. Lloyd, 'Installing the Awujalẹ', Ibadan, no. 12 (1960).

Yemoji river and passes through a number of villages and hamlets
where various sacrificial ceremonies are performed for him until
he reaches Imushin. At Imushin he meets the *Oloko*, the local ruler
who has travelled a mile from his palace to meet him. The *ọba*-
elect, in apparent astonishment at encountering him says: "I was
going to visit the *Oloko* at Idoko but I met him on the way."

After this episode he continues his journey towards Ilese where
he sleeps for the night. Next day, he continues his journey,
crosses Qwa river, and gets into Ijẹbu-Ode territory. He goes
through a number of important places in the town where certain
ceremonies are performed for him. The climax of the ceremony
comes when his followers surround the building of the *Apebi*, a
paramount Ijẹbu-Ode chief, and pull it down. It is also at this
point that he is first proclaimed the *ọba* (king) of the town. After
this the coronation ceremony takes place.

The Ijẹbu oral history, as now preserved in respect of Qbanta,
the founder of the *Awujalẹ* dynasty, says that Qbanta came from
Ifẹ. Before he came, Ijẹbuland, and in particular Ijẹbu-Ode, was
already well-populated. There were crowned rulers at Idoko and
four others ruled over Ijẹbu-Ode. Two waves of migration had
preceded Qbanta, namely that of Olu-Iwa, Ajẹbu, and Olode and
that of Arisu, the *ọba* of Ijasi. But they were merely fore-runners to
the real king, Qbanta. Immediately Qbanta came these loyal fore-
runners graciously handed over to him the reigns of power.
Qbanta's descendants, fifty-one of them, have since ruled Ijẹbuland as of right.[1]

Another version of the story says that although Qbanta came
from Ifẹ to Ijẹbu he was in fact not anxious to assume power. He
was content to be accepted as a noble migrant. But he found, on
settling down, that there were many warring factions in the
community, each centred on one of the rulers. He decided that the
community must be preserved, invited all the heads to a meeting,
and acted as a mediator (or is it that they themselves called him to
mediate?). This is the origin, the oral story says, of the title
Awujalẹ, for Qbanta was nicknamed *Awojailẹ* or *Amujailẹ* as a
result of his successful mediation.[2] Subsequently, in sheer admira-

---

[1] The present *Awujalẹ*, *Qba* Sikiru Adetọna II, is the 52nd *Awujalẹ* of Ijẹbu-
Ode. He was crowned in 1960.

[2] *Awojailẹ* means one who looks closely at the current quarrel; *Amujailẹ*, one
who knows intimately the cause of dispute. Each title thus means a kind of
mediator.

tion of his princely wisdom, the warring heads decided to transfer all effective power to him while they occupy subordinate positions. If the *Awujaḷe* installation rite as described above is compared with the story circulating about the advent of Ọbanta, it soon becomes obvious that the two do not agree. There is a definite attempt on the part of the oral story to oversimplify the events, and something of the decent euphemism and urban sophistication for which the Yoruba are remarkable has gone into the making. The oral story tends to emphasize two points, namely, that Ọbanta was not a conqueror or foreign aggressor and secondly that he belongs to the hard core of the Ijẹbu population and the two earlier migrations. In general the story seeks to emphasize the point that the Yoruba of this kingdom are one people and have always been so. But these claims are doubtful and have in fact been questioned.[1] It is virtually certain from what remains of the installation rites of the Awujaḷe that the army of his great ancestor, Ọbanta, overran the Ijẹbu kingdom and sacked many towns and villages. The tearing down of certain villages *en route* and in particular the *Apebi*'s palace at Ijẹbu-Ode during the installation ceremony is now only a relic of what must have been a major military operation. The encounter with the *Oloko* must have been an important psychological victory, for here was the emperor of 'three hundred and fifty-three towns and villages' feeling compelled to leave his great throne to meet a military adventurer a mile from home instead of receiving him royally at home, if indeed he were an agent of peace as the story says. At this time, the Oko were the most powerful in the land and the *Oloko* even kept a viceroy at Ijẹbu-Ode.

Thus in invading Ijẹbuland, Ọbanta had to reckon much with the Oko power, famous far and wide. But he must have been disappointed by the quality of the resistance since even the emperor turned himself easily into a suitor for peace. Ọbanta was quick to seize the advantage and henceforth real power passed to him while the *Oloko* went into obscurity.

The campaign at Ijẹbu-Ode must have been easy. The warring factions could not co-operate and they fell easy victims to their own unhealthy rivalry. Besides, Ọbanta must have had better military weapons and strategy and it was easy to vanquish the indigenous people armed with relatively primitive weapons. As

[1] See P. C. Lloyd, 'Sungbo's *eredo*' *Odu*, no. 7 (1959), 15-22.

Ọbanta had been conquering his way through, his ranks had become swollen and the sheer force of numbers he commanded was enough to overawe any adversary of the time. The *Olu-Igbo* had been slain at Ibu and his wife and god carried away. Ọbanta's followers are even reported to have described the people they found in certain parts of the land as 'men with tails like monkey's and men like coconut trees'.

The point about all this is that an apparently simple ceremony like the installation of an *ọba* hides within its rites considerable material about the history of the people in such a way as to express the people's original diversity as well as to indicate the process of unification. What is celebrated in this ceremony is the coming of a certain kind of rulership which has become permanent by virtue of its thoroughness and superiority to the existing system. The tactics which the adventurer adopted towards the various communities he conquered *en route* and at his destination show a great adaptation to the level of civilization or political wisdom of each. Thus at Igbo it was a straight battle with 'wild men'; at Oko it was more subtle diplomacy; and at Ijẹbu Ode it was a combination of physical force and ingenious manoeuvre.

If we accept this interpretation, then this installation ceremony can further illuminate the dark pre-Ọbanta past of these people. There is nothing to lead one to believe that the Ọbanta invasion was the first successful one in the land. On the contrary, it seems to be the last of a series, though probably the most successful. Thus even the Oko whom the Ọbanta hordes overthrew were probably not indigenous to the land. They too must have conquered earlier settlers, established a capital at Idoko, and ruled over as many of the scattered communities as they were able to bring under their sway until time overtook them. The Oko people sometimes even say that they migrated from the present Ekiti province.

But who were these earlier settlers? Were they followers of Olu-Iwa, Ajẹbu and Olode as the oral history says or were they the creators of the Agẹmọ culture? Our tentative suggestion is that the people who first made any appreciable settlement of the land were the creators of Agẹmọ culture. They were supplanted by the Olu-Iwa invaders who also held sway for a long time. They too were successfully invaded by two adventurers, Ajẹbu and Olode, whose achievements—the building of the Sungbo's *eredo* and the internal organization of Ijẹbu-Ode—have left a permanent impression on the land. Only after these did the Oko, and later the *Awujalẹ* hordes establish themselves.

So in Ijẹbu alone one can look back to at least five successive cultures. As for dates perhaps the first of these cultures is about five or ten thousand years old or even more, for it takes time for a people who were once strong to decay to such an extent as to induce foreign aggressors to their land.

The significance of this point for Yoruba heterogeneity is two-fold. First, there is the fact that one can count five political eras and migrations (for cultures exist only within their political contexts) among the Ijẹbu, a mere sub-group of the Yoruba, and that there are still pockets of these cultures in the land today. Secondly, other sub-groups of the Yoruba have not undergone identical experience with the Ijẹbu. With some one can only trace at present two or three such cultures, with others probably even more than five. But each experience must have been different in its own particular way and the sum total of the experiences is the measure of Yoruba heterogeneity.

It looks as if what the Yoruba *ọba*'s installation ceremony celebrates today is the coming of the monarchist Yoruba. Perhaps this is what is meant by the Yoruba legend which says that sixteen sons of Oduduwa left Ile Ifẹ on the same day and spread over Yoruba-land, their father giving each of them a crown and some other precious material—things which were easily recognized as belonging to royalty wherever they went and which induced the indigenous people to hand over power to them. Ifẹ, then, would be a type of political and cultural centre from where successive groups of warriors went out to extend their territory, colonize the indigenes, and engulf what is now Yorubaland with this new culture.

Moreover monarchism, as it is now conceived and practised in Yorubaland, is not an isolated phenomenon but a system rather widespread in West Africa, with little variation and local colour. A good example of this is the Ashanti kingship in Ghana. In the same way, accounts of installation ceremonies among some other West African peoples show striking similarities to the Yoruba practice. The oral traditions of these other West African monarchists also say much about migrations and conquests disguised as peaceful settlements. These stories which have basically the same format ought to lead one to investigate more their origin and will certainly throw some light on the past of the Yoruba. From a comparison with similar institutions among some other West African communities it should be possible to know more about the content of power of these migrants and that significant quality which made them, if they are in fact from the same source, victorious wherever they went and permanently accepted.

The ceremony of the *ọba*'s festival in Yorubaland and some other festivals associated with the ruler of the community can also be a fruitful source for Yoruba political history. Every Yoruba *ọba* has at least one annual festival and the form this festival takes often reflects the political circumstances which guided the establishment of the kingship. It might have been a situation that required a great fanfare and a show of power on a grand scale or one that warranted some secrecy and caution. The festival then usually took its subsequent character from this initial political fact.

Two contrasting examples of Yoruba *ọba*'s festivals—the *Ọdun Ọba* at Ode-Ondo and the *Obirẹn-Ojowu* at Ijẹbu-Ode will illustrate this point.[1] At the *ọba*'s festival in Ode-Ondo there is an elaborate celebration for eight days. But about a fortnight before the formal beginning of the festival drums keep sounding from the palace proclaiming royalty and a general festival-mood for all citizens. In the celebration itself on a particular day the *ọba* makes a tour of some parts of the town with all royalty and splendour. On two different dates during the festival the *ọba*, with all his entourage and all the Ondo chiefs, sits regally on certain ancient spots (which are now part of the main road at Oreretu and Odotu).[2] There the chiefs, the war chiefs, the political chiefs, and others dance according to their grades and rank and thus incidentally remind the community of the hierarchy of power.

The point about this pageantry from the angle of political history is that (if we may surmise that this aspect of the *ọba*'s celebration is of ancient origin and that it has remained relatively intact in form) it is a function of the political circumstances of the conquest of Ondo by the *Osemawe* aggressors and the pattern of the subjugation of the indigeneous people. As each of the chiefs dances he carries his matchet in an erect posture, dances from his seat to the

---

[1] See (i) Ulli Beier, 'The *Ọba*'s Festival, Ondo', *Nigeria Magazine*, no. 50 (1956), 238–59.

[2] The spot is now hardly physically distinctive. But, as in many ritual observances, the place exists in the mind of the people and the image comes to the fore at festival time.

king at the opposite end, and then back. Before the king he makes a pledge of loyalty and performs symbolic signs of what would be his fate if he were found disloyal. Each grade of chief makes a different set of symbolic pledges.

It may well be that the subjugation of Ode-Ondo was easy and complete. The *Osemawe* hordes, apart from being in multitudes must have been militarily far superior. The land was also probably sparsely populated by the indigenous Idoko people who were easily driven to the less fertile part of the land and have remained separate and relatively backward ever since. Perhaps the apparent ease and the completeness of the conquest also point to the age of this invasion. I think it will be found by and large from a historical study of Yoruba ceremonies that the early kingships and kingdoms hardly ever established a firm hold on the lands they claimed and that later ones, with a finer understanding of statecraft and better military ability, made more substantial and permanent gains. Whereas the earlier ones were compromises, the later ones easily triumphed over their indigenous adversaries and perpetuated their achievements in the splendour and finality of their ceremonies. It is the firm mastery of states in this latter era of state-building that was to be repeated and refashioned on a much larger scale in the Qyọ empire. In Qyọ, before decadence set in, it was not only the chiefs of Oyọ kingdom that paid homage to the *Alafin* at the *Bẹrẹ* royal ceremony but also some other Yoruba kings within the fold. Their representatives went to Qyọ and annually re-enacted the historical fact of their defeat and inferiority.

Of a different type is the *ọba*'s ceremony of *Obirẹn-Ojowu* in Ijẹbu-Ode. The ceremony also lasts for about eight days. The main features are three, namely, the bringing in of the Woro leaves of blessing, the carrying about of the Ojowu effigy and the public appearance of the *ọba*. Early on one of the days young women go to one of the nearby bushes and pluck certain leaves. They bring them in with songs and elaborate jubilation and deposit them at their household shrines and the more secluded parts of their houses. On the night before the public appearance of the *ọba*, the Ojowu effigy is carried by the *Olowa*[1] into the houses of important personages in the community. At each house, the dwellers come out and the *paterfamilias* takes the Ojowu and dances with it, the rest

[1] The effigy is in fact a piece of stone. At festival time it is painted in three or four colours—red, black, white, etc.

joining in. In the same way, the effigy is taken round the town and a type of homage or rite of acceptance is performed by each of the prominent people who carry it. The ceremony of the public appearance of the ọba is different from that of Ondo. It is a meeting with the Ojowu as well as a dance for the ọba. While the ọba goes from his palace (*ipebi*) to the dance arena (*Ojofa*) the *Olowa*, the carrier of the effigy, goes from his own quarters (Odo Esa) through certain shrines also to *Ojofa*. At *Ojofa*, unlike in the ọba's festival at Ondo, only the *Olowa* priest dances. He makes sixteen symbolic tours while the ọba is seated regally.

Thus the Ijẹbu ọba's festival is different from the Ondo one in two respects. First, it wears more the appearance of a ritual, the atmosphere being one of religious awe and ceremony. The presence of the supernatural is felt more and the noises which keep coming from the audience are in praise of this divine quality. Secondly, the festival takes more the form of the personal triumph of one man rather than that of a group. It looks as if the Ojowu effigy is a symbol of power, intrinsic and rooted in a man and in the dynasty he generated, rather than in a class of people as in the case of Ondo.

The story often told about the Ojowu is that it is an effigy which represents the spirit of the mother of Ọbanta. Ọbanta brought it and deposited it at Odo Esa and started the tradition of consulting it annually. He had brought the effigy from Igbo, a place overrun in his advance on Ijẹbu, and he treated it as a very precious possession. The effigy is said to breathe and to have been doing so for the past six hundred years since Awujalẹ landed in Ijẹbuland. Thus at least symbolically the Ojowu has come to be regarded as the fountain of power, the mother and spring of the dynasty. It has also shaped the character of Ijẹbu political life and made for stability, since the dynasty has been able to assert itself not merely by verbal divine claims but also through ceremonies which at least have all the appearance of divine sanctity.

Thus the king's festival, which is one of the major symbols of the apparent uniformity of Yoruba cultural life, fully investigated from community to community in Yorubaland, is likely, paradoxically, to reveal the immense heterogeneity of the people and their history as well as the diversity of the historical circumstances which have produced the apparent uniformity. It will also reveal the point that, in spite of appearance, the latest Yoruba conquerors had

to deal with people at varying levels of organization and sophistication. But they were armed with the same basic technique for sub-
jugating indigenes and this fact made for the limitations of their
success in certain places and its completeness in others.

There are also, in many Yoruba communities, certain observances which if properly investigated can yield material on political
history. Such a practice is the meeting of the ruler and a particular
priest of a community only once a year. In certain festivals, either
of the community or the king, there are such significant regular
events. A king and another chief whose political position is
relatively insignificant meet by arrangement and then part physically and symbolically till the following year. Such is the meeting of
the *Tami* and the *Awujalẹ* at the Agẹmọ festival at Ijẹbu-Ode, the
Ọlọja Idoko and the *Osemawe* in Ondo, the *Olukere* and *Ogoga* at
Ikere, the *Olobu* and *Olokuku* at Ilobu, the *Obalufẹ* and *Ajalọrun*
at Ijẹbu Ifẹ.

In many cases the priest-chiefs, like the *Olukere* and the *Oba-
lufe*,[1] bear names which sound more akin to the ownership of the
land than the names of the present kings and this raises the question whether many of the present kings were not simply Oduduwa
military officers who seized power from the former rulers. During
the meeting and festival it is the priest who sacrifices to earth and
the gods. The symbolic significance of this fact is that it is the
priest who knows the land and how to propitiate it and that although he has abdicated his political power his spiritual power is
still vital for the survival of the community. In many cases the rite
gives the impression that the priest-chief has in fact been cheated
of power and the yearly meeting and parting becomes something
of an atonement for the irrevocable seizure so that the indigenous
gods of the land may not revolt against the new political overlord.

One Yoruba ceremony that still retains vestiges of this old
political tactic is the Agẹmọ. Not only does the head *Tami* see the
Awujalẹ only once a year, even principal members of the same
Agẹmọ cult are not allowed to see one another more than once a
year. They cannot even meet casually or unofficially, and if they
do, each tries to destroy the other with dangerous incantations.
There are sixteen principal Agẹmọ priests,[2] each living in a separate

---

[1] *Olukẹrẹ* means owner of Ikẹrẹ or first man in Ikẹrẹ; *Obalufẹ* means the king
or chief at Ifẹ or the king or important person who owns Ifẹ.

[2] See Oyin Ogunba, op. cit., pp. 178–80.

village or town forming a ring round Ijẹbu-Ode, the seat of the *Awujalẹ*. Is this device a pointer to a cunning solution of a problem at a particular point in the political life of the community? Or is it, as the oral evidence sometimes says, that the priests were originally Ọbanta's military officers who were distributed over the land and put under sanctions lest they conspire against their leader? Did Ọbanta change the headship of a cult he found in the land and replace the leaders with men who are likely to be always loyal to him?

A full investigation of this aspect of Yoruba ceremonies is likely to reveal much about the type of solutions sought to important political matters at certain important eras of the history of the communities. It will also probably confirm our theory of the basic heterogeneousness of the Yoruba people, especially as it may yield material on the failure or relative success of this pattern of solutions in various communities.

There are also a number of Yoruba ceremonies which show, even more definitely, important events in the life of the communities at some distant date, but which have since been sanctified into ritual observances. Let us take a few examples of these. The first is the ceremony of symbolic parting between the *Dagburewe* of Idowa[1] and the *Awujalẹ* of Ijẹbu-Ode at the installation ceremony of the former. At this ceremony, the *Awujalẹ* journeys from his palace to a place called Mobalifon, two miles from Ijẹbu-Ode and the *Dagburewe* also journeys from his Idowa palace for three miles to Mobalifon. There, the two kings first face each other at close range and then suddenly turn their backs on each other and then walk away each to his palace. Neither of them must look back until he gets home and neither must see the other again.

The story that is usually told about the origin of this rite puts it in about the fifteenth or sixteenth century during the reign of the twelfth *Awujalẹ* of Ijẹbu-Ode. The king, the twelfth *Awujalẹ*, had fallen sick of some serious disease and had to be treated in a 'hospital' outside the town. Idowa (Ibudo Owa) was chosen as the hospital-site. In his absence, his younger brother was asked to act as regent and assume all the paraphernalia of authority, since it was unthinkable at the time to have an empty palace. He did and went further to assume the substance, rather than the mere shadow,

---

[1] For more details see Oyin Ogunba, 'Crowns and *Okute* at Idowa', *Nigeria Magazine*, no. 83, 249–61.

of power. Unfortunately (or perhaps fortunately) the elder brother soon recovered from his illness and was ready to return to the palace. But this became impossible because the younger one, in anticipation of the brother's death, had already assumed full power. (In this tradition one could not be an ex-king.) Thus the community was plunged into a serious dilemma of having two kings on their hand at the same time. To solve this the community advised the elder one to return to his hospital-home and try to live like a king there too. (After all a real king should not have fallen so sick!) But the incident was considered to be a very significant one, a major event that requires re-enactment and has thus been perpetuated into a ritual observance.

It may well be that, like many of the traditional stories, this one has been 'sweetened' to make it less offensive. Perhaps this was a palace revolution that drove the reigning king into exile permanently. Whatever it was, this ceremony, and its like all over Yorubaland, can be a beginning for a thorough investigation of Yoruba palace history and should yield material on many internecine power-struggles that must have engulfed Yoruba rulership at certain eras of their history.

Another such episode is that which has produced the Igogo festival at Qwọ. The festival lasts for seventeen days featuring a number of ceremonies including the blessing and release of new yams.[1] But central to this is the Oronsen episode. There had been jealousy on a large scale among the wives of the king (Ọlọwọ), with Oronsen, an extremely talented woman and the Ọlọwọ's favourite, as the centre and victim of jealous treatment. The other wives, led by Oluwa, conspired to unseat her and, seizing the unique opportunity of the Ọlọwọ's temporary absence on an expedition, broke her taboos and thus drove her out of the palace. The incident quickly assumed tragic proportions as Oronsen, disconcerted and mortified, would not come back unless certain conditions were fulfilled (including the execution of head wife, Oluwa). But it was impossible to fulfil such conditions and so Oronsen had to disappear finally into the unknown. The gravity of the event was not lost on the people, however, and every year since that time the Qwọ community, led by the Ọlọwọ himself who dresses up and plaits his hair like a woman, has always celebrated the Igogo festival to mark the event and placate Oronsen's offended spirit.

[1] Anon., 'Igogo Festival', *Nigeria Magazine*, no. 77 (1963), 90–104.

The Oronsen festival, judging by the quality and specialness of its ceremonies, must for some time have been celebrated differently from the new yam festival. But it must have been easy enough for the people at a later date to see a similarity between the purification rite which the Oronsen ceremony warranted and that of the new yam festival which is also a purification of the community before new crops are formally admitted. If we assume, reasonably, that the new yam festival must have preceded the Oronsen episode then the identification of the one with the other must also have been a significant political event in the life of the people.

This coming together of two originally different ceremonies is not peculiar to the Qwọ Oronsen festival. In fact there are instances in many other parts of Yorubaland. Another good example is the Ṣango festival and the whole concept of his apotheosis. The story about Ṣango, the legendary fourth king of Qyọ, is that he was a powerful, firm, and tyrannical ruler who had a passion for war and empire-building. But his generals later became tired of war and the unlimited sufferings of the citizens and counselled an end to such adventures. Ṣango would not yield and so his generals revolted and rose against him. Faced with imminent defeat and the prospect of an ignominious capture, Ṣango committed suicide, hanging himself on an *ayan*-tree.

It appears that Ṣango's sterling qualities came to be appreciated posthumously and so he was subsequently deified. He was appreciated as the spirit of adventure, tension, and unrest. In spite of his recklessness, he became in the mind of the people the personification of the principles of state-building and heroic exploits. With time, other qualities were added like generosity; he became the defender of the faith, punishing evil and all forms of public immorality; he became the conscience of the people, purifying the community through fire and dispensing supernatural justice. But there had been an earlier god, Jakuta, responsible for all these later qualities.[1] What probably happened was that at a point in history the two became identified as one and Jakuta became subsumed in the general Ṣango ceremony.

The point of investigation here should be to determine the process by which certain political events of magnitude come to be superimposed on certain ritual observances, which themselves must have had political origins, in such a way that the later event

---

[1] Idowu, op. cit., p. 69.

seems to swallow up the former though the former is still faintly recognizable. It may also determine whether these later events were the product of a general upheaval in the Yoruba country at a particular time which was so revolutionary as to impose a permanent change on the structure of ceremonial institutions.

By and large it will be found from a study of these ceremonies as a course for Yoruba political history, that the various units which make up the present Yoruba people have undergone sets of experience, sometimes widely different from one another. After the period of the upheaval of migrations and remigrations each community appears to have settled down to a local experience, developing its own character and tackling its own peculiar problems and thus fashioning its own ceremonies within the context of that experience. But the pattern of solution to problems has been similar from place to place in such a way as to give the whole Yoruba people a certain over-all general character in contrast with other neighbouring tribes. Thus, although this source will provide mostly local history it can, if conceived in the right dimension, also hint at the essential nature of Yoruba politics.

CULTURAL HISTORY

One basic principle of culture practice in relation to physical expression and artefacts is that a culture can only operate within the sum total of its experience. The corollary to this is that at the time of establishing an institution like a festival the type of costume devised for the *dramatis personae* is usually such as to be within the range of contemporary common usage. If we bear this point (and its corollary) in mind we can then make a few observations about the general drift of Yoruba cultural history as can be derived from certain aspects of Yoruba ceremonies.

One widespread assumption and belief today is that the Yoruba had always worn clothes. This is a point some writers have gloated over and used to support a theory of Yoruba cultural superiority to neighbouring tribes. But in certain Yoruba festivals including the *Edi* at Ile Ifẹ, some masquerades in Ekiti, and the Agẹmọ in Ijẹbu, the costume used by the principal characters is a huge quantity of raffia threads (sometimes running into thousands) worn from top to toe to make effective disguise. Also in many Yoruba communities the costume for Ògún festival is still the palm fronds, often scantily worn.

This raises the question whether in the distant past the everyday wear of the early Yoruba was no more than the meagre raffia thread or palm frond. Our point is that this is likely to be the case and further investigation may show that this practice has survived in areas like Ifẹ and Ekiti which are regarded as the earliest-settled spots in Yorubaland, or in an institution like the Agẹmo which is said to be of great antiquity. Somehow, in cultural institutions like the festival certain practices are resilient whereas others are subject to constant change, depending on the nature of the sanctions of each festival. Man in this land has probably been moving from pure ritual to ritual drama and so the more ancient ceremonies have worn better because of their more stringent sanctions.

In contrast to all these are the more modern costumes. Some of them, like the *Egungun* costume are made of the most modern velvet or damask and designed like a bishop's costume with cassock and surplice and some like an academic gown. But even here one might trace a history from the type of *Egungun* called *Aghọ* in Ondo who puts on animal skins, through the one who wears strips of red-coloured cloths, to the ultra-modern one who conspicuously advertises his affluence on himself. Some, like the Ekine costume in the Yoruba coastal communities, are made up of a huge assemblage of beautiful clothes and ornaments even to the point of gaudiness. At the time the Ekine type of costume came to the land it must have made a great impression. One myth still tells of an early competition between Agẹmọ and Ekine. It runs thus:

Ekine, a sea-goddess, came rather late to the land. But she arrived with great dignity and splendour and made a bid to be esteemed the greatest in the land. She gave public demonstrations of her brilliant colours and impressed many people who were ready to enthrone her. But there were also strong opponents who were against her frivolity and presumption. In particular Agẹmọ, the chameleon, who held the reins of power in the land, was apprehensive of the pretender and a struggle for supremacy ensued. To resolve this, a day was appointed for the two to show all their colours to determine who would be supreme. Ekine was quite confident she would win for she has all colours and all types of costumes imaginable and she came out with all of them. On the other side was Agẹmọ apparently bare and looking as if the day was already lost. Ekine started displaying her costumes first, for she was the protagonist of the competition. But each time she brought out and put on a new set of costumes she found that Agẹmọ, the chameleon, had exactly the same. She tried and tried many times, but it was the same and the chameleon always overtook her. She became frantic and desperate and invited costumes of all shapes from everywhere in the world and the same still happened. After some time, however, she exhausted all her stock. Then she despaired, for as yet Agẹmọ had not brought out any of his own colours but had won the competition by simply exhausting all the supplies of Ekine. Agẹmọ henceforth remained supreme.

One interpretation of this myth can be that at the time Ekine came to the land, the woven fabric, if worn at all, was the precious possession of only great men. But Ekine came with vast quantities of it, toned up the life of the community with colour and radiance and tended to steal the show from existing institutions. But Ekine never, nor ever could have had her way entirely, for while the people realized the importance of the brilliance of the new times they also appreciated the value of their 'old reliables'.

For our purpose the significance of all this is that just as the different ceremonies of a Yoruba community usually have their genesis in different eras of the community's history so do the costumes that are used to give physical expression to such ceremonies. Thus one can get an insight into the artistic life of the community from such an investigation. It will reveal a process from the rough-and-ready raffia threads to the magnificent fabric of today. Something can be gleaned of the time the people first began to put on clothes and the circumstances which brought about the revolution. One could know what the first clothes were like and whether they were in the form of the Yoruba *ibante*, as a writer has suggested.[1] One also wants to know when the first beaded garments and crowns which have since become the standard costume for the crowned head of a community were first introduced, for the early crowns were certainly not of beads and the early garments could hardly have been of beads either.[2]

The music and musical instruments of Yoruba ceremonies can also be a good source for Yoruba cultural history. There are usually three types of musical instruments in a Yoruba community, namely, clappers, usually two for each person and producing monotones; pot-like drums with one face and varying widely from the small *gbẹdu* drums to the huge *oro* and *igbin* drums; hour-glass

---

[1] Eve de Negri, 'Yoruba men's costume', *Nigeria Magazine*, no. 73, 4–12.

[2] The early crowns were of various materials including clay and metal. Pictures of some of them are to be published shortly.

cylindrical drums made up of *bata* and *dundun* drums. The clappers are the simplest of these instruments and do not require any special skill to operate. Usually they are used in connection with certain community festivals which are considered as old as the very foundation of the community. Such a festival is the ubiquitous *Oro* which, because of the extreme simplicity of its structure, is probably as old as man on this soil.

The pot-like drums, with their gong (bell) accompaniment must have been invented much later than the clappers. In fact it is possible to classify two periods here, namely, the period in which there were just gongs or when the gong was predominant as is still the case in festivals like the Agẹmọ today, and the period when the gong steadily disappeared until it came to the point where in many royal ceremonies only drums are used. The music produced became correspondingly more complex, and sophistication entered the community with the sixteen royal drums whose music is a structure of intricate relationships between the sixteen drums. But even with this growth in sophistication the music was still relatively simple as, in fact, it is today. Pot-like drums have a limited range of notes, usually two, and the music still had a tom-tom sound, in spite of the fact that the drums were sixteen.

The really revolutionary change in Yoruba ceremonial music came with the discovery or invention of the hour-glass cylindrical drums. The early ones must be the *bata* drums which still bear some resemblance to the pot-like drums in that one face is much bigger than the other. Can one say that this invention is another aspect of the genius of King Ṣango and also a significant contribution towards his inevitable apotheosis? The real *dundun* hour-glass drum probably came several centuries later and completed the musical revolution. Its supreme merit is its great adaptability. With a very wide range of notes, it could be made to produce any music, even to talk.

The point of all this is that from a study of the music and musical instruments of Yoruba ceremonies it is possible to construct a history of the growth of the music as well as the growth of the people's mind. Certain forms of music have been preserved over the centuries in certain ceremonies and the widely different qualities of ceremonial music within a Yoruba community can be a starting point in determining the age of each. By and large it will be found that it is only those ceremonies which have an innate dynamism, like certain Egungun festivals, that have changed with the times in the concept and quality of their music while others have remained conservative.

THE HISTORY OF RELIGION AND IDEAS

The high god in West Africa has often been thought of in the sense of a *deus remotus* or *deus otiosus*, a high god who has relegated his powers to subordinate gods and who lives in luxurious retirement like an absentee landlord. Mircea Eliade and Father O'Connell[1] among others have tried to explain the high god's relationship with and distance from man in terms of either the extreme purity of the godhead which should not be contaminated by human filth or the extreme energy and radiance of the supernatural which man cannot approach. Recently, Robin Horton[2] has expressed doubt about these high-sounding theories and noted, most significantly, that the so-called 'otiosity' is relative and certainly not universal in West Africa. For example, he says, the high god among the Kalabari people is certainly not 'otiose'.

In the case of the Yoruba there is evidence to show that the high god has not always been 'otiose' and that the present concept of an 'otiose' Olúdùmarè is a late development arising either out of a new philosophy in the land or as a result of direct and powerful immigration. The idea of a *deus otiosus* probably came in Oduduwa's train, like so many other such ideas. But there are still in Yorubaland today certain ceremonies which antedated Oduduwa and which show certain high gods who are by no means remote from man.

Such is the Agẹmọ high god with its cult and festival. During the festival Agẹmọ physically dwells with the people. A month before the festival a ceremony called *Ireku* (The Opening of the Gates) is performed to admit the high god into the human community. During his month-long stay all leaves and herbs are said to lose their potency in deference to the supreme god. At the celebration of the festival itself physical sacrifice is performed for the high god. This high god, rather than being in leisurely retirement, in fact

<hr/>

[1] James O'Connell, 'The Withdrawal of the High God in West African Religion: an essay in interpretation', *Man*, lxii, (May, 1962), 67–9.
[2] Robin Horton, 'The High God: a comment on Father O'Connell's paper', *Man*, lxii, (Sept. 1962), 137–40.

has ministerial functions on earth and is especially responsible for the upkeep of the community's land.

The presence of an 'enterprising' high god among the Yoruba people even today thus raises the question of the trend of the history of Yoruba religion. It seems unlikely that a people who have their gods within easy reach would still need to sacrifice a human being to communicate with him. In fact the whole idea of human sacrifice seems to tie up with the 'new times' in which the idea of the high god as an invisible, intangible being developed. In effect just as the monarch on earth reigned and was much superior to his lieutenants and the citizens, in the same way the high god reigned in heaven not just as a *primus inter pares* but as the author of earth and sole owner of heaven.

The new-fangled ideas of monarchy on earth and in heaven probably impressed the indigenous people (or is it that they were overawed into it?) to such an extent that in many places in Yorubaland it has completely displaced the former ideas. Where the success has not been so total it has managed to live side by side with the older idea. In such places the 'new faith' is usually the senior partner. Thus this source, on further investigation, should be able to yield some facts about the Yoruba development from the idea of the priest-king to that of the thoroughly secular one and also the process towards the theory of the divine right of kings.

Yoruba ritual subsists on a thorough-going principle of symbolic form. Such are the *Ikose*, the stamping of the feet to acknowledge the spirit of the ancients; the eating of the heart of a deceased king by the new one as a symbol of continuity in the tradition; and the use of burning torches to drive out evil spirits. An investigation into the origins and development of such symbolic forms, and in fact the whole of religion in this community as a system of symbolism, should be an interesting and rewarding exercise.

Assessing the Source

Yoruba ceremonies are rich as a source for Yoruba history. By and large the best and most significant of the Yoruba experiences seem to have been lived through her ceremonies, especially the festivals. The structure of a Yoruba festival is usually such as to accommodate and integrate easily subsequent experience, apart from the fact that new festivals are established from time to time. The result, therefore, is that as one goes through the ceremonies of a typical Yoruba community it is as if one is going through time itself with the dark past suddenly being illuminated and the present teeming with life.

But this is hardly to say that Yoruba ceremonies by themselves can give a full or even nearly-full picture of the richness of Yoruba history. These ceremonies, in spite of a contrary appearance, are notorious for their disregard of dates and for general imprecision. Also, as Ulli Beier has suggested, 'Yoruba religion appears to be kept alive not by ritual and dogma but by personalities. The gods exist through its priests.'[1] In such a system while there can be a gain in the richness of the history of such personalities, there is certainly a loss in precision and clear-cut models.

Yoruba ceremonies by themselves cannot yield the full result of historical investigation until they are compared with the ceremonies of some other West African tribes. One wants to examine the installation rites of some of these tribes and determine whether a general pattern emerges and so find the points of similarity and, if not, the set of circumstances which produced Yoruba uniqueness. One also wants to look into the multiplicity (sometimes duplication) of festival forms in Yorubaland and compare them with those of other tribes and find out whether the same obtains elsewhere and, if not, the reason.

A comparison of the 'properties' used at these ceremonies with those of other tribes would also help to establish facts of the cultural history more cogently. How widespread for example is the use of the raffia thread as costume and what has been responsible for its retention while others have changed face and form?

Is there something peculiar in the general pattern of the design of costumes over this wide region which can throw some light on Yoruba cultural history and help place Yoruba forms within the system? In the same way a comparison of the ceremonial drums and drummings of many tribes with the Yoruba practice would be useful in determining or confirming dates and trends. Each tribe is likely to show some variety and evolution which will help place in perspective the Yoruba story.

From the foregoing it sounds certain that the ceremonies of some other neighbouring African communities can also help as a source for Yoruba history, at least on the fringe. Although it is

[1] Ulli Beier, *A Year of Sacred Festivals in One Yoruba Town*, Nigeria Magazine Publication (1959), p. 13.

true to say with William Fagg that the dominant note in African art and ceremonies is the 'tribality', it is also important to know that forms of art and ceremonies do, many times, easily cut across tribal barriers.[1]

[1] William Fagg, *Tribes and forms in African Sculpture* (London, 1965).

CHAPTER VIII
Archaeology

FRANK WILLETT

ARCHAEOLOGY AND HISTORY

IT is usually considered necessary for a historian to be able to write well. Certainly many of the historical classics have become classics of literature too. A good historical article or book should be interesting to the non-historian. Of course the straight edition of a set of documents—the raw material on which the historian draws—is likely to be of less general interest. So it is with archaeology. Our documents are the material fragments left behind by our ancestors, which we recover by excavation and publish in reports and catalogues. These published reports are often a mass of charts and figures, lists of finds and analyses—difficult enough for an archaeologist to digest, and certainly off-putting to the historian. A number of African historians have asked me why archaeologists do not present their data in a more interesting way, in a form more usable by them. The point is, of course, that these are our collections of documents, our own edited but still relatively raw data. After we have prepared these, we can begin to study them to see what contribution they can make to the major task of historian and archaeologist alike, the reconstruction of man's past achievement. In other words, our excavation report is the transcription of our documents; when the archaeologist goes beyond this point to their interpretation, he will be writing history. I should like to ask historians who may have been put off by the forbidding appearance of archaeological reports to bear with us. The archaeology of the recent past in Africa is a fairly young study. It is only since the war that the history of African societies has become recognized as a valid field of research, and with this recognition, the archaeological investigation of these societies has grown. This being so, we are only now reaching the stage where enough data have been collected to permit us to attempt interpretations in more general historical terms. My recent book[1] has attempted to set the sculpture of Ifẹ in its historical as well as art-historical background, and this will undoubtedly be followed by many more such presentations of data recovered by archaeological techniques, but presented as a contribution to African history.

Although historians and archaeologists are both interested in the past, their approaches are rather different. It is therefore worthwhile to make some remarks about the nature of archaeological evidence. The archaeologist, of course, seeks evidence of human history, of man's development, of the economic basis of his society, and of his interaction with his environment. He looks for the material remains left behind by earlier men, and from them makes inferences about the non-material aspects of life in the past.

Because of the nature of his evidence the archaeologist tends to study communities rather than individuals, and thus his subject tends to have a social and economic rather than a political bias. His evidence is inevitably material, and therefore his interpretations tend to be basically materialistic. Nevertheless, it is evidence about people which he seeks, not about the things which he excavates. From their artifacts, we learn how people lived, and, by inference, their ideas and intentions. Kenneth Oakley has remarked that 'tools are fossilized ideas.' When we see some of the fragmentary remains which the archaeologist studies, it is as well to remember that these are indeed 'fossilized ideas', more than mere scraps of rubbish from an earlier age.

Of course, it is quite clear when we look at these remains that archaeology has some very severe limitations. Such evidence as the archaeologist can recover is entirely dependent on the accidents of survival. Stone, pottery, copper alloys, and so on survive, but many materials do not. In the African forests, iron usually decays away very rapidly, and wood hardly ever survives the white ant unless it has been carbonized. It is very rare to find animal bones, and yet much of our most valuable data in drier areas has come from the analysis of the animals which were eaten by the community. Very often the impermanent materials are those which could tell us most. How much we could learn of the history of African sculpture if only wood survived.

It is possible, however, to make inferences beyond the material evidence, but this needs to be done with great caution. Even

[1] Willett, 1967a.

Gordon Childe, probably the most brilliant prehistorian of his generation, has inferred the absence of chieftainship principally from the fact that all the huts in a given settlement are of the same size.[1] However, there are many modern communities in which the chief's hut is indistinguishable in size and contents from those of other villagers. In Africa, then, it is most important in interpreting archaeological data to employ carefully documented ethnographic parallels.

The need for recording the traditional ways of life before they finally disappear has been increasingly obvious to archaeologists. The study of the material aspects of traditional culture is considered old fashioned antiquarianism by social anthropologists, so that archaeologists are being forced to record this information for themselves. My own studies on modern Nigerian pottery were undertaken for the light they might throw on archaeological remains. One striking result was the demonstration that the pottery industry of Old Ọyọ had been transferred to Ilọrin after the collapse of the former city. The women potters had settled among or been taken by their former enemies and brought their traditions with them. Without ethnographic investigation, in a purely prehistoric context, with no oral traditions to guide us, we might well have concluded that the Ọyọs overran Ilọrin, rather than the opposite. 'Conventional history records primarily the movement of the men in a society; the pottery, on which the archaeologist relies, indicates the movement of their women folk. These movements may well be in opposite directions.'[2]

The archaeologist is particularly concerned with the influence of one society on another whether by trade, by war, by colonization, or by exchange of ideas, and in these circumstances, cooperation between historians and archaeologists can be most fruitful. The historian will often be able to supply information of a nature which is not preserved in the archaeological record, whilst the archaeologist will often be able to supply information about the society as a whole, its economic and social basis, and in particular, he should be able to provide evidence of dating which it may be possible to tie in with evidence obtained by oral tradition, for a great deal of his effort is devoted to the establishment of chronologies, whether relative or absolute. Both oral tradition and

[1] V. G. Childe, *Social Evolution* (London, 1951), pp. 87, 88, 90.
[2] Willett, 1961b, p. 77.

archaeological evidence in their own right produce merely relative chronologies, a sequence of events, but archaeology has developed a variety of ancillary techniques which can yield evidence of absolute dates. Indeed the most striking development in archaeology as a whole over the last two decades has been the remarkable proliferation of scientific techniques intended to help resolve our dating problems. It is in the need for a chronological framework which historians and archaeologists share, that one begins to appreciate the fact that the study of Yoruba history in particular affords a profitable field of co-operation between the two disciplines.

Sometimes archaeology is able to find evidence of absolute dating within its own data. In West Africa, this is usually a question of finding evidence of imports which are datable elsewhere. The most instructive imports of this type have been tobacco and maize, American crops which are unlikely to have been introduced before the first European contacts.[1] These vegetables of course do not themselves survive in the archaeological record. The evidence of tobacco is in the form of pottery smoking pipes; such evidence has provided the basis for chronology in Ghana from the seventeenth century onwards as a result of the work of Paul Ozanne[2] who has suggested to me that the supply of tobacco, sold in coastal trade from European ships, was probably exhausted before the ships reached Nigeria. This would certainly account for the fact that only one tobacco pipe has been found in an early context (seventeenth century)[3] though several were found in the excavation in the palace at Ilesha, apparently a nineteenth-century deposit. The ear or cob of maize was frequently used to decorate pottery so that this crop too is evidenced indirectly but reliably in the archaeological record. From the evidence of the maize impressed sherds, we are able to infer that a small number of the potsherd pavements made in Ifẹ were made later than the beginning of the sixteenth century. No such sherds however occur in the pavements at Ita

[1] Willett, 1962a, Stanton and Willett, 1963, but compare Jeffreys, 1963, Carter, 1963, 1964, who do not agree.
[2] P. Ozanne, 'Notes on the Early Historic Archaeology of Accra', *Transactions of the Historical Society of Ghana*, vi, (1962), 51–70; P. L. Shinnie and P. Ozanne, 'Excavations at Yendi Dabari', *Transactions of the Historical Society of Ghana*, vi, (1962) 87–118; P. Ozanne, 'The diffusion of smoking in West Africa', *Odu* N.S. ii, (1969), 29–42.
[3] Ozanne 1969, p. 36.

Yemoo which are now radiocarbon dated a few centuries earlier than this.

Probably the most widely used method of dating is radiocarbon. This has given a new dimension to archaeological research, and as numbers of radiocarbon dates have increased, we have been able to develop techniques for interpreting them. It is, for example, no longer considered advisable to rely on an isolated radiocarbon date. It is much better to have blocks of dates, whether two or three from the same horizon or a sequence in a succession of layers. Only in this way can we control the anomalies which arise from the fact that the radiocarbon date is calculated by a statistical technique. All future work will need to include financial provision for radiocarbon dating on a substantial scale as we must have sufficient dates to be able to handle them by statistical methods.[1] The dates so far available are discussed below.

More recently another technique has been developed which promises well for the help it can afford in solving some of the problems associated with Yoruba archaeology and in particular with the history of the art of Ifẹ: thermoluminescence. This has the advantage of operating directly on pottery (which includes terracotta) and can probably be used eventually on the cores inside brass castings to give us an indication of the age of these sculptures. Since none of the sculpture that has been discovered so far in Ifẹ was in a context of manufacture, even when we can date the period of deposition, this is the time of its abandonment, not of its manufacture. This is a complicating factor too in thermoluminescent dating. For this technique, it is necessary to collect a sample of the soil in which the specimen has been lying and this is used to calculate the length of time the specimen has been in that location. If the piece was already very old, the thermoluminscence date will not be the age of the piece. The specimens so far tested had been excavated before the technique was properly developed, but samples from the second shrine with terracotta sculptures at Ita Yemoo agree fairly well with the radiocarbon dates (one TL date

[1] Thurstan Shaw gives an annotated list of 72 radiocarbon dates from Nigeria in the *Journal of the Historical Society of Nigeria*, iv, 3 (1968), 453–65. In this he discusses the method itself and the interpretation of the resulting dates. He discusses the Iron Age dates also in *Current Anthropology*, x, 2–3 (1969), 226–9. Further dates are given in Willett 1971.

is A.D. 1170, two are A.D. 1420 producing an average of A.D. 1340 ± 150).[1]

YORUBA ARCHAEOLOGY SO FAR

Not all archaeological evidence is obtained by excavation. In Yorubaland in particular, a great many antiquities, especially terracotta and stone sculptures, have been found in other ways, usually still in use in local cults. Such finds are not discussed in this paper though references to them are included in the bibliography. Although the whole of Yorubaland is covered with sites which would repay archaeological investigation, relatively few so far have been excavated. The ancient city of Ifẹ has received most attention whilst excavations were conducted by the present writer at Old Ọyọ in 1956–7 and at Ilesha in 1959. The first person to excavate at Ifẹ was the German anthropologist Leo Frobenius who was there from 29 November 1910, until the middle of January in 1911, though he was only free to undertake investigations in the earlier part of this period. By modern standards, the record of the circumstances of his finds is utterly inadequate. Very little is said about the excavations he undertook, and they seem to have been simply to find objects rather than to find evidence. It is very difficult to be sure where he found most of the pieces which are now in the Museum für Völkerkunde in Berlin although at least one of the terracotta heads appears to have been found in the Olokun Grove. Some of the pieces which Frobenius obtained during his 1910 to 1911 expedition in Yorubaland are illustrated in more than one place. The captions to these illustrations do not consistently attribute the same find-spot to each piece. Some of the pieces are said to have been excavated at Old Ọyọ, some in Ọyọ, one near Ọfa, and some in Modakẹkẹ.[2] Moreover, the common finds such

---

[1] For a fuller account of thermoluminescence, see D. Brothwell and E. Higgs, *Science in Archaeology* (London, 1963), pp. 90–2; *Archaemometry*, v, (Oxford, 1962), 53–79; ix, (1966), 155–73; xi, (1969), 105–14; *MASCA News Letter* (Philadelphia) i, nos. 1 and 2, iii, no. 1, vi, no. 1. Details of thermoluminescence dates from Ifẹ are given in Willett 1971.

[2] For example:

Frobenius, 1912	Frobenius, 1923
i. opp. p. 312 Right: a carved board 'from the grave of a Shango priest, Ọyọ'.	Pl. 193 'Excavated in Modakeke'.
i. opp. p. 320 Left: Ifa tray 'from the ruins of Old Ọyọ'.	Pl. 192 'Excavated in Modakeke'.

as sherds of domestic pottery, crucible fragments, and so on, seem all to have disappeared, so that it would be quite impossible to attempt now to rewrite Frobenius's field-work in the form of a regular excavation report.

Nevertheless, it was Frobenius who first drew attention to the outstanding historical and archaeological importance of Ifẹ and to the important naturalistic sculpture found there, although his interpretation of its origin is no longer acceptable. Most of Frobenius's archaeological effort appears to have been expended in the Olokun Grove. He described his technique as 'burrowing'.[1] Certainly no archaeologist of the present day would be likely to adopt a similar method. Nevertheless, we are able to obtain from his account a general picture of his discoveries in the Olokun Grove. From the surface down to a depth of three-quarters of a metre, there was a very hard, compact soil containing what he called 'glazed potsherds', that is to say fragments of glass-making crucible. This overlay a red, homogeneous laterite with decomposed quartz. At a depth of two metres, there was a layer of pottery and at 5 metres, charcoal and ash. Through these layers, there were shafts 12 to 24 feet deep in the bottom of which he found glass-making crucibles together with other pots and terracotta sculptures. This is the site of the great industry which spread the blue glass *sẹgi* beads across West Africa. Some examples, found at Koumbi Saleh, Tegdaoust, and Gao, have been shown by X-ray fluorescence analysis to be identical with those found in Ifẹ.[2] It seems to have

Right: Fish shaped box 'from the ruins of Old Ọyọ'.	Pl. 194 'Excavated in Modakeke'.
i. p. 376 Ifà tray: no provenance given.	Pl. 191 'Excavated in Modakeke'.
i. p. 277 Iroke: no provenance given.	Pl. 175 'Excavated in Modakeke'.
ii. opp. p. 360 Ifà tray with birds 'from a grave near Offa'.	Pl. 189 'Excavated in Modakeke'.
ii. opp. p. 376 Carved boards 'from Yoruba temples'.	Pl. 184 'Excavated in Modakeke' (this is stylistically possible).

Modakẹkẹ is a section of Ifẹ where Ọyọ refugees had settled in the mid-nineteenth century. They had been forced to leave some months before Frobenius arrived, and he was able to collect a great deal of material from the ruined houses.

[1] Frobenius, 1913, p. 94.

[2] C. Davison, R. Giauque, and J. D. Clark: Two chemical groups of dichroic glass beads from West Africa, *Man. N. S. VI*, no. 4, Dec. 1971, pp. 645–59

been in the course of these excavations that Frobenius found some of the nine terracotta heads which are now in the Berlin Museum.[1] Because he found the local people impossible to employ as regular labour, he encouraged them to dig on their own account in the grove and elsewhere and paid them for their finds. Therefore, one cannot be sure whether most of the heads were found by Martius, the engineer assisting Frobenius in the digging, or whether they were found by the Ifẹ people themselves nor where any, except one, originated.

He does, however, record consistently the location where a number of other finds were made. He obtained some important terracotta sculpture on the site of the old palace which had already collapsed at the time of his visit. This included part of the representation of an elaborate stool group of characteristic Ifẹ type similar to the well-preserved one from the Iwinrin Grove[2] and to another fragmentary one, recently found at Akeran Compound in the centre of Ifẹ. There was also a very interesting and so far unique sculpture in quartz which appears to be the leg of a vessel;[3] this was found by one of his local workmen on the slopes of the hill leading up to the Ifà temple in the centre of Ifẹ.

Frobenius visited and described many of the shrines and groves in Ifẹ such as those for Qrẹ,[4] Ogun Ladin, the Qpas for Qranmiyan, and Ogun Esa, but the most famous find which Frobenius made in Ifẹ was the brass head known as Olokun which he tells us was dug up in the Olokun Grove during the second half of the nineteenth century. Naturally he tried to take this away from Ifẹ but was prevented. However it was shown by Underwood and Fagg in 1950 that the head which is now in the Ifẹ Museum is merely a reproduction of the one which Frobenius found, made by the modern technique of sand casting, a method completely unknown in ancient Ifẹ where the technique was that of 'lost-wax'

suggest that these beads, of their group A, are composed of glass which was originally manufactured in Europe and imported via the Arab world. Samples of glass from Ifẹ crucibles are still in process of analysis, but at present it looks as if the industry was a remelting one, rather than one which manufactured glass from raw materials.

[1] Illustrated in Frobenius, 1912, i, opp. pp. 104, 342, 344, 346; 1913, p. 105, pls. VI and VII, opp. pp. 318 and 320; Willett, 1967a, pls. 22, 29, 30, 60.

[2] Illustrated in Willett, 1960, p. V, and 1967a, pl. 76.

[3] Illustrated in Frobenius, 1912, i, 318; Willett, 1967a, pl. 63.

[4] Described earlier by Elgee, 1907, and Dennett, 1910. See also Murray and Willett, 1958.

casting which gives a far finer surface. We have no idea what has happened to the original head which Frobenius found; it has never come to light since. It is indeed strange that the metallic composition of the substitute head falls within the range of variation of the other brass heads from Ifẹ which were discovered only in 1938 and 1939.[1]

Because of the naturalism of the art, Frobenius thought that he had found traces of a west Mediterranean colony on the Atlantic coast of Africa which he guessed to have been founded in the thirteenth century B.C. and left without further Mediterranean influence after about 800 B.C. from which time it developed in an increasingly African manner. Of course this was only a guess based on the naturalistic appearance of the sculpture. Certainly no naturalistic sculpture had previously been found in Africa south of the Sahara. Indeed the serious study of the art of Africa was only just beginning.

For some time after Frobenius's visit, relatively little was done in Ifẹ. We do have a number of accounts by people like Talbot (1926) and Hambly (1935) which illustrate pieces from Ifẹ and augment our general fund of knowledge. The Ọni of Ifẹ, Sir Adesoji Aderemi, wrote an article, 'Notes on the City of Ifẹ' (1937), which published for the first time the copper mask known as Ọbalufọn and the first photograph of a potsherd pavement. The Ọni's contribution, however, has been much greater than this, for it was at his suggestion in 1934 that a great number of the antiquities which had hitherto been allowed to remain unprotected in the shrines were brought into the palace for greater safety, and his continuing efforts led eventually to the establishment of the Ifẹ Museum.

In 1938 and 1939, one of the most important single discoveries ever made in Ifẹ was uncovered. Whilst digging the foundation trenches for a building in Wunmonije Compound during the dry season of late 1938, thirteen brass heads of about life size were discovered. At the beginning of 1939, four more were found together with the upper part of a figure representing an ọni. These heads were in general similar to the one which Frobenius had already published from the Olokun Grove. There was, however, no Department of Antiquities in existence at the time, and all that could be done was to record the circumstances of discovery, which

[1] See Moss, 1949, and compare Barker, 1965.

was done both by William Bascom who was doing anthropological field-work in Ifẹ at the time and by Kenneth Murray who was later to become the first Director of Antiquities. Because of the limited open space around the find-spot, which is flanked by two-storey houses, the site is at present hardly suitable for excavation though it is to be hoped that one day it will be possible to investigate it more thoroughly.

The primary impact of this discovery was felt in the art world which was astonished to find what was evidently a significant tradition of naturalistic art in Africa.[1] Since the naturalism of these works was comparable to anything that ancient Egypt, Classical Greece and Rome, or Renaissance Europe had produced, it was assumed that they must have been made in one of these traditions. If they had been made in Africa at all, and it was quite clear that Africans were represented in many of the heads, then they must have been made by an artist working in one of these traditions, perhaps a wandering European. Such evidence as pointed to an African origin was scarcely considered although Kenneth Murray writing in 1941 demonstrated that Benin bronzes were being made before the Portuguese arrived and that the Ifẹ pieces appeared to be ancestral to them. He also showed that a similarity of style between the brasses and terracottas at Ifẹ indicated that they could not have been made very far away from the city itself and drew attention to the existence of naturalism in other African art traditions.

Mr. Murray made himself responsible for surveying the sites in Ifẹ which were known or thought to contain antiquities, and this valuable record is now preserved in the Department of Antiquities and has been of great help to archaeologists working in the city since then. In 1943, Mr. Murray was appointed Surveyor of Antiquities, and later a Government Archaeologist was appointed, Mr. Bernard Fagg, who made Ifẹ one of his first priorities and undertook in 1949 a preliminary season of investigations. A dozen well-shafts were dug in various parts of the city to test the nature and depth of the occupation deposit. The presence of someone in the town who was interested in antiquities led to the reporting

---

[1] Frobenius's discoveries led C. H. Read to publish in the *Burlington Magazine* in 1911, a plaster cast of an Ifẹ head which had been in the British Museum for a long time. Yet the art world took little notice.

of a small brass head from Wunmonije Compound[1] which was evidently the top of a staff of a type which was found at Ita Yemoo[2] some eight years later, and of some terracotta sculptures discovered at Abiri several miles away from Ifẹ.

Mr. Fagg visited the site at Abiri and recovered yet more sculpture of considerable importance. A number of pieces already known in Ifẹ itself were clearly not in the naturalistic style, but this site revealed the first evidence from finds made in the earth of naturalistic and stylized forms of human heads being used simultaneously in the same shrine. The fact that the pottery from which they were made was identical suggested that both had been manufactured at the same time.[3]

In the first five months of 1953, Bernard Fagg organized another season, this time assisted by his brother William of the British Museum and by John Goodwin from the University of Capetown. It was thus possible to increase archaeological effort on a number of sites at the same time. The work was divided between investigating certain shrines where it was expected that objects of Ifẹ art would lie buried in contexts which would throw some light on their use, and putting down shafts at random in the town in the hope of finding some evidence of brass casting. This latter hope was not achieved nor has any sign been discovered to date of the sites where the Ifẹ brasses were cast. The well-shafts, however, did provide a large series of pottery samples from all over Ifẹ and demonstrated the great variability of depth of occupation—in some case no more than one or two feet but occasionally going down to almost 28 feet. Conventional archaeological excavation in trenches has now revealed, however, that these greater depths were only obtained where there were already old pits underlying the general occupation level. The normal depth of accumulated occupation deposit in Ifẹ is only about 3 feet.

The investigations in the shrines, however, were more fruitful. The Grove of Osongongon Obamakin, which lies against the town wall on the western side of Modakẹkẹ, was explored. A number of pieces from here had been taken to the palace in 1943. They included a sculpture in granite of a calabash or pot with a sash

<hr />

[1] Illustrated in W. B. Fagg, 1950, fig. 1.

[2] Full-length photographs of these staffs are in Willett, 1959c, pl. VIa.

[3] See B. E. B. Fagg, 1949; W. B. Fagg, 1951, pl. 24; Willett, 1967a, p. 64 and pls. 24, 45, 61.

round its neck, the terracotta head said to be of Osongongon Obamakin,[1] and the incomplete representation in terracotta of a fettered man suffering from *elephantiasis scroti*,[2] The grove contained two minor shrines for Eshu and Ogun which excavation showed to consist of fairly recent votive pots presumably for palm wine. The main shrine, within the ruins of an old hut, contained fragments of terracotta figures. A fine terracotta head lay on its side next to an apparently modern food bowl. All the terracotta fragments found were within 18 inches of the ground surface and appeared to have been brought together relatively recently. Beneath them was a shaft almost 14 feet deep which contained pottery and charcoal. It was about 3 feet 3 inches in diameter at the botton although the top was narrower than this. It was thought that this might have been a burial pit from which the bones had decayed away.

The shrine for Ogun Ladin was also investigated. This lies inside the palace, and a number of antiquities are still visible; a large wrought-iron block of pointed pear shape, a granite mudfish, and a quartz cylinder.[3] They were found to overlie a pavement of potsherds set on edge with a pot inserted in the middle and covered with a broken terracotta ram's head. This pavement was left undisturbed, but a small cutting was made at the back of the shrine which revealed another potsherd pavement 18 inches lower, although in some places the upper pavement was found to lie on bed-rock. The lower pavement was of better quality than the first with the sherds arranged radially.

These potsherd pavements, which were not noticed by Frobenius, were found to occur all over the town of Ifẹ. They are especially common in the Ogbon Oya quarter close to the palace. Small discs of pottery about an inch in diameter had been frequently observed in the area around potsherd pavements. Some of these fine sherds were discovered in position in Ogbon Oya quarter overlying pavements, set vertically as a top dressing, producing a corduroy surface. Many of the pavements in this quarter were protected with cement curbs, and in laying one of these, a member

[1] Illustrated in Willett, 1967a, pl. 21.
[2] Illustrated in Willett, 1967a, pl. 40, and in R. Hoeppli, *Parasitic Diseases in Africa and the Western Hemisphere*, Acta Tropica Supplementum 10 (Basel 1969), p. X and pp. 204–5.
[3] Illustrated in Frobenius, 1912, i, 329; 1913, p. 303; Willett, 1967a, pl. 72.

of the Department of Antiquities staff, Haruna Al Rashid, discovered another group of terracotta sculptures which included
two human heads, one naturalistic and the other very stylized,
similar to those already mentioned from Abiri.
Excavations were also carried out in the Grove of Olokun
Walode. This appears to be a subsidiary grove for Olokun,
goddess of wealth, worshipped by the Walode family. At a depth
of only a few inches, in the centre of the shrine, several fragments of
terracotta sculpture were found, all from different figures. A
fragmentary head of very great beauty was discovered, one of the
finest examples of the naturalistic style of Ifẹ art.[1] In contrast to
it, there was also found a very small head with grotesque ears as
large as its face.[2] This has a rather eroded surface whereas the
former head is almost as fresh as when it was made, despite the
fact that it has been broken. The other finds included the foot of a
bush cow, the left thighs of two different kneeling figures, a hand
holding a bowl, a right hand holding a cutlass, a large fragment of a
right foot, and about a dozen other fragments, some of them with
elaborate bead ornamentation. Their fragmentary nature and
varying conditions of preservation showed quite clearly that they
had been brought from elsewhere and placed together in this
shrine. A fragment of a glass-making crucible was found with them
and suggests the possibility that they had been originally found in
the Olokun Grove itself. Some inches below these fragments there
lay a much-eroded patch of potsherd pavement which had evidently become buried by the accumulation of soil some time
before the terracotta sculptures were laid in position. It was
thought likely that the fragments had been brought together at
some time in the nineteenth century during the reoccupation of
Ifẹ after one of the two evacuations caused by the Modakẹkẹ Wars.

Further work was done at the Olokun Grove itself during the
1953 season. The grove covers a very extensive area to the north of
Ifẹ and has been greatly disturbed apparently in the search for
beads. Many of the bell-shaped chambers which originally
composed it were located, and seventy well-shafts were dug in the
hope of locating an undisturbed chamber. This aim, however, was
not achieved, but Frobenius's suggestion that these chambers

---

[1] Illustrated in [Murray and Fagg], 1955, p. 4; Willett 1967a, pl. 31.
[2] Illustrated in B. E. B. Fagg, 1959, fig. 5.

were probably burial pits was regarded as being an entirely satisfactory interpretation.

Close to this grove, at Elesije, a chamber of similar type was also excavated. This and a vertical shaft beside it were both entirely filled with recent skeletons, some pottery, and a large number of modern beads. It was considered that this was a burial chamber of the Olokun Grove type which had been plundered and then reused for the burial of smallpox victims.

Some work was also done at the Iwinrin Grove which had already produced the large collection of terracotta figures of approximately life size that formed the core of the original collection in the Ifẹ Museum. A recent hut had been built in the grove to protect them, and the floor was found to contain many fragments of terracotta mixed with loose earth. A number of well-shafts were dug around the outside of the hut without any significant discoveries. William Fagg, however, working on the material from this grove was able to show that many of the fragments combined to make a fine terracotta stool group which is now regarded as one of the most important achievements of Ifẹ art. The central seated figure was later found to have been flanked by a pair of attendants of almost life size and possibly modelled as a single piece of terracotta. The group may well be the largest single terracotta object ever made in Africa.

During this season's excavations at the Iwinrin Grove, a disc of blue-green glass about $\frac{3}{4}$ inch in diameter with a red centre set in a strip of cuprous metal was found. Four more were found during the writer's excavations there in 1959. It now seems very likely that these are decorations from a wooden box stool which is the prototype of the circular stools in terracotta, in bronze and in stone in Ifẹ.[1] Further work conducted by the writer in 1959 also located a potsherd pavement close to the hut.

Whilst the excavations were proceeding in these various sites, Mr. Fagg also reconstructed the Ọpa Ọranmiyan after excavating the area around it. It was found that this stone column had originally been erected about 20 feet away from its present site though no burial pit was located. The excavation, therefore, refuted the tradition that the column marks the site of Ọranmiyan's grave. Behind the staff, however, there is a grove for Ọranmiyan con-

---

[1] See B. E. B. Fagg and W. B. Fagg, 1960; Willett, 1961c; 1967a, pp. 82-4.

taining a mound which has not been excavated. Of course, it is highly likely that Qranmiyan was not an individual but rather a mythical embodiment of the heroic spirit which inspired the Ifẹ in their days of expansion.[1] From the time of these excavations onwards, finds have been made all over Ifẹ and district and have regularly been brought into the Ifẹ Museum. The most spectacular of these was a group of brass castings found in November 1957, at Ita Yemoo. There were seven castings altogether: the figure of an Qni a little over 18 inches in height; a royal pair with their arms and legs interlocked just over 11 inches in height; an elaborate vessel less than 5 inches high in the form of a pot resting on a round stool with its loop supported on a rectangular stool and the figure of a queen curled round the pot holding a staff in her hand; two staffs of the type which she holds, just under a foot in length topped with human heads (one of them gagged); and finally two ovoid mace-heads, each bearing two gagged heads.[2] All these were in the usual naturalistic style of Ifẹ brass casting, but the proportions of the four human figures shown at full length reveal an important characteristic of African as opposed to European sculptural tradition, i.e. the head occupies a quarter of the overall height of the figure and the legs occupy considerably less than half. This confirmed the suggestion which William Fagg had originally made when he saw the fragmentary figure from Wunmonije Compound, that these would have been the proportions of that figure had it been complete.

Excavations showed that the brasses had lain on a potsherd pavement, but most of it had been destroyed by the labourers who had found them. Close by, however, within the foundation trenches of the building which was being erected, a complete pavement was revealed, which was preserved, as it was the first of these pavements ever to be found intact. Close to the original site where the brasses were found, another shrine was discovered which contained terracotta sculpture lying on a potsherd pavement. Much of this had been dug away in the building of two houses, one of which was later purchased and demolished and the fragments of sculpture recovered from inside the bricks. Much of the sculpture, however, is still missing and may be supposed to be inside the bricks of the

[1] This is discussed further in Willett, 1967a, pp. 124–5.
[2] These are illustrated in Willett, 1959b; c; 1967a, pls. 6, 9, 10, III–VI.

two-storey house which is still standing on the site. From the material which was discovered, it was quite clear that at least seven figures, mostly of about two-thirds life size, had been standing on this shrine. Apparently these had been complete until the shrine was abandoned. Their condition suggested that they had been exposed to the weather for a short time. Presumably they had originally stood in a mud-walled house and the thatched roof had been burnt off before the rain finally brought down the walls and the figures.[1]

It was discovered during the 1957–8 and 1958–9 seasons that the whole area around Ita Yemoo showed evidence of occupation, particularly in the form of potsherd pavements. Much of the site was purchased eventually as an archaeological reserve, but major excavations could not be undertaken until the department had acquired the land. It was finally possible to investigate further in 1962–3. The pavement found in 1957–8 had a depression at one corner which was investigated during this second main season. It was found that a large pit lay underneath it, though this did not seem to be the cause of the subsidence because a pavement made of quartz pebbles which lay 14 inches beneath the potsherd pavement was still perfectly level. The dip in the pavement had evidently been deliberately made. Charcoal from near the top of the pit gave a radiocarbon date of A.D. 1470 ± 100 (M-2117) whilst a sample from the bottom gave a date of A.D. 960 ± 130 (BM-261).

During this season, another shrine containing terracotta sculpture was located in the centre of an open courtyard with a paved veranda around it. This shrine contained parts of two sculptures, which appeared to have been already fragmentary at the time the site was abandoned.[2] Charcoal in the same layer yielded dates of A.D. 1060 ± 130 (BM-262) and A.D. 1150 ± 200 (M-2119) which encourage us to reject the fifteenth-century date from beneath the pavement just mentioned (as also does the twelfth-century date which accompanied sculptures over a pavement at Lafogido, quoted below: I-4911).

A trench 60 feet long and 8 feet wide was dug across the town wall in order to establish the relations between the occupation deposit at Ita Yemoo and what appeared at the time to be the only accurately dated antiquity. It was generally believed in Ifẹ that

---

[1] Willett, 1959c, provided an interim report in this season's work.
[2] Illustrated in Willett, 1967a, pl. 65.

the 'outer' town wall was constructed by the Ǫni Abeweila about 1848/9, but Ozanne has shown that the work of this Ǫni was confined to two short stretches of wall north and south of Modakękę.[1] The wall we sectioned, according to Ozanne, was first constructed during the second medieval phase and reconstructed during his second modern phase, though the excavation gave no evidence at all of two phases of construction. It was found that the ditch of the town wall was dug into hard natural clay and had convex sides. It had been kept repeatedly cleaned out which had made the bottom of the ditch very narrow and steep. The material which had been removed was redeposited on the outside of the wall where it overlay the old land surface in which the mounds of cultivation could easily be detected. Dug down from this surface was a well which provided a radiocarbon date of A.D. 850 ± 120 (M-2121) presumably due to the charcoal being already ancient when it was buried (a presumption which is supported by the analysis of the pottery which seems to be the oldest on the site; perhaps an old rubbish dump was used to fill in the well), for a nearby pit, which appeared from the stratigraphical evidence to be older, yielded a radiocarbon date of A.D. 1350 ± 100 (M-2120). It seemed likely that the top of the earthen bank was over twenty feet above the bottom of the ditch as originally constructed. There had been considerable disturbance in the central part of the bank, but it seemed to be an earthwork rather than a mud-brick wall. No sign of timber facing or strengthening was detected. The same land surface was found buried beneath the wall and deeper still another potsherd pavement was located which was overlain by what was probably the remains of the building in which the pavement had originally been constructed. Beneath this pavement was more occupation deposit, charcoal from which produced a radiocarbon date of A.D. 1160 ± 130 (BM-269). This layer corresponded to the one through which was cut the pit dated A.D. 1350 ± 100 (M-2120). These dates thus support each other. At a greater depth still there lay a small fragment of yet another pavement. Underneath this again was a large pit about 15 feet in diameter which had been cut into by the ditch. This was filled with alternate light and dark layers which might conceivably represent alternate dry and wet season rubbish. Near the base of this, a human skull was found. Whilst this pit was open, a well had been dug nearby; it was later cut through by the

[1] Ozanne, 1969.

ditch of the town wall. The complexity of the stratification of this trench afforded us a great deal of satisfaction. For a long time, it was feared that normal stratigraphy was not present in the archaeological deposits of Ifẹ. Certainly the upper levels showed very little differentiation. Even on this site, the soil above and below the potsherd pavements seemed to be hardly distinguishable.

Substantial samples of the potsherd pavements on this and many other sites in Ifẹ are being analysed for the evidence they may afford of the duration of the 'pavement period' of Ifẹ.[1] No evidence of maize impressions has been found in those from Ita Yemoo, which is in conformity with the radiocarbon dates. The earliest radiocarbon date, A.D. 850 ± 120 seems to come from earlier material from outside the excavated area, but the pit dated A.D. 1350 ± 100 cuts through a deposit dated A.D. 1160 ± 130, which itself underlies a pavement, whilst a date of A.D. 960 ± 130 underlay another. These dates, however, conflict with the date of A.D. 1470 ± 100 which for the moment has to be regarded as anomalous. Over the pavement, and representing the date of abandonment of the shrine with terracotta sculptures already old, broken and incomplete, we have dates of A.D. 1060 ± 130 and A.D. 1150 ± 200. The main activity on the site thus appears to have been from the tenth to the fourteenth centuries A.D., the wall itself having been constructed later than the fourteenth century. The classical period of naturalistic Ifẹ sculpture is thus confirmed as being earlier than the first European contacts, and possibly having begun several centuries earlier.

During 1958–9, a football pitch was laid out at the Catholic Mission in Ifẹ, and this in turn revealed more potsherd pavements, one of which was at that time unique although similar ones have been found since. It consisted of a pavement laid out with rows of potsherds set on edge forming rectangles, the spaces in between being set with quartz pebbles.[2] This pavement too has been preserved. A cutting here revealed for the first time that the town wall had been constructed after the collapse of the houses containing potsherd pavements. The most interesting find was a grave overlaid with very many cooking pots (iṣasun) with groups of cowrie shells interspersed among them. The bowls had probably contained food although no traces of this remained. They were of a

---

[1] Some of the basic problems involved are discussed in Willett, 1967b.
[2] Illustrated in Willett, 1960, pl. VIII; 1967a, pl. 66, figs. 16, 17.

black ware with incised decoration similar in character to the fine wares from Old Ọyọ, a tradition which continues in the modern pottery of Ilọrin. The burial was probably the head of a family from Old Ọyọ who had settled in Modakẹkẹ and whose family continued to bring offerings to his grave.

The extent and distribution of the potsherd pavements to which we have made frequent allusion (they have been found at distances of up to four miles from the centre of the town) make it quite clear that at the time that these pavements were made, Ifẹ was a far more extensive town than it now is. By the mid-nineteenth century, when the town walls reached their present form, the city had almost certainly contracted to within these limits although there may well have been some hardy folk who still continued to live outside its protection.

Before we had radiocarbon dates, most of the dating evidence for Ifẹ came from Benin where the oral traditions refer to the introduction of brass casting from Ifẹ towards the end of the fourteenth century. It was, therefore, considered worthwhile to investigate a site in Ifẹ which has very strong connections with Benin, namely *Ọrun Ọba Ado*. It is from this site that Ọranmiyan is reputed to have set out to found the Yoruba dynasty in Benin, and it is to here that the heads of the kings of Benin were brought for burial. One of the late Dr. R. E. Bradbury's informants accompanied the head of King Adolo when it was brought from Benin to Ifẹ in 1888, the last occasion on which the tradition was kept. Towards the end of the dry season of 1960–1, preliminary investigations on the site located eleven pits which appeared to have been intended for the burial of these heads. At the end of the year, in the ensuing dry season, two trenches were laid out so that six of the pits could be totally excavated.[1] An interesting series of pottery was discovered, some of it unlike any that had been previously found in Ifẹ, but no signs of the heads of the kings were located although some animal bones were recovered. It seems very probable that only nail parings and hair clippings from the corpse were taken to Ifẹ for burial. One of the pits (no. 1) had been sealed in with a small potsherd pavement whilst a fragment of a terracotta sculpture of a recumbent animal, possibly a cow (though the head was broken off, so we cannot be sure) was recovered from the top filling of

---

[1] A photograph of some of these pits is printed upside-down in the *Annual Report* of the Department of Antiquities for 1958–62, p. 59.

another pit. Charcoal from this site has produced the following sequence of dates:

Pit XI: A.D. 560 ± 130 (BM-265);
Pit III: A.D. 800 ± 120 (M-2114);
Pit V: A.D. 800 ± 120 (M-2115);
Pit VI: A.D. 940 ± 150 (M-2116);
Pit VI: A.D. 990 ± 130 (BM-264).

These suggest that the site was in use earlier than Ita Yemoo, an interpretation which is supported by the conspicuous differences in the pottery from the two sites.

Several other sites have been investigated in Ifẹ, usually aimed at discovering the context from which pieces brought into the museum were recovered. One of these was behind number 3, Iyekere Street in Ifẹ where a bronze D-shaped pendant plaque was discovered.[1] This was in the Benin style and had clearly been imported from there. The discovery was not reported to the museum until twenty years afterwards, but an excavation was conducted here which showed that, assuming the memory of the finder was accurate, it had been deposited in the late nineteenth century.

Working from the University of Ifẹ, the late Oliver Myers undertook two excavations in Ifẹ. The first was at Igbo Obameri near the Mokuro Road close to Ita Yemoo. Here inside a grove are the remains of mud buildings which had formerly been a temple. In front of one stood a stone column dedicated to Ogun although it was evidently set in the ground upside-down. Myers examined this and found that the original tip had been broken off. Presumably this accounts for its inversion. In the principal room of the shrine, there was a mound of earth in which were found a large number of fragments of many different terracotta sculptures which had probably at some time in the past been found in other contexts and brought into this shrine for safe keeping and perhaps worship.[2] A radiocarbon date of A.D. 1730 ± 100 (M-1686) has been furnished by the University of Michigan for charcoal which underlay the shrine and appears to come from an earlier occupation of the whole area. This figure must be construed as referring to the earlier occupation rather than to the time of construction of the

---

[1] Illustrated in Willett, 1967a, pl. 90.
[2] A particularly unusual piece is illustrated in Willett, 1967a, pl. 67 and fig. 5.

shrine although it appears to come from material incorporated in its walls.[1]

Myers's second excavation was at Oduduwa College, Ifẹ, where at the beginning of 1966, a workman digging to enlarge the fish-pond found a terracotta head. In clearing the area for excavation, another terracotta head was found in the side of an old spoil pit. A number of potsherd pavements were located which showed that there must have been a series of buildings along the side of the stream which had been dammed to produce the fish-ponds. The location of the site, just outside the town walls and down the slope from them, suggests that there may well be a substantial accumulation of occupation material because the central part of Ifẹ is subject to great erosion, and at the foot of a slope, there is more likely to be aggradation. Furthermore, since the site is close to an old stream, it is very likely to be waterlogged and affords the possibility that organic remains may be preserved. It is hoped that this promising site will be investigated further.[2]

In 1969, Ekpo Eyo excavated a shrine at Lafogido immediately behind the Palace in the centre of Ifẹ, and according to tradition, the burial-place of the Ọni Lafogido, the first ọni to break the tradition of burial outside the city wall at Igbo Odi. The site consisted of a number of terracotta sculptures, of animal heads placed upon globular water-pots set in rows opposed to each other on the edges of a rectangular potsherd pavement. A radiocarbon date of A.D. 1110 ± 95 (I-4911) was obtained from charcoal overlying the pavement. During the same season's work, Eyo investigated the site of discovery of a fine classical head at Odo Ogbe Street in the Ilare quarter of the town. The head seemed to have been placed there around A.D. 1630 ± 95 (I-4669) after discovery elsewhere, but beneath the site he located grave pits containing human bones. Charcoal from the bottom of one pit furnished a radiocarbon date of A.D. 1095 ± 90 (I-4670).[3]

In 1951 Eyo had assisted Miss L. V. Hodgson in the excavation of a site at Apomu Forest Reserve, ten miles south of Ondo which produced a unique series of sculptures which he has described and

---

[1] Myers's interim report, 1967a, should be read in conjunction with letters from J. B. Griffin and F. Willett in *The West African Archaeological Newsletter*, vii, (1967), 4–6.

[2] Interim report is Myers, 1967b.

[3] Eyo, 1970a and b. I am grateful to Mr. Eyo for his permission to quote these dates from his letter to the author dated 28 July 1970.

illustrated.[1] They have some affinity to certain highly stylized heads which are contemporary with the classical Ifẹ naturalistic sculptures. The Apomu site has not been dated. However, the contemporaneity of the highly stylized and the naturalistic sculptures in Ifẹ itself is confirmed by the fact that at a site near Abategba, fourteen miles from Ifẹ along the Ondo road, a group of evidently late pieces includes crude copies of both styles.[2] Ọmọtọsọ Eluyẹmi excavated two sites in 1960 at Egbejoda which have produced no less than 75 terracotta heads in a post-Classical style, together with a few pieces which resemble those from Apomu, which is probably, therefore to be considered post-Classical too. No report on the site has been published at the time of writing.

In view of the importance of Ifẹ in Yoruba tradition and quite clearly in the art history of West Africa as a whole, it is perhaps not surprising that most of the archaeological work that has been done in Yorubaland has been concentrated there. Only three other Yoruba sites have received any excavation, Ọwọ, Old Ọyọ[3] and Ilesha. (Other excavations have been conducted within the area of Yorubaland, but these have been on sites of Stone Age date entirely, and so are not relevant to the present discussion.)

In 1970 Chief J. D. Akeredolu reported that a surveyor had dug up some fragments of terracotta sculpture at Egberen Street in Ọwọ, some hundred miles from Ifẹ by modern road, and eighty from Benin. The modern culture of Ọwọ is basically Yoruba but shows an evident overlay of Benin features. Many of the ivory carvings from Benin were carved by Ọwọ artists so the influence seems to have been mutual. The sculptures excavated at the site by Ekpo Eyo early in 1971,[4] show strong affinities with the naturalistic art of Classical Ifẹ, but have emphases which relate also to Benin. Especially remarkable are the sculptures of a crouched leopard with a human leg in its mouth and of a basket filled with the heads of human sacrificial victims. Radiocarbon dating confirms that they belong to the time when the technique of bronze casting is reputed to have been introduced to Benin from Ifẹ.[5]

[1] Eyo, 1968.
[2] Willett, 1967a, pp. 66–7, pls. 55, 56, where the site is referred to as 'Ondo Road'.
[3] Frobenius, 1949, p. 104, mentions employing people to excavate in the ruins of Old Ọyọ, but he has left no record.
[4] See Eyo, 1972.
[5] See Willett 1967a and 1970a.

The investigations which I conducted at Old Ọyọ in 1956–7 were of an essentially preliminary nature. The first purpose was to establish whether or not this was the site visited by Lander and Clapperton, whether indeed it was Old Ọyọ. Most of the effort was expended in surveying the site and discovering its nature, relatively little excavation being undertaken. The site of the Mejiro Cave was excavated, and a deep layer of Yoruba occupation material was found to overlie a microlithic stone industry of pre-Yoruba date.[1] A section through the remains of a compound close to the palace had to be abandoned when the water supply finally dried up. In addition, a number of well-shafts were dug in the search for water to extend our time on the site, and the material from these was kept as archaeological evidence. A great deal of surface collecting was also undertaken so that we have a large series of pottery from Old Ọyọ which has turned out to be of great value. One type of pottery, very characteristic of Old Ọyọ, I have described as fine grey/black ware.[2] Pottery of this type has been found on all the other sites where I have conducted investigations providing an effective dating horizon approximating to the time of the collapse of Old Ọyọ when refugees spread out all over Yorubaland taking their pottery traditions with them. At the site in the palace at Ilesha, one of our first indications of date was a large fragment of pot of a type which could be interpreted as having been developed from the fine grey/black ware of Old Ọyọ.[3] Later we were able to get confirmation of the date of the site as being approximately the third quarter of the nineteenth century which bore out the interpretation based on the pottery. An investigation is in progress at the moment on a series of examples of pottery of this type from Old Ọyọ itself and from several other sites to determine the composition of the clay so that we may establish whether or not the sherds represent pots which were traded from Old Ọyọ or whether they were made locally in the Old Ọyọ tradition by refugees. The other fine-quality ware from Old Ọyọ I have called the 'Diogun ware. This has a sandy paste, is fawny-grey to brown in colour, and is very well fired and quite hard, though the surface is not burnished. The decoration of this

---

[1] Reported by Willett: The microlithic industry from Old Ọyọ, Western Nigeria, *Actes du IVᵉ congrès panafricain de préhistoire et de l'étude du quaternaire* (Tervuren, 1962), ii, 261–72.

[2] Willett, 1961b, p. 76 and fig. 8.

[3] Willett, 1961a, p. 9.

pottery consists of impressed triangles forming a variety of raised zigzag motifs. The forms of these pots are particularly beautiful, especially some complex fluted rims which are very characteristic.[1] This type of pottery, however, has not been discovered outside of Old Ọyọ. There are in addition coarse wares which are less helpful in our study of cultural contact between one site and another. The two styles of fine ware, however, are so very different and distinctive that it almost suggests that there were two different populations at Old Ọyọ. Whilst this is not impossible, it is perhaps more likely that two phases of occupation are represented. All the fragments of 'Diogun ware were recovered by surface collecting, but since there has been extensive erosion at Old Ọyọ, it is possible that these wares represent the earlier occupation of the city before its evacuation to Igboho, and that the fine grey/black ware was developed only after the return. We cannot answer this without further excavations at Old Ọyọ itself and also at Igboho.

In 1959, workmen, levelling the ground to build the Post Office telephone exchange in an area that had formerly been part of the palace in the centre of Ilesha, disturbed a deposit containing a number of sculptures in fired clay. We cannot call them strictly terracotta because they had not been fired to the consistency of pottery, and are, moreover, solid. Mr. Ulli Beier drew my attention to this site, and a hurried investigation was made on the day before I had to proceed on leave. In October, the site was excavated. A large pit was revealed containing about 200 sculptures. Some were representations of whole figures in a squatting position; others represented merely heads. They were usually on bases shaped like a Christmas pudding. In many cases, these bases alone made without any sculptures were found, and there were other types which had the same form as many of the heads without having the face indicated. Occasionally these objects were sculpted as heads without any base. Where human characters were shown, the style resembled modern Yoruba sculpture. The eyes were globular and bulging with the eyelid clearly indicated; the lips flat and protrusive; the ears composed of a flat disc with a small knob at one edge representing the tragus.[2] A number of pieces from Ifẹ

---

[1] Willett 1961b, p. 75 and fig. 7.
[2] Willett, 1961a illustrates the different types. See also Willett, 1967a, pl. 107 and fig. 40, and *Annual Report* of the Department of Antiquities (1958–62), p. 65. A detailed excavation report is almost complete.

have been found which appear to show a stylistic progression in the direction of Yoruba sculpture, and there are two figures in the Ifẹ grove of Igbodio which are in a style very similar to the Ilesha pieces.[1] These sculptures form a link between the art of classical Ifẹ and modern Yoruba sculpture for the Ilesha sculptures belong to the period of time from which we have well-documented pieces in museum collections, the third quarter of the nineteenth century. What we now need are links in the other direction to show us how the naturalism of classical Ifẹ arose. It seems to have come from the same sculptural tradition as that of Nok, but the details of this evolution are still obscure.[2]

The labourers had removed the mound which had covered the upper part of the Ilesha site, and, in consequence, the relationship between the mound and the various pits composing the site and to some extent between the pits themselves had been obscured by this removal of the upper levels. Beneath the pit containing the sculptures, a grave was found with traces of a human skeleton. Beside the first pit was another, 7 feet deep from the surface to which the site had been levelled. This pit contained dark brown clay which had clearly been thrown in by the basketful and may have been a storage pit for clay for the manufacture of the figures. Another pit, oval in plan and expanding at the bottom, cut through this brown clay. This turned out to be a royal grave pit. The king was a very tall, powerfully built man of about forty. He wore a necklace of blue glass (sẹgi) and red stone (okun) beads. On his left forearm, he wore a massive bronze bracelet and eleven thinner bracelets on his right forearm. Beside him were two iron daggers with bronze fittings; the wooden handle of one survived on which one could easily see knot-work carving. The king's head had been very carefully removed after death and placed on his chest. With him in the grave were two men, two women, and two individuals aged between thirteen and seventeen whose sex could not be determined, and three children between six and twelve. Individual bones of some of the skeletons were scattered about the grave pit so it is clear that these people were not buried

[1] Illustrated in Willett, 1967a, pl. 108.
[2] The most recent discussion of the problem is in Willett, 1967a, pp. 119–28, where it is related to the question of the origins of the Yoruba themselves. The site of Yelwa RS 63/32 has produced terracotta sculptures which may be offshoots of the Nok tradition, associated with radiocarbon dates of the first to seventh centuries (C. T. Shaw, *Antiquity*, xliii, (1969), 196).

alive with the ọba. Several of them wore bronze bracelets and beads, and in the grave we discovered not only pots but an ivory trumpet, cowrie shells, and some bones of a goat or sheep. Since this grave cut through the pit containing the brown clay, it must be younger than the clay pit. A discussion with the late Ọwa of Ijesha and his chiefs revealed that only two ọwas had been buried in the palace, Atakunmọsa and his son Ggẹgbaje. Their reigns were calculated as having been around the third quarter of the nineteenth century so that the rest of the site must have preceded this, though the pottery associated with the fired-clay sculptures suggests that they were not much earlier than the burial of the owa.

FUTURE WORK

The excavation at Ilesha provides an example of the way in which historical evidence in the form of oral tradition can be of help to the archaeologist. Without such evidence to furnish dates, the archaeologist of the recent past would be in considerable difficulty. Similarly where normal historical resources are limited or incomplete, archaeology can be of great value in filling in the gaps for the historian. Indeed the area of Yorubaland offers us a very rich field of co-operation between archaeologists and historians.[1]

One pressing problem that confronts us both is that of the origin of the various elements which compose Yoruba culture. How much of it was due to outside influence, and how much of it was invented and developed locally is a problem which cannot be easily answered. It is my personal belief that we should make far more searching investigations inside Yorubaland before we start to discuss too deeply the questions of outside origins or influences. Where we work in areas of relative ignorance, it is only too easy to turn to fields of knowledge and presume that characteristics we find in our less well-known areas must have come from the better-known areas where they have already been described. This tendency has caused many characteristics of African culture, especially the institution of divine kingship, to be traced back to ancient Egypt. However, in our ignorance of dates for features of West African culture, it is not difficult to argue the opposite case, that a great deal of Egyptian culture had its origins in Africa south of the Sahara. Without a chronological framework in which these

[1] This has been discussed Willett, 1969.

possible connections can be fitted, there is no point in wasting effort in wild surmise. What is needed first of all is a chronological framework. Only then can we possibly make estimates of the direction of cultural influence.[1]

Clearly, archaeologists and historians share this need for a chronology in many areas. Some of the most interesting aspects of Yoruba history are known to us only from oral tradition; indeed in the case of the foundation of Ifẹ itself and the traditional stories of the gods who lived there in the early days, it would be more accurate to speak of myth. Here there are no external sources which can furnish even a skeleton chronology for the historian; archaeology alone can find the answers. The archaeologist should normally be able to establish the date of the foundation of a site and the sequence and duration of its occupation. In large cities like those of Yorubaland, however, he is faced with a very difficult problem for he needs to excavate extensively if he is to discover, for example, the ancient town plan, and yet the greater part, if not the whole, of his site will be covered by modern buildings. This, of course, makes the search for the earliest deposits a very chancy matter. In Ifẹ itself, we have found only 6 to 8 inches of occupation material below the level of the potsherd pavements, except where ancient pits have been dug, yet the radiocarbon dates indicate that Ifẹ was occupied by A.D. 800 if not from A.D. 560.

Even the interpretation of European documents is fraught with difficulty. Alan Ryder[2] suggested that the Ifẹ where we have been conducting our excavations, although it is known as Ile Ifẹ (the home Ifẹ), is not the Ifẹ referred to by D'Aveiro but a later one. In July 1967, I attempted to locate possible earlier sites of Ifẹ. I visited two in Kabba Division, Oke Ifẹ and Ifẹ Odo which are adjacent to each other. The traditions I collected there made it quite clear that their founder came from Ile Ifẹ though I was unable to establish just how long ago. These sites would in any case, be suitable for excavation, which might demonstrate the date of their foundation although a longer investigation of the oral tradition might well be as rewarding. These towns are roughly

[1] A very cogent discussion of this general problem is H. S. Lewis, 'Ethnology and Culture History', in C. Gabel and B. R. Bennett, *Reconstructing African Culture History* (Boston, 1967). The question of the relationship between Egyptian art and that of the rest of Africa is discussed in Willett, 1971a, pp. 109–14.

[2] 'A reconsideration of the Ifẹ–Benin relationship', *J.A.H.*, vi, (1965), 25–37.

north of Benin and not east as they need to be to fit Ryder's hypothesis. I also visited the Ifẹ in Igala close to Abejukolo. Here the brother of the reigning *onu* was very well informed about the succession of the *onus* there. It was quite clear that the occupation of that site had begun only in the middle of the eighteenth century. No reference was made at all to Ile Ifẹ, but they claimed to have come from another Ifẹ beyond the Benue. This one I have not been able to locate, but the evidence that I have collected neither confirms nor refutes Ryder's hypothesis. There may conceivably be an older Ifẹ where the art objects of the classical period were made and from which they were brought to Ile Ifẹ, but their vast numbers and now the radiocarbon dates make this highly improbable.[1] We are however examining the local sources of clay to see whether it is possible to demonstrate that the terracotta sculptures or the cores of the brass-castings were locally made. In any case it is quite clear that there is an abundance of data still to be recovered from the soil in Ile Ifẹ.

These are early days yet in the investigation of the history of Yorubaland. Archaeological distribution maps in West Africa still show the distribution of effort by individual archaeologists rather than that of ancient cultures. As time goes on, many of the blank areas will be filled in, and we may look forward to a much more fruitful period of interpretation. The investigation of the recent past will probably call for a new breed of archaeologist and historian; he will be trained in both disciplines, an archaeologist who can use oral tradition, a historian who can undertake excavations. By introducing archaeology into history courses in African universities, it should be possible to build up an élite scattered throughout the country who will be interested in their own past and able to record and survey the antiquities of their own areas. Since many of the graduates of Nigerian universities will be returning to teach in schools, they in turn will be able to encourage similar interests among the young people of the country. In this way, the general public will be educated to the need to preserve antiquities, and we may look forward to the day when little or no historical evidence is destroyed without being adequately recorded. But long before that millennium is reached, we must pass from the stage of merely collecting data to that of interpreting them, for, as Sir Mortimer Wheeler has told us, 'archaeology and

[1] See Willett, 1970a.

history are alike frustrate unless they contribute to the vital *reconstruction of Man's past achievement*, in other words aspire to interpretation as well as to mere transliteration.'[1]

[1] *Alms for Oblivion, An Antiquary's Scrapbook* (London, 1966), p. 115. Italics are in the original.

CHAPTER IX
Art in Metal

DENIS WILLIAMS

IRON

This stone was the anvil of Lade, the smith. Lade was the mightiest smith of the past. When he died Ogun changed all his tools to stone. The stone in the Ọni's palace is Lade's anvil, and its name is Ogun-Lade. It was washed out of the earth in a season of rains at the exact time when the Koran was brought to the land.[1]

Like many other heathen nations the Yoruba have their traditions about the creation and the deluge. It is their belief that at the creation men fed on wood and water, that they had a long projecting mouth, that the bat was originally a creature in human form and was a blacksmith by trade, and that with his instrument he reduced men's mouths to their present shape, for which cause he was condemned to lose the human form and to assume that of a beast.[2]

Sokoti Alagbẹdẹ Ọrun was a spirit who dwelled in heaven and was expelled for bad works and condemned to dwell thereafter among men. He became a blacksmith.[3]

THE meteoric sources of early iron led the Egyptians to regard the metal as imbued with the blasting powers of the thunderbolt— expressed in their mortuary rite of the Opening of the Mouth.[4] Among the Yoruba exists a traditional relationship between Ṣango —the *oriṣa* of thunder and lightning, and Ogun—the *oriṣa* of war and of iron; the thunder-axe is used in the cult worship of Ṣango as well as of Ogun. When lightning strikes a village the dispossessed must seek refuge in a blacksmith's forge.[5] In the tradition recorded by Frobenius the Ogun-Lade, like those stone celts which the thunder-god hurls during his visits among men, was 'washed out of the earth'. We have no evidence that meteoric iron was ever

[1] L. Frobenius, *The Voice of Africa*, vol. i (London, 1913), p. 302.
[2] S. Johnson, *The History of the Yorubas* (Lagos, 1921), p. 35.
[3] An Oṣogbo tradition collected by the author.
[4] G. A. Wainwright, 'The Coming of Iron', *Antiquity*, x, 11.
[5] S. Johnson, op. cit., p. 35.

used by the Yoruba as it was in other parts of the continent. The association of Ogun with the thunder-axe might more plausibly be connected with the apparently prior appellative of the *oriṣa*—god of war, indicating perhaps a neolithic weaponry before the coming of iron, an idea seemingly borne out by the persistent worship of this *oriṣa* in stone, by the conversion of iron into stone in Frobenius's myth from Ifẹ, by the propitiation of Ogun in Ọyọ kingship ritual,[1] and by the tradition in which Ogun is remembered only as a warrior.[2] The second myth stresses the revolutionary role of iron in food production and the commonweal, and here we might note its significance among forest peoples in supplementing an inherent protein deficiency in their food of starchy roots, while the third underlines the divine origin of the smith, a tradition which perhaps acknowledges the foreign origin of iron. These traditions, and particularly the association with the thunder-god, Ṣango, whose double-axe motif recalls a complex of lightning and thunder myths of Mediterranean antiquity, suggest for the apotheosis of Ogun as god of war a period well before the coming of iron—a period in which, as the fiery *oriṣa* of destruction, the Yoruba peoples embodied in him such concepts of natural energy—impersonal devastation, superhuman destruction—as they had previously symbolized by the double axe in Ṣango, the terrible third *Alafin* of Ọyọ.

So it seems likely that the coming of iron was apprehended among the Yoruba within a pre-existing *oriṣa* system in which the potency of the unfamiliar metal was explained in terms of the blasting powers of the thunder-axe of the *oriṣa* Ṣango, whose thunder mythology and its associated iconography in the janus-headed thunder-axe and in the sacred ram might well in turn be of Nilotic and Mediterranean antiquity. Most renderings of the *oṣe Ṣango* are in wood, though examples occur too in brass and in iron. For the iconography of the thunderbolt sign as it arose in prehistoric Egypt, its development through Pharaonic times as the names of the sky-god, Min, his relationship with Amun, Zeus, and sky-gods in Asia Minor, Wainwright gives a full picture.[3] He does not distinguish separate symbols for the lightning and

---

[1] Ibid., p. 45.
[2] At Ire village, his 'home'.
[3] G. A. Wainwright, 'The Emblem of Min', *Jour. Egyptian Archaeology* (1931), 185 ff.

thunder attributes of these gods; among the Yoruba Wescott and Morton-Williams describe an independent lightning-motif associated with the *laba Ṣango*.[1] A connection between the thunderbolt and the iron deity among the Greeks is indicated in the myth in which Zeus, worshipped in the thunderbolt, gave birth to Hephaestus the blacksmith god—one of the twelve great gods of Olympus; and Palmer relates the name of the petty market-broker of the Hausa, Dan Baranda, who 'faces both ways' to make a living by battening on buyer and seller alike, to the Greek deity of ancient Crete, Zeus Labrandeus. Both names come from the sacred double-headed axe which by the Hausa is called *Barandami*.[2]

The iconography of the double-headed axe in the Ṣango cult-sculpture of the Yoruba thus suggests a cultural context of Nilotic and Mediterranean antiquity; its thunder associations in the worship of Ogun indicate that the coming of iron among the Yoruba was apprehended in a pre-existing *orişa* system in which impersonal natural energy had been symbolized in the fiery nature of their tempestuous third *Alafin*.

The Coming of Iron among the Yorubas

On presumptive evidence only Mauny dates the coming of iron to the Western Sudan at *c.* 300 B.C.,[3] and the date is repeated by Goody and others though it cannot confidently be established even for the Meroë, which we know to have been smelting during the first century B.C.[4] It is possible that smelting technique might have diffused from Meroë to East and West Africa, and a degree of material evidence seems to support the hypothesis, but iron-

---

[1] J. Wescott and P. Morton-Williams, 'The Symbolism and Ritual Context of the Yoruba Laba Ṣango', *Jour. Royal Anthr. Inst.*, xcii, pt. 1 (Jan.–June 1962).

[2] Sir Richmond Palmer, *The Bornu Sahara and Sudan* (London, 1936), p. 2.

[3] R. Mauny, 'Histoire des metaux en Afrique occidentale', *Bull. IFAN*, xiv, no. 11 (1952), 578.

[3] An unsupported antiquity is sometimes claimed for this industry; see A. J. Arkell, *A History of the Sudan to 1821* (London, 1961), p. 130, who suggests that iron might have been worked in the Sudan before it was worked in Egypt; the industry is dated to 700 B.C. by L. Aitcheson, *A History of Metals* (1960), p. 137; is claimed to have antedated that of Egypt, R. Forbes, *Studies in Ancient Technology*, viii (Leiden, 1964), p. 121; and even that it was the source of Egyptian knowledge, T. A. Rickard, *Jour. Royal Anthr. Inst.* lxxi (1941). None of these claims has any foundation in evidence. Certain temples of the palace of Amanishakete, 45–12 B.C., are erected on mounds of iron slag which might have strewn the Meroitic landscape for considerable periods before her reign, and iron objects excavated at this site speak for a mature industry, but firm earlier dates are still wanting.

smelting among the Yoruba appears to be much more clearly related to influences exercised across the Sahara at a date unlikely to have affected the Western Sudan much before the first century A.D.[1] The Nok culture of Northern Nigeria is at present thought to have been working iron between 500 B.C. and A.D. 200[2] and Mauny believes that by A.D. 500 the knowledge had come to affect most areas of the Guinea forest.[3] On the basis of oral tradition a similar date has been proposed for the Congo.[4] Yoruba connection with Saharan-born iron techniques is exemplified in the design of the typical iron-smelting furnace of Western Nigeria. This is a domed furnace of identical design to furnaces occurring elsewhere within the great triangle described by the buckle of the Niger and the Guinea littoral, and nowhere else in tropical Africa (fig. 1). Such a furnace was still in use among the Koranko of Sierra Leone in 1920, where it was recorded by Dixey.[5] In Upper Guinea it was recorded by Campbell in 1910,[6] along the course of the Upper Niger by Desplagnes in 1907,[7] among the Mossi of Upper Volta in 1937 by Francis-Boeuf,[8] and in Ashanti by Wild in 1931.[9] The Sierra Leone type was described as long ago as 1825 by Laing.[10] Until about 1925

[1] The evidence lies in the comparative study of furnace designs. A 'Meroitic' type is widespread throughout tropical Africa to as far south as Zambia, and covering all West Africa. Arkell believes that Christian Beja from the Bayuda desert (Sudan Republic) might have introduced iron-working in the Ennedi hills where he excavated an iron-smelting furnace. A. J. Arkell, *Wanyanga* (Oxford 1964), p. 15. The north-south route may have carried the domed furnace of the Late European Iron Age inherited by the Romans from the La Tene Celts. See ch. XI, 'Iron and the Gods', of my forthcoming book *Icon and Image—A Study of Sacred and Secular Forms in African Classical Art*.

[2] B. E. B. Fagg, 'Radiocarbon Dates for the Nok Culture', *Africa*, xxxv (Jan. 1965). For iron at Nok see B. Fagg, *Man*, July 56: 95.

[3] R. Mauny, *Tableau géographique de l'ouest africain au moyen age*, IFAN (Dakar, 1961), p. 315.

[4] G. A. Wainwright,: 'Pharaonic Survivals between Lake Chad and the West Coast', *Jour. Egyptian Archaeology*, xxxv (1949).

[5] F. Dixey, 'Primitive Iron Ore Smelting Methods in West Africa', *The Mining Magazine* (Oct. 1920), 213.

[6] J. M. Campbell, 'Native Iron Smelting in Haute-Guinée', *Inst. Mining and Metallurgy*, no. 7.

[7] L. Desplagnes, *Le Plateau Central Nigerian* (Paris, 1907), fig. 165.

[8] L. Francis-Boeuf, 'L'Industrie Autochthone du Fer', *Bull. Com. D'Etudes Hist. et Scientifiques de L'A.O.F.*, xx (1937), 404, 464.

[9] R. Wild, 'An Unusual Type of Primitive Iron-Smelting Furnace at Abomposu, Ashanti', *Gold Coast Review*, ii, no. 5 (1931). See also, R. J. Forbes, *Geog. Review*, no. 23 (1933), 234.

[10] A. G. Laing, *Travels in the Timanee, Kooranko, and Soolima Countries in Western Africa* (London, 1825), fig. 107.

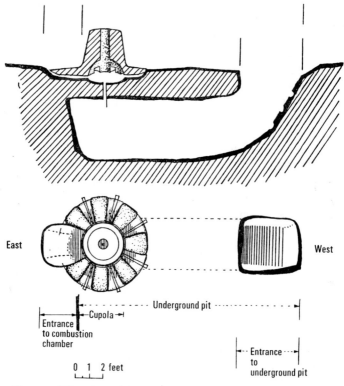

East

West

Underground pit

Cupola

Entrance
to combustion
chamber

0 1 2 feet

Entrance
to
underground pit

FIG. 1. The domed furnace, Isundunrin, Western Nigeria.

batteries of this domed furnace provided centres of extensive iron-
working among the Yoruba at sites which determine the most
easterly distribution of the design, but already at the end of the
nineteenth century the industry had begun to die out: 'here and
there all over the country the furnaces are being closed, and soon
will doubts begin to be expressed as to whether Yorubas ever knew
the art of smelting iron from the ores.'[1] A correspondent to a Lagos
newspaper of 1904 was astounded to discover the existence of the
industry not far from Ọyọ:

'Sir, I wonder if anyone in Lagos ever heard of this wonderful industry,
for I am pretty certain that no one has ever visited these works and
watched the process of burning common stone into iron. It was my
privilege last week, by permission of the Aremo, to visit the village where

[1] S. Johnson, op. cit., pp. 119 ff.

the largest iron-works of the Yoruba country are carried on. There are eleven furnaces in full blast, and a staff of one hundred men, women and boys engaged in this work. . . .' ¹

In the same year Bellamy published a scientific description of an Ọyọ iron industry.² The present author was unable to locate this site by name but it is possible that it might be the same as that described in the *Lagos Weekly Record*. In the village of Laagbe just outside Ọyọ still stand today the ruins of several domed furnaces overgrown by thick bush; these may well be the remains of the 'eleven furnaces in full blast' which at the turn of the century needed some hundred men to keep them going. The following description of the Laagbe site is from the author's field notebook dated 25 November 1964:

The furnace is situated in the bush about ten minutes walk from Laagbe village, which is itself about twenty miles from Ọyọ. The site is clearly marked off a narrow bush-track by a grove of sere-sere trees which have grown up where the ironworkers' cottages originally stood. A thick carpet of leaves covered any traces that might yet remain of iron slag, tuyères, etc. The furnace itself is badly ruined; nothing remains of it but a portion of the combustion chamber, about three feet high. This appears to be the original height judging from the curvature of the inside of the cupola, though persons present claimed it was higher. Vent holes and counterports have vanished or are buried in the soil, though native descriptions define a structure exactly like that of Isundunrin 1, the entrance to the underground gallery being about 16 feet from the counterports (Isundunrin 1, 15 feet). Three house-posts still stand on the north side. A few feet away on this side are remains of a large (10 foot diameter) storage bin where charcoal was kept during the smelt. This appears to have stood outside the building. The 'eleven furnaces' mentioned in the *Lagos Weekly Record* of 5 March 1904 are said by local inhabitants to be scattered over some area, now mostly bush, or to have been destroyed in the layout of the nearby Government Agricultural Scheme; others might have perished at the hands of hunters fearful of their harbouring snakes.

The name Ọla Igbe mentioned by Bellamy would seem to have been contracted over the years to Laagbe, the present name. Later at Ọyọ, the daughter of the old iron-worker was found, a woman of some sixty odd years. Specimens of the best iron produced in the industry are still

¹ *Lagos Weekly Record*, 5 Mar. 1904. (Univ. Ibadan Library, bound with *Lagos Standard*.)

² C. V. Bellamy, 'A West African Smelting House, with Analysis of Specimens by W. F. Harboard', *Jour. Iron and Steel Industry*, lxvi, no. 2 (1904), 99–126.

preserved in her family's Ogun shrine along with the staff of the *Alagbẹdẹ* and smaller Ogun (anthropomorphic) staff. The larger staff, about four feet high, is non-figurative. Smelted iron still held in the shrine appeared more purely metallic than other examples of local iron I have examined. The old woman claimed that in the old days her family-works supplied Ọyọ, Iwo, and Ibadan with iron. The family came originally from Ogbomọṣọ.

Without being requested to do so she then described the main points in the design of the furnace and in the processes of smelting. Her account, naturally, was more descriptive of the part women played—pounding the ore, washing it in the river, bearing it to the furnace—in exactly the detail recorded for them by Bellamy. A smelt took a day and a half.

In the process of recollection she produced two fragments of tuyère from inside the house. Neither with these nor with the metal objects in the shrine would she part for any money; they are still fresh with sacrificial offerings. Similarly at Laagbe village a piece of the traditional iron, and a stone, forms the visible contents of the Ogun shrine, which is under a tree. These are likewise still in ritual use and covered with sacrifices. The owners refused to consider selling at any price.

As a young woman she had worked in the furnace, so that assuming her present age to be about sixty-five the furnace would have been alight around 1920. The date for Isundunrin is estimated at 1925. Because Ogun is felt to be present in the metal all ironwork of a ritual nature and for work in agriculture and hunting must be 'virgin', i.e. iron not previously heated. This virgin iron is held to be 'active' and must therefore be placated by sacrifice, especially tools and weapons, which could in this state harm the owner. The tool or weapon is not considered 'tame' until it has been used white. For this reason European iron, despite the quantities in which it entered Nigeria in the slave-trade, was resisted for use in tools and weapons (as several writers testify) almost to the present day. So the 'dating' of art objects by identifying them as made of native or of imported iron would seem to hold out no possibilities.

This review of the historical implications of oral and written sources for Yoruba iron might end with Johnson's twilight appraisal of the state of the industry at the end of the nineteenth century.

Certain districts are rich in iron ores; its iron production gave its name to the city of Ilọrin, from *Ilọ irin*, iron grinding, also to Ẹlẹta, a district of Ibadan, *Eta* being the term for iron ore. Certain districts in the

Ekiti province are also famous for their iron ores from which good steel was made, such as Oke Mesi. Before the period of intercourse with Europeans, all articles made of iron and steel, from weapons of war to pins and needles were of home manufacture; but the cheaper and more finished articles of European make, especially cutlery, though less durable, are fast displacing home-made wares. Charcoal from hard-wood, and the shells of palm-nuts are the materials generally used for generating the great heat required for the furnace, which is kept going all the year round. Iron rods and bars of European commerce being cheaper are fast displacing home-made products, and here and there all over the country the furnaces are being closed . . ."[1]

It is extremely doubtful that steel was ever consciously made by the Yoruba. Though the traditional domed furnace was at times capable of generating temperatures in excess of 1,500°C, liquid metal produced at such temperatures was regarded by the smith as 'spoiled'.[2] Such liquid iron is a prerequisite in the production of true steel. But in traditional practice repeated hammering and quenching of the smelted bloom in the smithy to remove impurities produced a hardening of the metal through the absorption of small quantities of carbon which resulted in a toughness approaching that of steel;[3] for this reason farmers until quite recent times preferred native to imported agricultural tools. Johnson's reference to the home production of domestic items of iron manufacture must be complemented by the documented importation to West Africa of a wide range of made-up piece-goods of iron and steel from the fifteenth century onwards. Far the most important of iron imports during this period is the European iron bar which came in as a result of the organization and expansion of the slave-trade in

---

[1] For iron in traditional Yoruba armament see R. S. Smith, 'Yoruba Armament', *J.A.H.* viii (1967), 87–106.

[2] S. Johnson, loc. cit. A controlled smelt was observed by the author at the traditional smelting village of Isundunrin, near Ejigbo, in association with the Department of Physics of the University of Ifẹ. This furnace, now entirely reconstituted, is believed to be the last remaining example of a tradition that might be very many centuries old.

[3] P. A. Talbot, 'The blacksmith apparently knew how to harden, temper, and weld'. *Peoples of Southern Nigeria*, iii (Oxford, 1926), p. 924. A contemporary description of Yoruba iron-smelting is given in the same place. 'Sometimes however Negroes produce steel, either by accident or design. I have encountered several references to tempering and puddling—that is, lessening the carbon content by reheating, and both Bellamy and Stanley have published accounts of Negro steel manufacture and analyses of the product.' W. Cline, *African Mining and Metallurgy* (Wisconsin, 1937), p. 30.

the mid-seventeenth century, and profoundly affected the development of a native iron industry and ritual imagery in the Yoruba iron arts.

The Ritualizing of Iron among the Yoruba

Note that all the Iron for Guinea is of the very same size and weight as described in the description of Nigritia, and is called at London by the name of Voyage Iron, and is the only sort used all over the coasts of North and South Guinea.[1]

A Barr is a denomination given to a Certaine Quantitie of Goods of any Kind, which Quantitie was of equal value among the natives to a Barr of Iron when this river was first traded to. Thus a pound of Fringe is a Barr, two pounds of gunpowder is a Barr, and each species of Trading Goods has a Quantitie in it called a Barr; therefore their way of reckoning is by Barrs.[2]

The most current goods to purchase slaves at New Calabar, in 1704, were iron bars, copper bars, of which two sorts, a great quantity especially of the iron.[3]

Such a bar was flat, 9 feet long, 2 inches wide, and half an inch thick; it was divided into twelve lengths of $7\frac{1}{2}$ inches each, each of these cuts then being subdivided into three; the resulting portion was considered just enough for fashioning into an African hoe.[4] In Dapper's time thirty-two or thirty-three of these weighed about ten quintal, i.e. roughly 35 pounds each.[5] Though the metal was smelted in parts of the Guinea forest from possibly as early as c. A.D. 500, inefficient methods of extraction resulted in an almost universal iron hunger which was met by Europeans with the importation of 'bits' and 'wedges' and odd made-up articles during

[1] J. Barbot, *Description of the Coast of Guinea* (London, 1732), p. 45.

[2] F. Moore in E. Donnan, *Documents Illustrative of the History of the Slave Trade to America*, ii, p. 396.

[3] J. Barbot, *Supplement*, Churchill v, p. 464.

[4] Le Sieur Brüe, in T. Astley, *Voyages and Travels* (London, 1746), p. 119. The tablet $2\frac{1}{2}$ inches by 2 inches by $\frac{1}{2}$ inch seems accurate enough, though for this the original division would have been into more than twelve parts. The author has examined at Warri in the Niger Delta an iron bar 12 feet by 4 inches by 4 inches claimed by its owner, Chief Sam Warri of Agbassa-Warri, to be a specimen of European trade iron. In the same collection is held a nude iron figurine claimed to have been made by the present Chief's grandfather.

[5] O. Dapper, *Description de l'Afrique* (Amsterdam, 1686), p. 300. A quintal was a Portuguese measure of weight equivalent to four *arrobas*; an *arroba* equalled 32 lb. A. F. C. Ryder, 'An Early Portuguese Trading Voyage to the Forcados River', *J.H.S.N.* i. no. 4 (1959).

Plates

NOTES ON PLATES

PLATE 1. A bowl used to contain palm-kernels used in Ifa divination (*agere Ifa*). The white substance filling the incisions may indicate that it was used for divination in the cult of one of the 'white gods'. Its height is about ten inches. It was obtained from a dealer in Ibadan who could not identify its place of origin. It is now on exhibition in Lagos Museum. It was probably made in Ọyọ province and seems to be of some antiquity. The little carving is harmoniously and intricately carved and the details are most beautifully finished. Part of the base has been destroyed.

It illustrates two women sitting on stools side by side and playing with their hands on standing drums which taper to a narrow base. The skins of the drums are tightened by pegs, not by wedges as in many southern drums. A girl holds the drums. The hair-style is not usually seen in Yoruba carvings. The women wear heavy plugs in their ears and strings of beads on their necks, wrists, and ankles. The triple face-marks are of the type known as *abaja*. The broad stripes on the breasts and arms are similar to the body marks known as *ẹyọ* used by the royal family of Ọyọ. (See Johnson, *A History of the Yorubas* (Lagos, 1921), p. 150, and Abraham, *A Dictionary of Modern Yoruba* (Lander, 1958), under *ila*, sections 2 and 3.)

PLATE 2. A double Ifa bowl, the property of the *Olubara* of Ibara. It combines an *agere Ifa* used to hold the palm-kernels with an *ọpọn Ifa* used to hold the *ikin*, *ọpẹlẹ*, and other materials for divination. The *agere*, its cover, and the chain joining the two together, are a *tour de force* of woodcarving as all are carved from one block of wood. The *ọpọn* is decorated with a band of interlaced pattern. In the centre a man rides on horseback; the details of the harness and bit are carefully illustrated. On his right a woman with a head-tie feeds a child; another woman with a child on her back seems to be dancing: she is followed by a hunter with a gun and cap. On his left is an *Egungun* escort (*atọkun*) with a cudgel and a whip from which the bark has been partly peeled in a spiral; behind him is an *Egungun* masquer whose cloth is held by a child masquer; these are followed by a *bata* drummer. The figures carry the triple *abaja* marks on the cheeks which, in this area, are used by the Egbado people; they also have triple marks on their foreheads.

A carving of the same school, though not perhaps by the same hand, is illustrated in William Fagg, *Nigerian Images* (London, 1963), pl. 82; the two carvings differ very slightly in the treatment of lips and nostrils.

PLATE 3. Detail of a door in Abẹokuta photographed in 1957. The figures represent two women with head-ties and wrappers tied round their waists; they carry in their left hands the tongued bells known as *aja*. One woman holds what seems to be a brass staff, the other holds a cola-nut. A soldier wears a hunter's vest with cowry-shell charms; he holds a gun and a rope which is tied round the waist of a prisoner. Three of the figures carry *abaja* marks on the cheeks but the soldier is marked with vertical *pele* marks. The women have double chevron marks on their foreheads.

PLATE 4. An *Ogboni* drum at Ęşęta-Ekiti. Height about forty-eight inches. The style is that of the Ikǫle-Igbirra school and the drum was probably carved early in this century. There are about forty figures represented on the drum, none of which seems to be explicitly related to the *Ogboni* cult. There are two large standing figures of women; one places her hands on the heads of two children or assistants; the other holds two staffs. Other figures represent soldiers or hunters, a warrior on horseback, a woman carrying two children, a man holding two dogs tied to a rope (this motif is repeated several times). Among the animals represented are: a baboon eating a corn cob; a dog with an animal (a hare?) in its mouth standing on what seems to be a cat but may be a leopard (cats are rarely represented in carvings); doves; a horse; lizards; mudfish. The upper rim is decorated with a strip of *ibǫ* pattern.

PLATE 5. A tray collected by Wieckmann in the seventeenth century. It is now in Ulm Museum, Germany. It is not certain that it is Yoruba work but is similar to a Yoruba Ifa divination tray. Similarities are the head surmounting the tray, and the fringe of decorative motifs surrounding the plain surface of the board; the tripartite division, however, is unusual. The closely knit design and the decorative surface-patterns are reminiscent of the hieratic form of Ijebu Yoruba carving referred to in the section in this chapter on 'Variation' and in the notes to figures 2 and 3. A careful comparison of this work with works in the hieratic ijebu style would be of interest (cf. William Fagg and Margaret Plass, *African Sculpture* (London and New York, 1964)).

1. *Agere Ifa*

2. Ifa bowl from Ibara

4. Ogboni drum from Ekiti

3. Detail of an Abẹokuta door

5. A tray from Ulm Museum, Germany

the sixteenth century and well into the seventeenth, at which latter date the situation was capitalized upon with the introduction of the iron bar as demands from the West Indian plantations resulted in the organization and expansion of the slave-trade.[1]

A certain amount of oral and material evidence suggests that the second appellative of Ogun—god of iron, was ascribed at a period when the social and military significance of the metal came to be linked with its increased availability. At Ire, his 'home', Ogun is remembered only as a warrior; there are no traditions of iron-working and iron-smelting. The present *Onire* (1965) recites a list of twenty-nine kings in succession from Ogundahunsi, the first *Onire*, who was the son of Ogun, which might suggest that for this part of Yorubaland the metal was not in significant use in c. 1530.[2] If iron remained unimportant at Ire around this date this state of affairs would accord with that apparently prevailing in parts of the Gold Coast at the same time where, as Towerson's accounts suggest, the demand for European iron appears to have arisen during his first and second voyages—between 1555 and 1561.[3] We might remember too that for parts of the Gold Coast the archaeological record indicates the continued use of stone implements into the fifteenth century.[4]

The illustration of a hunter's doublet at fig. 2 incorporates a memory of iron in its purely magical function. Along with various 'medicines' efficacious in meeting the hazards of war and of the

---

[1] The whole subject of the supply of iron to the West Coast is treated in my forthcoming book *Icon and Image*.

[2] Calculating fifteen years to a reign. But it has seriously been pointed out that this method of applying a mean reign to Yoruba king-lists is inherently full of pitfalls, taking into consideration such hazards as changes in the manner of succession. The king-list was related to me by the *Onire* supported by his priests and elders. Another for five adjacent towns including Ire is contained in the *Oye Intelligence Report, 1933*. In this the Ire list comprises only twenty-two names, the first seven sovereigns being said to have ruled at a nearby site before Ire was settled. The names can be collated in only a few cases, different parts of a single king's name having apparently been used for the same monarch in the two versions. The report gives no sources. It was kindly supplied by Mr. John Picton of the Nigerian Antiquities Service.

[3] In his voyage of 1555 he found that 'people desired most to have basons and cloth; some would buy trifles as knives, horsetails, horns; some of the men going ashore sold a cap, a dagger, a hat, etc.' No mention of iron, which however figures in his trade list of 1561, 'some wedges of iron, swords, daggers, hammers, short pieces of iron. . .' In T. Astley, *Voyages and Travels*, i, pp. 157–76.

[4] P. Ozanne, *The Iron Age in Ghana*, unpubl. MS. Inst. African Studies, University of Ghana (by permission).

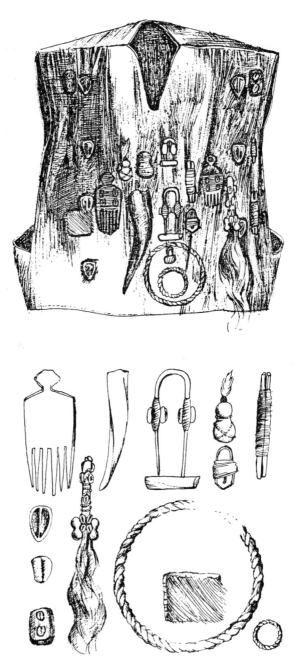

FIG. 2. Hunter's doublet with 'medicines'.

hunt are the double-pronged *aba* stuck into a bit of wood on which, in combat, the warrior or hunter recites incantations before unclasping it and pointing the two sharp prongs in the direction of the adversary. Its effect is to produce surrender or flight on the part of the latter. When not in use its power is neutralized by the points being stuck into a tree. The large iron torque (*ifunpa*) functions in much the same way as the *aba*. Worn on the upper arm it can be manipulated to produce choking in an enemy. In the small skin purse (*apętę*) is contained a finger-ring of iron twisted into the shape of the *aba*, which confers power on the warrior in hand-to-hand combat. The horn (* așę*) likewise contains three metal pins, one each of copper, brass, and iron, any of which the hunter might use as a pick for transferring 'medicines' to his tongue with curses meant to deliver the adversary into his hands.

The magical potency of iron associated with Ogun as god of war appears to have been complemented at some stage with a range of his type-symbols referring principally to a European period. Such are the *gaman*, and *gbana* (both characterized by the incorporation of European iron chain), the slave-manacle of obvious European connections, the hunter's amulet (incorporating the *ędan Ogun* of a style which has been dated to *c.* 1640–1830),[1] the European firearm (not common in Nigeria until the later nineteenth century[2]), the European padlock, a *Balogun's* pendant of cognate iconography to the *ędan Ogun*, pincers or tongs of a European prototype, a European sabre, etc. These type-motifs are all particularly associated with Ogun, and point to attributes ascribed to him after the period of European supplementation of the metal. It is possible

[1] D. Williams, 'The Iconology of the Yoruba *Edan Ogboni*', *Africa*, xxxiv (1964). At Warri in the Delta, where there are no traditions of iron-smelting, war is said to have been waged with 'medicines'. Arrows were of wood, as occasionally was also the case among the Yoruba. Examples of the latter of a generation ago are described as having been carved from the palm branch and dipped into a concoction made up from the heads of poisonous snakes exactly as recorded in the twelfth century Tohfut ul Alabi (Palmer, *Sudanese Memoirs*, i, p. 90: 'They shoot arrows poisoned with the venom of a yellow snake; lit with that venom within an hour flesh drops from bone even in the case of an elephant or other beast'). See also Diego Gomes, *De la première découverte de la Guinée* (Bissau, 1959). The Yoruba bow was made from the *Aringo*, or the *Erin*, trees, both noted for toughness and pliability. The potency of the poison was graded according to the size of the quarry from doses suitable for small birds to those for large animals and human beings. Iron-tipped arrows were used contemporaneously with poisoned ones of reed. (Informant, D. Adeniji of Iwo.)

[2] A. Ajayi and R. Smith, *Yoruba Warfare in the Nineteenth Century* (Cambridge, op. cit., i, 1964), p. 17.

that it is at this period that he came to be known as the god of iron, as the revolutionary effects of the metal came to be appreciated in the Yoruba economy. Where an iron hunger is everywhere attested by sixteenth-century travellers along the west coast, we find by the end of the seventeenth century, fifty or so years after the introduction of the European iron bar, that the local people were now producing surplus equipment for trade. Where in 1588 James Welch had taken to Benin 'ironwork of sundry sorts',[1] by the opening years of the eighteenth century the Bini were producing 'implements for fishing, ploughing and otherwise preparing the land'.[2] Though stone tools persisted in parts of the Gold Coast into the fifteenth century, by the end of the seventeenth we hear of sections of the people there 'forging all sorts of war arms that they want, guns only excepted, as well as whatever is required in their agriculture and housekeeping'.[3] Around this time (1708) an Act of Parliament to settle the trade to Africa deprived the Royal African Company of monopoly rights and threw the trade open to any of the subjects of His Majesty's Realm of England, with a resultant improvement in the quality and quantity of iron reaching the West African market.[4] It is from this period that come the magnificent ceremonial iron cutlasses of the Ashanti now in the Wallace Collection, London, and in the Copenhagen National Museum. Similar cutlasses were made by the Yoruba from locally smelted iron into quite recent times. Such is the *ida Qranyan* which is taken to Ile Ifẹ on the death of an *Alafin* and reconsecrated at the grave of Qranyan before being brought back for the installation of each new *Alafin*.[5]

The Sacred Iron Figurines of the Yoruba
With the ritualizing of iron comes the genesis of form in the

---

[1] In E. Donnan, op. cit., i, p. 202.
[2] The Dutch traveller DR, in Bosman, ibid.
[3] T. Astley, op. cit., p. 305.
[4] E. Donnan, op. cit., i, p. 421; ii, p. 96.
[5] S. Johnson, op. cit., p. 45; R. S. Smith, *Yoruba Armament*, p. 93. The present weapon, examined by the author in 1965, is obviously not very old; the sanctions of kingship involved might be regarded as independent of the particular weapon in which it is vested, and there is perhaps nothing incongruous in the weapon being renewed from time to time. A similar sanction of kingship is held by the reigning sovereign at the small Ekiti village of Orin; this sword by contrast (Apeluwa's sword), claimed to have been brought from Ifẹ, seems of extreme age—its anthropomorphic brass pommel and guard are worn smooth with use so that the Janus-head configuration is now hardly decipherable.

sacred iron figurines. Its role in food production and the common-weal is reflected in the emergence of a group of forest cults in which an iron imagery is obligatory. Such are Qsanyin, Erinlẹ, Oginyan, Oriṣa Oko. Iron takes its place in a scheme in which the materials of art are held to be imbued with particular spiritual attributes.

'Wood was the first material used in carving—at the time of the very first *oriṣas*, Oriṣa nla, and Qbatala.'

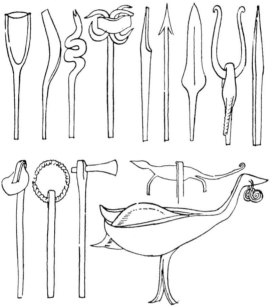

FIG. 3.   Ritual Iron Staff for the cult of Erinlẹ.

'Lead represents the white oriṣas—Oriṣa nla, Qbatala, Qbalufọn, white being primary.'

'Iron came next with Ogun, Qsanyin and Erinlẹ. All these are represented by birds: Ogun-Ajibowu's bird, the blacksmith bird; Qsanyin—the Ologeesa bird; and Erinlẹ—the Aluko, or *kowee* (with crest).'

'Brass is for the Ogboni, it does not change:
The *ẹdan* does not die, rocks never crumble,
The *ogiri sakan* does not die from year to year.
I become the hill, I become the rock beneath the sea,
I die no more.
May it please God that I become like the rock beneath the sea.'[1]

[1] Informants: The *Onigbẹti* of Igbẹti, and David Adeniji of Iwo.

The tradition might indicate the sequence in which these metals appeared among the Yoruba. Lead, the easiest of all metals to extract from its ore, might have been known in West Africa since early antiquity. It occurs in Nigeria and was possibly, like tin,

FIG. 4. Ritual Iron Staff for cult of Ọsanyin.

worked from very remote times. Its quality of 'purity' may have been adopted into a pre-existing cult system in which the relative *oriṣa* were worshipped in wood, though in West Africa it is tempting to regard wood-carving as a specifically iron-age phenomenon: at any rate its wide variety of cult forms strongly implies the possession of iron tools, particularly when the miniature size of most African wood-carving is taken into account. For iron we are not justified in thinking of dates much before *c.* A.D. 500 for the Guinea forest, but as we have seen, Ogun might already then have been apotheosized as god of war—certain of his type-symbols surviving today (such as the *kumo* and the *orukumo*) strongly suggest a neolithic weaponry. The bird-motif, common to the plastic

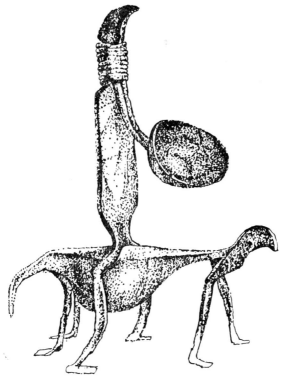

FIG. 5.   Iron figurine from Ogom Shrine, Qfa.

imagery of Ogun, Qsanyin, and Erinlẹ, underlines the association of these iron cults with the productive and healing life of the forest; it is likely that the adoption of these cults followed upon the increased availability of the metal after the sixteenth century, and represent abstract concepts generated in man's relation to his environment. Brass in tropical Africa is everywhere an iron age phenomenon and among the Yoruba was never independently ritualized. For its imperishability it is sacred to the worship of earth in the *Ogboni* system, and in it have been created the finest masterpieces of the Yoruba plastic genius. Oral tradition claims that the *ǫdan Ogboni* was first whittled from palm-stalks.[1]

Skills developed in fashioning cult-stereotypes to the various

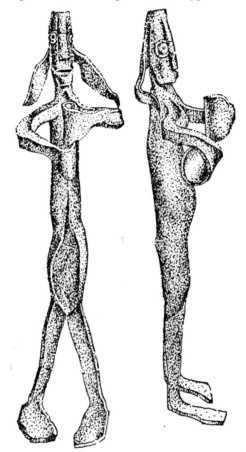

FIG. 6.   Iron figurine from Ogom Shrine, Ǫfa.

forest gods in whose imagery the use of iron is obligatory would have placed at the disposal of the smith that range of forms and a mastery of their use which would result in the unique sacred iron sculpture of the Yoruba, for the repertory of forms to be encoun-

[1] D. Williams, 'The Iconology . . .' R. Horton similarly found among the Kalabari that specific trees possessed specific spiritual attributes which deter-mined their choice for different types of sculpture, cf. *Kalabari Sculpture*, Nigeria Antiquities Service (1965).

tered in the *ọṣun Ọsanyin*, the *ọṣun Erinlẹ*, the *oṣe Orìṣa Oko*, and
Oginyan are specific in their representation of the beasts and crea-
tures of the forest as well as of the tools and implements developed
in subduing it to the needs of man (figs. 3, 4). From these skills
would grow the magnificent iron sculpture of the Yoruba and the
related virtuoso pieces of the Fon of Dahomey[1] (figs. 5, 6).

COPPER BRONZE & GOLD

Carthaginian participation in the gold trade of the Western
Sudan until Roman times does not have the significance for us
which it might, for whatever the merchandise they traded—per-
fume, precious stones, Greek pottery—it is unlikely to have been
the brass which was to distinguish the cargoes of the caravan trade
of a later day. Following on their appearance in North Africa, Arab
eyes begin to search the southern horizon for the city of gold
towards which they mounted their first expedition in 734;[2] but not
for another half-century, in 780, would written records relate a
definite connection between the Mediterranean trade entrepôt of
Tahert (Tiaret) and the central and Western Sudan, whither trade
routes now led to Gao on the Niger, and to Ghana; and half a
century later still Ghana first appears on Arab maps.[3]

The caravan trade did not go in one direction only; 'The
Negroes come up from their country and take away the salt from
there.'[4] They may even have been acquainted from the earliest
times with the exotic wares of the North African bazaars. In this
way we can perhaps explain the presence of copper objects south of
the Sahara—trinketry and miscellaneous trivia—which begin to

---

[1] That the famous Dahomean example representing the god of iron, Gu
(obviously related to the Yoruba Ogun), evolved from the cult-imagery associated
with this god among the Fon (as also among the Yoruba) is suggested by the
assembly of type-motifs which constitute the theme of the head-dress—cutlass,
hoe, digging-stick, fish-hook, etc. Other such staffs on which figurative motifs
appear are wrought exclusively to the royal ancestors—a tradition which seemingly goes back to the calabash of offerings used in mortuary rites; their various
elements name specific attributes of the ancestor (*noms forts*) and partake of his
being. See P. Mercier, *Les Ase de Musée d'Abomey*, IFAN Catalogue, viii (1952),
11 ff.

[2] R. Mauny, 'Etat Actuelle de la Question de Ghana', *Bull. IFAN*, xiii, 1–2
(1952), 464.

[3] T. Lewicki, 'L'Etat nord-Africain de Tahert et ses relations avec Le Soudan
Occidental à la fin du viiie siècle', *Cahiers d'Etudes Africains*, ii, no. 8 (1962).

[4] H. A. R. Gibb, *Ibn Battuta* (London, 1957), p. 317.

appear there, apparently, only towards the close of the first millenium A.D.[1] Within the Niger buckle occur a number of sites in which neolithic remains and iron objects have been found in association; the same area yields fine filigree copper jewellery and bronze objects, which leads to the conclusion that these sites represent two historical stages, the latter suggesting an association with Old Ghana at its apogee, between the tenth and eleventh centuries, a culture in which brass and iron appear on the breastplates of horses, on horse-bits, sabres, lances, arrows, hatchets, and various other sophisticated weapons and implements.[2] Excavation at Kumbi Saleh (Old Ghana) has confirmed the splendour and sophistication of a city divided into two sections, one inhabited by proud and wealthy Arab traders from the Maghreb occupying Mediterranean-type stone houses uncommon then in the Western Sudan, the other by the black kings of Ghana bound to their traditional religion and beliefs. It is in this relationship that we might perhaps seek the beginnings of *cire-perdue* casting of objects and trinkets in gold— as a treasure of ritual cast gold figurines found in Tripoli in 1929 perhaps attests. It is worthy of note that the confident Arab culture of Ghana has so far yielded to the spade few objects of the bronze caster's art which can unequivocally be regarded as of local manufacture. Copper trinkets from sites all over the region of the period are mostly rude representations hammered into the shapes of birds and lizards, etc., with ornamental items such as crotals, bracelets, and rings. It would seem that though hammered copper and brass were used for small ornaments in a local industry the more ambitious type of object in cast brass or bronze continued to be imported from the Maghreb. Very valuable at this date (*c.* A.D. 1000) is an articulated bronze bracelet excavated at Killi by Desplagnes (fig. 7a). Similar articulated bronze bracelets will occur in a variety of forms throughout the Guinea forest to the Niger Delta, but at dates still very much in the future (fig. 7b). The evidence is interesting in pointing to the path of influence followed in the dissemination of at least one source of the *cire-perdue* technique practised in West Africa, though we should be on our guard against equating the distribution of manufactured objects too closely with the distribution of technique. These bracelets appear to have been

[1] E. Bovill, *The Golden Trade of the Moors* (Oxford), p. 69 speaks of brass imports to Ghana in the ninth century.
[2] L. Desplagnes, op. cit., pp. 15 ff.

used as currency throughout the region and were the precursors of
the Portuguese manilla introduced in the fifteenth century with such
effect on the growth of the brass industries of the Guinea forest.
Ibn Battuta (1354) describes an important copper currency produced in an industry at Takedda, the copper locally mined being
'cast into bars a span and a half in length' and used in the southern
markets to buy slaves, millet, butter, and wheat.[1] Such casting was

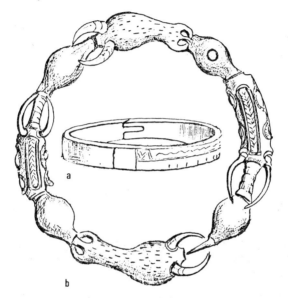

FIG. 7. (a) Articulated brass bracelet, Killi, Upper Niger.
(b) Articulated brass bracelet, Niger Delta.

done in open stone or clay moulds of a type today common in the
forest region (fig. 8). A specimen was excavated at an Ifẹ site in
1966. Ibn Battuta's observation is possibly the earliest written
source for the casting of copper in the Western Sudan, and though
the process employed is a far cry from the technique of *cire-
perdue* casting, the mining, smelting, and casting of copper into
ingots for a local trade is of importance in the history of the Guinea
bronze for it implies the use of much the same range of tools and
equipment necessary in bronze smithing—furnace, bellows,
moulds, and iron tools for handling the liquid metal. Of particular
interest is the fact that the ingot produced in the Saharan open

[1] H. A. R. Gibb, op. cit., p. 356.

mould was bent into the bracelets and torques, today a common feature of Yoruba and other African bronzes, but far more important the description of Ibn Battuta's open mould establishes a *terminus a quo* for the working of copper in the Nigerian area, for the ingots purchased (and they were brought into Borgu) would be worked in one form or another by their buyers. Whether the metal was also at this date worked by alloying with zinc to make brass, or

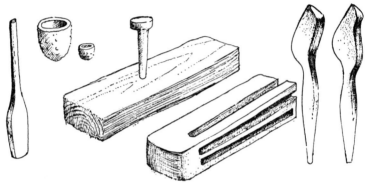

FIG. 8.   Open brass casting mould and other smith's equipment.

with tin to make bronze we do not know. These two processes would imply a knowledge of techniques for casting the alloy produced—which would be made for no other purpose.

The sequence seems to have occurred in the founding of the 'Sao' culture of Lake Chad in which, according to local tradition, two separate groups of immigrants brought respectively copper jewellery, and the metallurgy of iron and of bronze. The 'Sao' culture is considered to have lasted from the eleventh to the fourteenth century;[1] its bronze industry might have affected Nigeria in the dispersal of smiths after the Islamic conquests of the sixteenth century—Muslim interdiction against graven images is thought to have spread Sao techniques among the Hausa and Kanuri, where to the present the itinerant smith is a tradition;[2] the iconography of the Yoruba and the Bini bronze certainly speaks for northern connections[3] (fig. 9). Certainly at some stage after the tenth

[1] J. P. Lebeuf, *Archaeologie Tchadienne* (Paris, 1962), p. 126.
[2] J. P. Lebeuf, op. cit., p. 114.
[3] D. Williams, *Icon and Image* (unpublished MS.).

century, possibly some time after this date, the primary working of copper by hammering into images and perhaps implements was succeeded by the casting of cupreous alloys: the evidence to hand

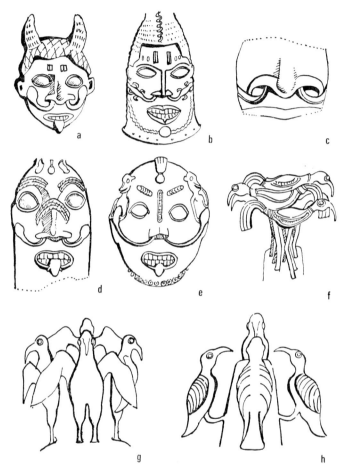

FIG. 9.   a-e: Jebba, Benin, Ifẹ, Benin (?), Yoruba. f-h: Tada, Benin, Yoruba.

provides no reason for looking further back than this to account for the rise of the bronze industries of tropical Africa.

These naked facts we may consider in seeking a temporal framework for the emergence of bronze casting industries south of the Sahara: that (a) beginning with Al Hussein (950) we have written evidence of trade copper entering Old Ghana (although at this date the metal seems to have been worked only by hammering), and that (b) copper ingots reaching Nigeria from a mine at Takedda in the Sahara in 1354 were cast there in moulds such as are today still used by the Nigerian smith. That in these four hundred years the art of *cire-perdue* casting was possibly learnt in the area is suggested by the gold hoard from Tripoli already mentioned. For how long the open mould of Ibn Battuta's day has been employed in the south we cannot say; its presence there is merely cited as material evidence for the connection of these industries with those of the Western Sudan and the Mediterranean, and as establishing a *terminus a quo* for the working of copper in Nigeria.

To the south it is generally claimed that bronze was being cast at Ifẹ early in the period at dates variously given as the twelfth, thirteenth, or fourteenth centuries; and it is from Ifẹ that the technique is believed to have been learnt at Benin. But plausible as these dates might seem within the period, we must observe that they are based entirely on oral tradition and tendered in every case with very uncertain supporting evidence. The Ifẹ–Benin succession in bronze casting is open to serious doubt.

Iconographic evidence indicates that at some stage in their bronze histories the art of Ifẹ and that of Benin were contemporaneous. The Bini bronze can fairly confidently be dated to the four hundred years between 1485 and 1897[1] so that could the tradition of an Ifẹ authorship for the Bini industry be found acceptable Ifẹ tutelage would have taken place towards the end of the fifteenth century or early in the sixteenth. But those works of art which most convincingly connect Ifẹ with Benin are demonstrably datable to the mid-seventeenth century.[2] It is worth noting too that of the very few Bini bronzes so far analysed at least one bears a lead-zinc composition very similar to a certain group of Ifẹ bronzes. Tada bronzes similarly attributed to an unsupported early date are now demonstrably to be dated no earlier than the mid-seventeenth century.[3] From the picture of the Nigerian bronze as a whole it seems unlikely that a significant figurative bronze industry existed anywhere in the country much before the closing years of the

[1] For analyses of bronze casting moulds and cores and the evidence to be extracted from these, see D. Williams, 'Bronze casting Moulds, Cores, and the Study of Classical Techniques', *Lagos Notes and Records*, i, no. 1 (June, 1967).

[2] D. Williams, *Icon and Image* (unpublished MS.).

[3] For dating techniques in the African bronze see *Icon and Image*.

fifteenth century, and into this picture we would need to fit the evidence for Ifẹ as more knowledge of this mysterious school comes to light. As for the Ifẹ–Benin succession in bronze casting, recent analysis of mould- and core-stuff does not seem to support the tradition.

Of far more importance to the history of art and the study of aesthetics is the Yoruba sacred bronze—bronzes particularly in the cult imagery of the *Ogboni*, of Ogun, and Ọbalufọn. Metaphysical concepts responsible for the realization of sacred form in this genre make them unique in all African art. An important style-cycle in the Ogboni bronze is datable to the period 1640–1830.[1] Imagery in this cycle was at some stage adopted in the cult of Ogun—possibly with the ascription of his second appellative—god of iron—which as we have seen is most plausibly to be referred to a period *c.* 1530–*c.* 1650 connected with increased availability of the metal.

The school most impressively associated with the *Ogboni* sacred bronze is that at Ijẹbu-Ode, which might indeed be the author of the genre. Certainly the art was borne therefrom to Abẹokuta, and quite late—'about three generations ago' on the evidence of the descendants of the original smith, Alatiṣe Ogundipẹ. Another tradition at Abẹokuta refers a separate influence in brass casting to immigrants from Ọyọ-Ile; this tradition centres in the Kẹhinde family, Oke Ṣaje, Abẹokuta. Technical distinctions in casting method seem to support separate origins for these two traditions. The smiths of Abẹokuta have developed a local sacred imagery of great originality and vividness and continue in practice where today the furnaces of the Ijẹbu smith are cold and his superlatively grave and holy achievements in bronze art decorate the museum show-cases of the world. As to the age of the Ijẹbu industry nothing conclusive can at this stage be said, though the written record attests to the importation of brass there around 1506–8. But it would be misguided necessarily to associate such brass imports with the existence of an industry.[2]

The possibility exists that a school of bronze existed at Ọyọ-Ile, though no extant work can unequivocally be attributed to such a school. At Igboho the author has examined a heroic-size brass mask

---

[1] D. Williams, 'Iconology of the Yoruba *Edan Ogboni*', *Africa*, xxxiv, no. 2 (April, 1964).
[2] Periera: *Esmeraldo de Situ Orbis* (Bissau, 1956), p. 131.

claimed to be of this industry. It is made to *oriṣa* Ṣango and is used annually in rites associated with the royal *bere* festival. A similar mask of great beauty was subsequently examined at (new) Qyǫ, made likewise to *oriṣa* Ṣango and used in the annual *bere* festival. The masks are of similar size and iconography though the latter example is incomparably the finer. Both are called *Alakoro*, a title of uncertain significance.[1] An armlet claimed to have been made at Qyǫ-Ile is reported by Meyerovitch[2] and Johnson speaks of '100 brass posts' removed from the palace at Qyǫ-Ile by the Emir of Ilǫrin after its fall, and elsewhere of the 'seven silver doors' of the *Qba* Qnisilę.[3] Metal work of some kind was certainly carried on at Qyǫ-Ile, as attested to by a crucible excavated at the ancient town site by Willett.[4] Clapperton mentions metal objects in the market-place, but does not record their provenance.

Yoruba smiths at Qbǫ-Aiyegunle near Ilǫrin are masters of a bronze imagery of quite distinct originality in technique and perhaps in its historical connections. Their technical ancestry seems directly linked with early industries in the Chad region; aesthetically their forms are those of the finely wrought filigree gold objects from Ghana and the Ivory Coast, and these seem in turn associated with old industries in the head waters of the Niger and further afield to the Mediterranean.[5]

All Yoruba bronzes seem related to these nodal industries—those at Ifę, at Ijębu, at Abęokuta, and at Qbǫ, in the last of which the tradition of the travelling smith has spread form and technique far and wide as it may well have done in the others.

[1] See D. Williams, 'Two brass masks from Qyǫ Ile', *Odu* n.s. iii, no. 1 (1966). *Alakoro* means 'He who has *akoro*'—a sort of chiefly head-gear. At Qyǫ, the *Ęṣǫ* (war-chiefs) were sometimes referred to as *Alakoro* (see Johnson, op. cit., p. 73).
[2] *Man* (March–April, 1941).
[3] Johnson, op. cit., pp. 176, 259.
[4] 'Excavation at Old Qyǫ: An interim report', *J.H.S.N.* ii, no. 1 (1960).
[5] D. Williams, *Icon and Image*.

CHAPTER X
Art in Wood

FATHER K. F. CARROLL

THIS chapter attempts to describe both the scope and limits of Yoruba woodcarving as a historical source. Carvings made in the early years of this century are available in abundance, but those over a hundred years old are rare. There are, fortunately, a few carvings preserved in European collections which date as far back as the seventeenth century. Yoruba carving illustrates the life of the people in detail and over the last three centuries there seems to have been no major change in its style or subject-matter. It enables the historian to build up a detailed picture of the dress, weapons, tools, utensils, ornaments, occupations, and ceremonial of the Yoruba people in the last few centuries. Yoruba carving, however, is not concerned with individuals or events. As a source, therefore, it is of value not as a chronicle but as a record of the cultural background.

The nature of Yoruba carving

The historian of this area is fortunate in having as a source, not the austere art of so many areas of Africa, but an art of profuse illustration. I will describe some characteristics of Yoruba carving likely to be of interest to the historian.

1. Yoruba carving presents detailed illustration of the traditional culture—the life of the farm, the village, the palace, and the cults. It is an art of the people and there is no separate style identified with the court or religious ceremonial. Its selection of themes and emphases, therefore, presents a picture of Yoruba culture made by the whole people and not by the court or priests alone.

2. It presents types not individuals. The carving made to commemorate the accession of an *Alafin* of Qyọ did not attempt to portray him as an individual.[1] An *Egungun* mask used to

---

[1] There is a figure in Lagos Museum of a horse-rider carrying a spear. It was kept in the *Alafin's* Ṣango shrine at Koso near Qyọ and is said to have come from

commemorate a deceased person does not portray his personal characteristics, though the carrier of the mask may do so by voice and gesture. Ibeji figures made in remembrance of dead twins make no attempt to portray them as persons. The carver, in fact, does not normally intend that his figures be identified by name. Even the oriṣa are rarely if ever represented directly. Eṣu is the only common exception.

The people do sometimes identify a carving as Ṣango, Ọbatala, Oduduwa, etc., but there is usually nothing in the carving to support the identification. The carver's usual intention in these cases is to portray a worshipper. Frobenius, writing early in this century states bluntly that the people are usually mistaken in taking such images as representations of the oriṣa itself.[1]

In northern Yoruba, Elempe, the mythical warrior king of the Nupe people, is often identified by name and the carver intends this identification.[2] Philip Allison also suggests that two of the European figures in carvings made by Ọlọwẹ of Ise-Ekiti were intended to represent Reeve Tucker, the first travelling commissioner to reach Ekiti, and Captain Ambrose (fig. 1). Usually, however, Europeans are represented as types and not as individuals.[3]

Ọyọ-ile. A new figure is supposed to have been made for each *Alafin*. (cf. note by P. A. Allison, 6 Oct. 1960, in the photographic index of the museum.)

We find examples of portraiture at two extremes of Yoruba art, the brass heads of Ifẹ and modern carved figures at Ọwọ. However, there is no evidence of genuine portraiture in traditional Yoruba woodcarving. See F. Willett, 'On the Funeral Effigies of Ọwọ and Benin and the Interpretation of the Life-Size Bronze Heads from Ifẹ, Nigeria', *Man*, i, no. 1 (1966).

[1] '. . . the figures and other figments and symbols are never actually representations of the Gods, but rather of priests and others engaged in sacrificial or other ceremonial in honour of some particular deity.' (Frobenius, *The Voice of Africa* (London, 1913), p. 196.)

'Je ne connais que très peu de figurations qui soit réellement l'image d'un dieu. Dans la plupart des cas c'est par erreur que les indigènes prennent ces figurations pour l'image d'un dieu.' Frobenius, *Mythologie de l'Atlantide* (Paris, 1949).

[2] Bandele, a carver of Osi-Ilọrin, says that in his area Elempe is represented wearing a special type of helmet made of leather and brass. See K. F. Carroll, *Yoruba Religious Carving* (London, 1967), pl. 27, p. 31. There is a large figure in the *afin* at Ila known as Elempe. The original made by Fakẹyẹ is in the Lagos Museum.

[3] Cf. P. A. Allison, 'The First Travelling Commissioners of Ekiti Country' *Nigerian Field*, xvii, no. 3 (1952).

Lander brought home a stool from Borgu after his 1830 expedition. This is now in the British Museum and is illustrated in R. & J. Lander, *Journal of an*

FIG. I.   Two figures of Europeans on horseback from a door by Ọlọwẹ
of Ise Ekiti in Lagos Museum. Allison tentatively identified the figures as
Captain Ambrose and Commissioner Reeve-Tucker (Cf. Allison, 1952).
The faces are carefully characterized but the rest of the figures, especially
the horses, are blocked out impressionistically.

Expedition to Explore the Course and Termination of the Niger (London 1832),
pp. 226–30. Lander describes the stool as follows: 'The form is nearly square;
the two principal sides are each supported by four little wooden figures of men;
and another of large dimension, seated on a clumsy representation of a hippopotamus, is placed between them. This important personage is attended by his
musicians, and guarded by soldiers, some armed with muskets, and others with
bows and arrows, who formed the legs of the stool.' All these carvings are clearly
in the Yoruba style. The 'hippopotamus' is actually a horse though the carver
has given it cloven hooves; Yoruba carvers sometimes make the same mistake in
modern times.

A separate figure in the British Museum, seemingly collected at the same
time, shows a beautifully carved representation of a European on horseback
dressed in a cut-away frock-coat, wearing a cravat and what may be a cloth or
a wig on his head. The face is a forceful caricature of a European and shows a
small turned-up nose and a massive jaw. One is tempted to see in this figure a
portrait of Clapperton or Lander. However, it is unlikely that the carving
represents any particular individual. White men had already been typed in the
minds of carvers and people, as witness Clapperton's description of a masquerade in old Ọyọ depicting a sickly-looking white man. (H. Clapperton, *Journal of
Second Expedition into the Interior of Africa* (London, 1829), pp. 55–6.)

3. Carvings frequently illustrate incidents and anecdotes of traditional life: a woman sits at her loom with a baby on her back; a king presides over the execution of prisoners; a northern warrior rides on horseback with a captive tied to the harness. The carver does not attempt to build up a series of anecdotes into a sustained narrative whether of a story, a myth, or legend, or a historical event. In fact, the illustrations carved on an object are frequently not even linked by a common theme. The illustrations on an Ijẹbu *Ogboni* drum may refer directly to the *Ogboni* cult, but those on an Ekiti *Ogboni* drum may illustrate figures and anecdotes of everyday village life or of other cults (Plate 4).

4. The subject matter of carvings is confined almost entirely to man, his accessories, and the animals with which he comes into particular contact. In modern times objects of prestige, such as lorries, aeroplanes, and iron-sheeted houses, may be illustrated in their own right. Architecture and scenery are represented only incidentally and symbolically in relation to the living figures: a man climbs a palm-tree; a box-like palace encloses the king and his courtiers. Yoruba carving does not provide a source for the study of traditional architecture, village lay-out, topography, or vegetation.

5. It is not possible at present to offer an assured interpretation and analysis of Yoruba carving as an expression of the people's philosophy and religious belief. African carvings have frequently been interpreted in abstract terms without any attempt to discover the people's own interpretation. In Yoruba country study of such interpretation has scarcely begun.[1] The museums commonly record the date of collection and place of origin of a carving and more rarely the name of the carver and its function. But records of the people's explanation and interpretation of the figures and anecdotes illustrated, or of the proverbs, songs, prayers, or praise-chants which may be associated with the object, scarcely exist.

The antiquity of Yoruba carving

The life of a woodcarving in a tropical village is short. Even carvings made of hardwood have a life of scarcely a century.

---

[1] For incomplete studies of such interpretations, see: J. D. Clarke, 'Three Yoruba Fertility Ceremonies', *Journal of the Royal Anthropological Institute* (1944): H. U. Beier, *Sacred Wood Carvings* (Lagos, 1957), 'Festival of the Images', *Nigeria Magazine*, no. 45 (1954), 'Ori oke Festival', *Nigeria Magazine*, no. 60 (1958), and 'Gelede Masks', *Odu*, no. 6 (1958).

Agents of destruction are: fire sweeping through the thatched compounds, decay due to termite or other insect infestation and wet and dry rot; loss and destruction in warfare; neglect or deliberate destruction by Muslim or Christian converts; destruction by witch-hunting cults and by government officials (for example the burning of implements of the smallpox cult).[1]

Collection and export was probably the most important agent of preservation before the creation of Nigerian museums, though export is now closely controlled. William Fagg has pointed out that African traditional art has become, like European classical art, the patrimony of the whole world.[2] It is not, therefore, to be regretted that so many overseas museums should have representative collections of African carvings, including those of the Yoruba, the most prolific of all African carving areas. It is, however, to be regretted that there are few, if any, Yoruba carvings made before the middle of the last century in Nigerian collections, though Lagos Museum is rich in carvings made within the last sixty or seventy years. It may be possible to build up a representative collection of older carvings by exchange. Even records and illustrations of the older carvings in the world's museums are not easily available and a complete illustrated catalogue of carvings older than a century would be valuable to Nigerian scholars.[3]

Records

I have mentioned the fragmentary nature of the records con-

[1] There are very few examples of carvings for the smallpox cult in Nigeria, presumably because of the banning of the cult by the Government early in the century.

Some idea of the loss and destruction of carvings can be gained by the following quotation: 'Before the Modeke war, Ilife must have been a unique example of the old-world style of timber architecture in the hundreds of sculptured beams which we hauled out of lofts and barns . . . at that time, viz. 1894, the greater portion of the temples and houses must still have been decorated in an unusually striking and beautiful way.' (Frobenius, op. cit., p. 81.)

Much of Frobenius's own invaluable collection seems to have become the victim of war in Europe.

[2] '. . . the tribal art of Africa does not belong to Africa any more than ancient Greek art belongs to Greece. Both now belong to the world . . .' From the script of a talk given by William Fagg at the First World Festival of Negro Arts, Dakar.

[3] Joan Wescott gives some idea of the older material available in various collections in her illustrated pamphlet, *Yoruba Art in German and Swiss Museums* (Ibadan, 1958). The Nigerian dealers who have been busily engaged in the last few years in collecting Yoruba carvings for sale to collectors have indeed saved many from decay or destruction, but they present them for sale without any record of provenance or function.

cerning Yoruba carving. The creation of fuller records is a work of importance and urgency. The tradition of woodcarving has come close to extinction as few carvers working in the traditional situations have apprentices. Moreover, the rites in which many carvings were used are being transformed where they are not being discontinued.

A perfect knowledge of Yoruba, often in deep dialectical forms, is essential for a full understanding and efficient collection of detailed information about the carvings, their interpretation, and accompanying chants. Because of the difficulty and frequent impossibility of precise translation of word and idiom, it is preferable that these records be made first in vernacular.[1] This task can only be carried out adequately by Yoruba scholars.

Types of object carved

Typical objects carved by Yoruba craftsmen are: doors, veranda-posts, masks, free-standing figures, drums, ornamental spears, bowls, trays, stools, mirror-frames, and *ayo* playing-boards. All these objects, whether secular or religious, may represent figures and anecdotes of Yoruba life.

Variation

Yoruba carving is not homogeneous and there is considerable variation in style, in subject-matter illustrated, and in type of object carved. Carving records and illustrates the direct and in-direct influences of nearby cultures, for example that of the Bini on Ọwọ, of the Fọn and Egun on west Yoruba groups, of the Afenmai and Nupe on north-east and eastern Yoruba, and of the Ijọ on Ijẹbu. It is of obvious interest to historians to investigate such variations and influences.

Though there is no area of Yoruba country where the life-observing and life-illustrating spirit is not dominant in the carving tradition as a whole, exceptions can be found in certain types of carving. For example, the face or 'pot' of eastern masks (Ijẹṣa, Ondo, Ekiti) is relatively abstract in relation to its own

[1] A first fruit of Yoruba scholarship in the production of carefully edited Yoruba oral texts is *The Content and Form of Yoruba Ìjálá*, by S. A. Babalọla (Oxford, 1962). Analogous works on the songs, chants, prayers, and stories connected with carving are needed. Babalọla's texts are not explicitly related to carving but valuable traditional comment can be found on pp. 198–200 and 331–2.

superstructure and Yoruba carving in general. Many carvings in
Ijẹbu area (figs. 2 and 3) are dominated by a strongly decorative
feeling and commonly use a limited range of hieratic subjects. The
agbo masks of the Ekine water-spirit cult (fig. 4) in the same area
closely imitate the stylistic abstraction, horizontal forms, and
subject-matter of the Ekine masks of the Ijọ people.[1] However,
other anomalous Yoruba carvings cannot be so easily explained:
e.g. the long horizontal masks at Ọyọ and Egosi in Ekiti.[2]

FIG. 2. Ifa bowl collected in
Ijẹbu-Ode in 1958; now in
the British Museum. The
bottom of the bowl shows a
highly decorative use of the
interlaced pattern known as
ibọ. The upper section creates
a carefully interlocking design
based on the human face and
figure. This motif is similar to,
though not identical with,
the large decorative figures
found on *Ogboni* drums in
Ijẹbu.

Carvings also record the relative importance of various cults
in different areas of Yoruba land. For example, the importance
of Ṣango and Egungun cults in central and west Yoruba is shown
by the profusion of carvings made for them, but carvings for these
cults in eastern Yoruba districts are relatively rare. Masks for the
Gẹlẹdẹ cult are found in great numbers in Ẹgbado, Aworí, Ketu,
and Ọhori districts but are not found in nearby areas. The *Gẹlẹdẹ*
cult does not seem to have been diffused even into the neighbouring
areas of Ẹgba and Ijẹbu though mask-forms similar to those of the
Gẹlẹdẹ cult are to be found in Ikorodu and Ijẹbu-Rẹmọ (fig. 5).

The influence of Europe is shown in the cross-bows, guns, and
military and police uniform illustrated in many carvings. Carvings
also illustrate details of Muslim-carried culture traits, such as

[1] See Horton, *The Gods as Guests* (Lagos, 1960), *Kalabari Sculpture* (Lagos,
1965). Carroll, op. cit., pl. 14 and note.
[2] For illustration of the long horizontal type of mask see Carroll, op. cit., p. 51.
Masks for the *Olojufoforo* ceremony in Osi-Ilọrin area resemble some forms of
Nupe mask; see ibid., pls. 66, 72. Another unusual mask form is illustrated in
Beier, op. cit., (1957) pl. 28B.

FIG. 3. Detail of an Ijẹbu door, the exact provenance being unknown. The door is now in Lagos Museum. It shows the highly decorative style found in many Ijẹbu carvings for the *Ogboni* (*Oṣugbo*) cult. A similar style is shown in the *Ifa* tray stated by Frobenius to have come from the ruins of old Ọyọ (Frobenius, op. cit., plate opposite, p. 292). For comments on the accuracy of Frobenius' records see Frank Willett, *African Art*, London 1971, page 92 and note 82). Compare also the tray in the Ulm Museum collected in the seventeenth century, plate 5.

In the lower half of the illustration finely treated *ibọ* patterns are shown. Above from upper left to right are: a bow and arrow; a figure of Eṣu with his thumb in his mouth, spear in hand, and cap projecting at the rear. Below him is a ram. To the right there is a kneeling figure of a woman with a scarf and sash (?) holding a pair of *ẹdan Ogboni*. In front of her is a standing woman (the breasts are not represented) holding two metal armlets; the head-dress and hair are treated decoratively. She seems to have a large pendant in her ear. To her left there is a kneeling figure of Eṣu holding a staff and having a small gourd attached to his hair.

All the other panels of this door are similarly illustrated with decorative figures.

decorated scabbards and cavalry harness, the hour-glass tone-drum, and related forms, and the interlaced patterns known as *ibọ*. These drums have non-Yoruba names even in areas where they are now fully integrated into the social life of the people and are used in pagan ceremonies (as *dundun* in the *Egungun* and *bata* in the Ṣango cults). In many areas, however, they seem to be clearly

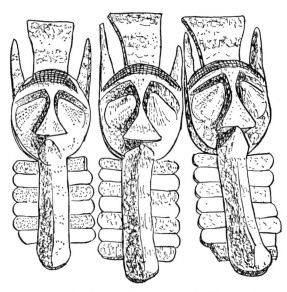

FIG. 4. An *agbo* mask of the Ijẹbu Ekinẹ cult. The masks are used in threes. This form is called *Igodo* (the *oriki* being *ọlọmọ pẹu pẹu*) and was made in Ibeju near Ẹpẹ in 1960. The agbo masks are similar in style to the masks of the Ijọ people who also have a water-spirit cult called Ekinẹ. For comparison with these Ijẹbu masks see Horton, op. cit., pls. 30, 39, 43, 59, 68–71.

foreign and peripheral to the pagan cults, which use other drums in their ceremonies.[1] The particular species of interlaced pattern based on a simple geometric plan, known as *ibọ* by the Yoruba,

[1] Non-Yoruba names used for the drums are *gangan, kanango, koso*; identical or similar names are used by the Hausa. Nouns beginning with a consonant are usually non-Yoruba in origin. It would seem that not only the hour-glass drum (*dundun, gangan*) but the other narrow drums carried by a strap, such as *bata* and *koso*, are recognized as of northern origin. See Laoye I, *Timi* of Ẹdẹ, 'Yoruba Drums', *Odu*, no. 7 (1959); A. King, *Yoruba Sacred Music from Ekiti* (Ibadan, 1961); O. W. Ames, 'Hausa Drums of Zaria'. *Ibadan* xxi (1965).

seems to have been diffused in Africa by Muslim influence
though the patterns themselves are probably pre-Muslim.[1]

Other media

The relatively short life of woodcarving suggests that the historian should look to the more permanent media for illustrations of

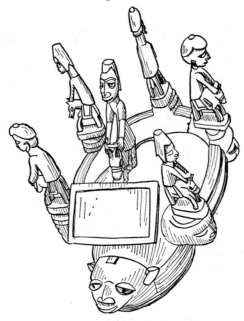

FIG. 5. A mask from Ikorodu for the Magbo cult. It is in the Lagos
Museum. The form is closer to that of Gẹlẹdẹ than the typical Magbo
mask. The heavy features of the horse riders are typical of certain types
of Ijẹbu carving. Masks for Magbo and for Agẹmọ cults in Ijẹbu are more
typical of the Yoruba carvers' interest in everyday life than either the
decorative or hieratic art illustrated in figures 2–4.

the old Yoruba culture. Terracotta, stone, ivory and brass, have
all been used by the Yoruba craftsmen. Unfortunately, these arts

[1] Interlaced patterns are ultimately based on patterns created by such crafts
as basketry and metal filigree. The various interlaced patterns of the widespread
African species are distinguished by the sobriety of their basic geometric plan and
lie at the opposite extreme to the exuberant, free-flowing forms of Scandinavian
and Celtic interlaced patterns. Yoruba craftsmen, such as embroiderers and
bead-workers, though not carvers, cut templates of these patterns in leather or
card and they were probably carried far along the trails of Africa in this form.

do not seem to have been in any way as prolific as Yoruba wood-carving.[1] Moreover, they are not nearly as extensive in illustrative scope as woodcarving. An exception is found in certain orna-mented pots which have adopted the style and life-illustrating power of woodcarving. There are few examples of these in collections at present but it could be hoped that many more, including those of some antiquity, may be collected and pres-served.[2]

Ibeji figurines

The great number of *ibeji* figurines in the villages and in collections suggests that they might be used in the history of woodcarving in a way analogous to the use of pottery in archaeo-logy.

The little carvings are easily collected and are usually well preserved and often of relative antiquity. With due caution they can often be dated with some accuracy as they are usually made soon after the death of a twin.[3] Their basic similarity in size and form makes it relatively easy to identify the work of individual carvers or schools of carving and it should be possible to use them as a control in the historical and stylistic analysis of Yoruba carving. Moreover, details such as hair-style and facial and body markings provide material for study. Theoretically, facial marks are linked with area and lineage, though as worked out in practice the situation is somewhat confused and no one has yet presented a definitive description of the system.[4] As the *ibeji* figures carry the record back well over a century they are of obvious historical interest.

[1] It is possible that brass plaques analogous to those of Benin may have been used by the Yoruba though no examples have yet come to light. See Babaḷọla, op. cit., p. 34. Also, in this book, Denis Williams, p. 164.

[2] For an illustration of such a pot in Lagos Museum, see *Nigeria Magazine* (September 1962), 20.

[3] If we find an *ibeji* figurine kept by a woman of about sixty who says it was made for her grandmother's twin we could estimate its age as about one hundred years. However, miscalculation is possible on several counts; for example, the twin of the grandmother may not have died until a mature age (though in fact most twins die in infancy), again, the image may have been destroyed in a fire and a new one made many years later to replace the original.

[4] P. C. Lloyd, 'The Yoruba Lineage', *Africa*, xxv, no. 3 (1955).

CHAPTER XI
The Yoruba Language in Yoruba History

ABIỌDUN ADETUGBỌ

WHAT contributions can a deep study of the Yoruba language make to Yoruba ethnohistory and what type of linguistic evidence is relevant to historical studies? These are two of the questions the history-minded linguist poses to himself. Anthropologists and ethnohistorians have often watched the progress of linguistics with interest in the hope that historical linguistics would provide a worthwhile hypothesis and theory concerning the laws of the evolution of language, lines of culture transmission and diffusion, the basis of genetic classification, etc.

In a well-thought-out paper, 'Linguistics as an instrument of Prehistory', Swadesh[1] enumerates three ways in which linguistics can make contributions to prehistory:

(a) by establishing facts concerning common origin and subsequent divergence of languages, implying earlier unity and subsequent separations of peoples;

(b) by discovering diffused features among languages, which bear evidence of prehistoric culture contacts; and

(c) by reconstructing the vocabulary of old stages of languages in order to bring out suggestions of the physical environment and content of prehistoric cultures.

These goals may seem somewhat ambitious to the layman and even to some linguists, especially when it is remembered that outside Indo-European and New World linguistics not much progress has been made apart from the establishment of genetic relationships among languages.

Language studies fall into two main categories—the synchronic or descriptive and the diachronic or historical. Historical linguistics forms the base from which inferences of an ethnohistorical nature

---

[1] Morris, Swadesh, 'Linguistics as an Instrument of Prehistory', *Southwestern Journal of Anthropology*, xxvi (1959).

are usually drawn. Historical linguistics itself presupposes a thorough understanding of the present state of the language discussed.

Historical linguistics studies language change on two axes: time and space. Language, like any other human institution, changes in time. A comparison of one's speech habits with those of one's grandparents will make this change easily recognizable. It is this change in time that makes it difficult for us to understand, say, the language of earlier ritual songs and poems, Chaucer, and sometimes even our own parents.

Language change in space is responsible for the existence of dialects of the same language. Even though dialects of the same language are by and large mutually intelligible, we still recognize that a person speaking a dialect different from our own speaks with an 'accent'.

The main task of historical linguistics in all its branches, in the comparative reconstructive model, in dialectology, etc., is the study of this change in language with a view to establishing the degrees of divergence between two stages of a language, whether temporal or spatial, and accounting for the evolution of the different stages. Historical linguistics thereby hopes to be able to gain some insight into the changes in which human institutions have been involved, and which are necessarily reflected in the people's language.

Yoruba linguistic research has progressed much within this century, with Bamgboṣe's full-scale descriptive study, *A Grammar of Yoruba*[1] marking a complete reversal from the traditional English-language-oriented Yoruba grammars to a structural, theory-oriented analysis. Bamgboṣe has, of course, his forerunners in Ida Ward, Siertsema, and Abraham,[2] to mention a few, who even with their limitations as foreigners to the language have made valuable contributions.

Most Yoruba linguistic research has, however, been of the synchronic descriptive type whose worth is limited from an historical point of view. Along the historical linguistics axis, a few word-lists exist and so do some history-oriented studies. Among

---

[1] A. Bamgboṣe, *A Grammar of Yoruba* (Cambridge, 1965).

[2] Of note among the descriptive works on Yoruba are: Rowlands, 'Types of Word Junction in Yoruba', *BSOAS* XVI, ii (1954), 376–87; B. Siertsema, 'Problems of Phonemic Interpretation' I and II, *Lingus* (1958 and 1959). I. Ward, *An Introduction to the Yoruba Language* (Cambridge, 1952).

these are Greenberg's use of some Yoruba language forms in his comparative approach to a hypothesis of African language classifications in *The Languages of Africa*; Armstrong's use of similar material in *The Study of West African Languages* and 'Glottochronology and African Linguistics'; Lucas's *The Yoruba Language: Its Structure and Relationship to Other Languages*; and the present writer's 'The Yoruba Language in Western Nigeria: Its Major Dialect Areas'.[1] These are the sort of works we feel can make contributions to history. While both Armstrong and Greenberg have their bases in the comparative reconstructive linguistic approach, Lucas's work can at best be classified as folk etymology. The present writer's work is dialectological in nature.

GENETIC RELATIONSHIP AND ITS SIGNIFICANCE
FOR YORUBA HISTORY

In *The Languages of Africa*, Greenberg classifies Yoruba as belonging to the Kwa subgroup of the Niger-Kordofanian language phylum. The Kwa family includes the following languages: Kru, Baule, Twi, Ga, Ewe, Fon, Yoruba, Edo, Nupe, Igbo, Idoma, Ijǫ, Efik, to mention the best known among the eighty or so languages extending from around Liberia to the Cross River in Nigeria.

Greenberg mentions three fundamental principles that helped him arrive at his classifications. They are:

(a) sole reliance in comparison on resemblances involving sound-meaning correspondences;

(b) mass comparison of languages *contra* isolated comparisons between pairs of languages;

(c) reliance on linguistic criteria only.

Greenberg's first fundamental principle: reliance on a comparison of sound-meaning correspondences among the languages he has classified as Kwa, has something to do with the comparative method, the most potent of techniques in linguistic prehistory. When one is confronted with two or more distinct languages suspected of being related, the comparative method is used either to confirm this suspected relationship and to arrive at the common ancestor of the languages, or to show that one's suspicion has no basis. A common ancestor is postulated for genetically related languages since these languages are merely the present continua-

[1] For bibliography on the early studies see P. Hair, *The Early Study of Nigerian Languages* (Cambridge, 1966).

tions of what at some earlier period were dialects of the same
language.

Greenberg, in arriving at the Kwa family hypothesis, demon-
strates that the languages of this family have a great number of
shared correspondences. The scope of Greenberg's work is not
limited to Kwa alone, and the result is that documentation of these
shared features for Kwa is understandably small. We give below
some of the cognates in Kwa according to Armstrong.[1]

1. *be* (in a place)
   Twi   – Wọ̀
   Yoruba   – Wà
   Idoma   – Bá

2. *come*
   Twi   – bà
   Ewe   – và
   Fon   – wán
   Yoruba   – wá, bọ̀
   Itṣekiri – wá
   Igbo   – byá

3. *cut off*
   Yoruba   – bẹ́
   Igbo   – bẹ́
   Idoma   – bẹ́
   Ewe   – bẹ́

4. *child, to bear a child*
   Ewe   – ví
   Fon   – vǐ
   Yoruba   – bí
   Itṣekiri – bí
   Bini   – biẹ
   Epie   – bie
   Idoma   – bí

5. *ten*
   Ewe   – èwó
   Fon   – wǒ
   Yoruba   – ẹ̀wá
   Itṣekiri – mẹ́ẹ̀gwá
   Igala   – ẹ̀gwá

   Idoma   – ìgwó

6. *goat*
   Yoruba   – ewúrẹ́
   Igala   – éwó
   Igbira   – ẹ́vú
   Igbo   – éwú
   Bini   – ewe
   Idoma   – ẹ̀wù

7. *garment*
   Ewe   – àwù
   Fon   – àwù
   Yoruba   – ẹ̀wù
   Bini   – ẹ̀wù

8. *this*
   Twi   – èyí
   Yoruba   – èyí
   Itṣekiri – ẹ̀yí
   Igala   – ei

9. *shoot*
   Yoruba   – ta
   Itṣekiri – ta
   Igala   – é-ta
   Bini   – sa
   Idoma   – tá

10. *stone*
   Yoruba   – òkúta
   Nupe   – tákùn
   Igbira   – ịrẹ́ta
   Igbo   – òkúte

[1] R. Armstrong, *The Study of West African Languages* (Ibadan, 1964).

11. *arrive*

Twi	– du
Ewe	– dé
Yoruba	– dé
Epie	– té
Efik	– dí

12. *know*

Yoruba	– mọ̀
Igala	– mà
Igbo	– má

13. *count*

Yoruba	– kà
Itṣekiri	– kà
Bini	– ká
Idoma	– kà

14. *die*

Twi	– wù
Ewe	– kú
Yoruba	– kú
Bini	– wú
Idoma	– kwú

15. *person*

Twi	– ní
Ewe	– amẹ
Yoruba	– ẹni
Itṣekiri	– ọnẹ
Igbo	– ónyé
Igala	– onẹ
Idoma	– ọnyẹ

Provided with such a list as the foregoing, no linguistic sophistication is needed to discover the close correspondences in forms and meanings among the languages cited. Were we dealing with comparisons between forms in two languages, we might be tempted to explain away these correspondences as due either to chance, diffusion, or borrowing from one language to another. With the number of the languages involved, however, to explain these sound-meaning correspondences as due to either chance or borrowing would be preposterous, and this is the essence of Greenberg's second fundamental principle: mass comparison.

The importance of mass comparison as against isolated comparison between two pairs of languages is twofold: it eliminates reasonable doubt as to the possibility of making conclusions of such a wide nature as Greenberg has drawn for African languages, and secondly it eliminates arbitrariness in the classification of these languages into genetic groups. The importance of resemblances cutting through a wide spectrum of languages is that it eliminates chance or borrowing as explanations; the data and the evidence thus allow no other inference than that of genetic relationship.

It is worth noting here that there may be four types of resemblances among languages:

(a) Universal resemblances shared by all languages and

therefore inherent in the definition of language, e.g. that all human language is vocal;

(b) convergent resemblances which are parallels that emerge among languages without historical contact, for example, onomatopoeia;

(c) diffusional resemblances which are features of one language extended over another; and

(d) genetic resemblances which result if two or more languages retain corresponding features of an earlier language from which they are derived.

The sound-meaning correspondences shown earlier are peculiar to the languages mentioned and therefore not universal; they do not arise as a result of convergent development of the languages because the forms are *a priori* basic to the individual languages; they are non-diffusional resemblances because of the very wide range of languages in which they occur.

Greenberg's final fundamental principal is self-explanatory: that languages should be classified exclusively on linguistic evidence.

From the point of view of many linguists there seems to be enough justification, evidentially and methodologically, for grouping together the far-flung languages spoken from Liberia to Southern Nigeria as belonging to one language family—the Kwa. It is also to be remembered that the Kwa language family is itself only one unit among the eleven units of language families which show interrelationships and are called the Niger-Kordofanian language phylum.

The implications for Yoruba origins in the genetic interrelationship among the Kwa languages and the languages belonging to the Niger-Kordofanian phylum are immense. First of all, it means that the hundred million or more peoples who live in West, East, and Central Africa and who today speak about 600 different languages might have been at an earlier prehistoric period closer together than they now are. That is, the different languages spoken today might have been, at that period, mutually intelligible dialects with varying degrees of divergence from one another. If this were the case, then the prehistory of these peoples and their origins must belong together. It will therefore be futile to isolate one of the 600 or so groups and posit for it an origin without reference to the history of the other groups.

Secondly, if, as has been done, we posit an origin for Yoruba people outside their present *locale* it is only reasonable that we posit a similar, geographically contiguous place as the origin of all the people who speak the languages within the Kwa family.

And thirdly, we have to mention the time-depth factor in the divergence of languages. The belief that is current among the Yorubas is that they migrated to their present home from somewhere in the Middle East or lower Egypt in different waves between the seventh and eleventh centuries A.D. The history of known cases of language-differentiation makes it improbable that the time-depth in the differentiation of Edo from Yoruba would be less than 3,000 years. And when one thinks of Yoruba as one out of about eight languages within the Kwa family, one also has to reckon with a greater time-depth to account for the divergence among these far-flung languages.

If we accept the genetic relationship posited for the Kwa languages and accept also the time lapse that underlies the differentiation of Edo and Yoruba, we shall also have to adopt the view that our theories of Yoruba origins are in need of revision. If on the basis of the posited Yoruba immigration to West Africa from somewhere else, we also have to posit that the Kwa peoples migrated to West Africa from a similar place as the Yorubas, then we have to conclude that the major differentiations that set their languages apart one from the other must predate the migrations. But our historians are neither agreed on the migrations of the Kwa peoples other than the Yorubas nor are they ready to posit for all these peoples the same ancestral home. A rejection of the migration theory is probable in the light of the linguistic evidence. It is perhaps unlikely that the shared linguistic features among these languages were acquired outside Africa, especially when these resemblances include the designations for tropical flora and animals. The time-depth in the differentiations of the languages too would compel us to posit contact among the peoples for upwards of 3,000 years.

The establishment of genetic relationship among languages is not the main purpose of historical linguistics nor is it all that language study can contribute to prehistory. We have elaborated here on the place of Yoruba among African languages because it is the area on which much agreement has been reached in African language studies. Genetic classification of language is itself a means to an end: the goal of establishing the prototype from which the related languages have diverged, thereby ascertaining the physical environment and content of the earlier cultural unity of the now different peoples.

Admittedly African linguistics is only now coming into its own and very little has yet been done in reconstructing the earlier stages of our languages. But linguistic reconstruction is a very potent instrument of prehistory. In the Yoruba case, however, we shall still have to wait for some time before our results can be of any use.

YORUBA DIALECTS

The Yoruba language is a dialect *continuum* but has a *koine* known as Standard Yoruba or Modern Yoruba. This standardized form of Yoruba is causing a recession of geographical speech-variants among the educated. Standard Yoruba is, however, only a part of the Yoruba language; it is not the Yoruba language: the Yoruba language being an aggregate of all the dialects (including the *koine*) spoken within the Yoruba linguistic area. Because of the shared features among all the dialects which allow for some degree of mutual intelligibility, the Yoruba language *qua* language is an aggregate, and not the sum total, of all the dialects it subsumes. Standard Yoruba has a place of honour among Yoruba dialects because to a very large extent it is probably the only dialect which is more or less socially defined; the other dialects being geographically delimited.

Dialectology seeks to characterize the nature, cause, and course of discontinuities within a linguistic area. It studies language on the axes of both time and space: time for the establishment of change and space for an account of how the geographical variants within a language area are distributed. It may thus be seen that as an instrument of history, dialectology contains its own seeds of success. Its 'explanations' for the change in linguistic features as contact, migration, diffusion, and the entailment of the features themselves within a linguistic structure do have historical implications.

Dialectology's relevance to history may be immense as demonstrated in Marvin Herzog's *The Yiddish Language in Northern Poland: Its Geography and History* (Bloomington, 1965) and Uriel Weinreich's *Language and Culture Atlas of Ashkenazic Jewry* (in preparation).[1] The two works do not only show the convergence of language change and cultural discontinuity but also a documentation of the approximate epochs in which the changes took place, and these are corroborated by historical records. Admittedly, the scope of the historical relevance of dialect studies to history is more limited than that of the wider comparative-reconstruction method and its depth of historical explanation smaller than that offered by the genetic classification of languages; nevertheless dialect studies offer more convincing evidence of the internal history of a people, their migrations, etc., and here we may be on surer ground because of the relatively smaller time-depth we need in accounting for the differentiations within the language area.

In the Yoruba case, however, we come to grips with the same problems enumerated earlier: lack of any deep study of Yoruba dialects and the infancy of dialectology of the Yoruba linguistic area. We shall attempt here only a summary of some of the findings and groupings of Yoruba dialects contained in 'The Yoruba Language in Western Nigeria: Its Major Dialect Areas'.

On the basis of linguistic and ethnohistorical criteria, the Yoruba language in Western Nigeria falls into three major dialect groupings: North-West Yoruba (NWY), South-East Yoruba (SEY), and Central Yoruba (CY). Each major dialect grouping is characterized by some features of homogeneity but also has within it some features with restricted distribution which delimit what we may term minor dialect subdivisions within the major dialect area. We shall enumerate first some of the general features of differentiations which set off the major dialect areas from one another, and later we shall be able to mention some of the historical implications of the linguistic features of divergence.

North-West Yoruba (NWY) comprises the Ọyọ, Ọṣun, Ibadan, and the northern parts of the Ẹgba areas and is historically a part of the Ọyọ Empire. Here, lineage and descent are unilineal and agnatic; traditional government is based on a division of power between civil and war chiefs. Linguistically, negation is expressed usually with {kò}, tense and aspect distinctions are made largely by the use of 'preverbs': {Ń} for the continuative aspect, {yíò} and {á} for the indefinite tense, etc. In the phonology Proto-Yoruba (PY) /gh/ and /gw/ have merged and become /w/; the upper

---

[1] Uriel Weinreich has done tremendous work in Structural Dialectology. The Yiddish Atlas is forthcoming.

mid-oral vowels /i/ and /ụ/ were raised and merged with the high oral vowels /i/ and /u/ respectively; so also were the nasal counterparts of the upper mid-vowels, i.e. /in/ and /un/ raised and merged with the high nasal vowels /in/ and /un/ respectively; furthermore, the sibilants /S/ and /Ṣ/ are confused, except in the Abẹokuta area.

South-East Yoruba (SEY) consists of Ondo, Qwọ, Ikalẹ, Ilajẹ, and Ijẹbu areas and was probably for a long time a part of the Benin Empire. Lineage and descent are in many parts multilineal and cognatic; traditional government operates through a system of graded societies and a three-tier chieftaincy system, the NWY division of titles into war and civil being unknown. Linguistically, SEY is less innovating than NWY: negation and tense-aspect distinctions are made by pronoun vowel change and tone change; PY /gh/ and /gw/ are retained; PY upper mid-nasal vowels /ịn/ and /ụn/ which in NWY were raised to and merged with /in/ and /un/ respectively have been lowered to /ẹn/ and /ọn/ respectively.[1]

Central Yoruba (CY) is made up of Ifẹ, Ilesha, and Ekiti areas and is characterized by a series of transitional phenomena. It shares many of the ethnographical features of SEY and to a large extent the lexicon of NWY. In other respects, it is unique. It polarizes negativeness and positiveness in its singular pronouns and retains relics of the PY system of vowel harmony whereby the co-occurrence of vowels in successive syllables of the morpheme (word) is determined by features of tenseness and laxness. In its vowel systems, it is the least innovating of the three dialects groups.

Historical Implications of Dialect Differentiation

Each feature of dialect differentiation has its own history but this history does not lie completely in the linguist's field. Dialect differentiation and recognition straddle linguistics and ethnography. The best results in explicating the features of dialect history must of necessity come from the joint venture of specialists in linguistics and anthropology. The conclusions of historical value that the linguist can draw relate mostly to the relative chronology of the developments of the features of dialect diverg-

---

[1] We follow closely the conventions of Yoruba orthography. Some dialectal sounds are, however, not accounted for in the orthography. Such sounds are gh, a velar fricative [γ]; i and ụ, which are lax high vowels, front and back respectively.

ence. Extrapolating from these, he may deduce other sociological factors such as the amount of coherence that inheres in the linguistic habits of a particular area, the contact and/or discontinuity that may be responsible for divergences. Also the structure of the features of divergence will itself be able to give the analyst some clues as to probable migrations and their routes.

We draw attention here to the analysis of only a few elements of dialect divergence in Yoruba as the scope of this chapter does not permit a full-scale discussion of Yoruba dialects. We should warn, however, that this limitation in the scope of the evidence presented necessarily affects the reliability of the historical implications arising from it. To isolate a dialect feature and base upon it conclusions of an historical nature must be unconvincing because only an interplay of the distribution of the features of differentiation, the relative positions of different isoglosses, and a comparison of the *loci* of the bundling of both linguistic and ethnographic isoglosses and isogrades, will yield us the clear picture on which the validity of our claims rests. We prefer, however, offering some of the evidence to not offering any at all.

Pronoun and Pronominal[1] Differences among the Dialects

We find a few differences among the different dialect groups. These are:

(a) coalescence of the terms for second and third person plural pronouns and pronominals in SEY as against their separation in both NWY and CY;

(b) absence of the pronoun of respect in SEY *contra* its presence in the other dialects;

(c) the operation of vowel-harmony rules on the level of grammar in the singular pronouns of CY and its absence in both NWY and SEY;

(d) the polarization of positiveness and negativeness in the singular pronouns of CY and SEY;

(e) the use of the pronoun as tense signaller in both CY and SEY as against the use of preverbs in NWY.

(a) It is to be noted that the dialects spoken in Okeigbo, Ondo

---

[1] Following Bamgboṣe we distinguish between pronouns and pronominals in Yoruba. We call the pronouns those forms which traditionally are known as the short pronouns. Correspondingly the traditional long pronouns we now call the pronominals. See Bamgboṣe, *A Grammar of Yoruba*, pp. 106–7.

and environs, the whole of Okitipupa, and Qwọ divisions, lack the opposition between second and third person plural pronouns. Thus the opposition in NWY between ẹ wá 'you (pl.) came', and wọ́n wá, 'they came', is not made use of in SEY, both forms having coalesced to àn án wá, 'you (pl.)/they came'.

Allied with this coalescence of the second and third person plural pronouns is the absence of the pronoun of respect in the same dialects. In all dialects of NWY in the Ijẹbu areas of SEY, in Ifẹ-Ilesha and parts of Ekiti division of CY the second and third person plurals are the pronouns of respect both in formal and in colloquial speech. Thus in addressing an elderly person a NWY youth usually says: ẹ̀yin ni, 'it is you (pl.)', instead of ìwọ ni, 'it is you (sing.)', which is considered rude. In those areas of SEY and CY which lack the pronoun of respect, an elderly person is always addressed in the second person singular, /ùwọ/. Even the third person plural pronoun is being used as a respect form for singular references in NWY. Asked about the where-abouts of his mother an Qyọ boy usually says wọ́n wà nílé, 'they are at home', instead of ó wà nílé, 'she is at home'. The so-called majestic plural, i.e. the use of the first person plural pronoun for singular reference is also prevalent in the areas with the pronoun of respect.

We may note that the absence of the pronoun of respect in some areas of SEY is due to the coalescence of the terms for second and third person plural pronoun. Were the SEY speaker to use the fused form of the second and third person plural as the pronoun of respect, he would probably be left with a coalescence of three or more distinctions.

We suggest that the coalescence of the second and third plural pronouns was a movement from the SEY areas westwards towards both the CY and NWY areas. The advance of the diffusion was checked by its collision with the eastward expanding use of the pronoun of respect. The emergence of the plural of respect in NWY areas may be due to or influenced by the introduction of the English language in Western Nigeria in the last century. (Nigerian English abounds in displaced pronouns as respect forms of address in deference to age and status.) In turn, this new respect function for the plural pronouns may be seen as the stabilizing factor which prevented the falling together of the second and third person plural pronouns of NWY and CY.

In the singular pronouns of CY, vowel-harmony rules are operative, that is, these pronouns have two forms each and which form is used is determined by the tenseness or laxness of the vowel of the predicate verb to which the subject pronoun is assimilated. Thus we have:

tense verb /ri/ 'to see'	lax verb /ra/ 'to buy'
mo rí 'I saw'	mọ rà 'I bought'
(w) o ri 'you saw'	(w) ọ rà 'you bought'
o rí 'he-she-it saw'	ọ́ rà 'he-she-it bought'

The operation of vowel harmony on the level of grammar as seen above is not unique to CY dialects as we find relics even in the Ọyọ dialect of NWY. The average Ọyọ man says *ọ́ lọ* 'he went' but *ó rí* 'he saw'. This pronoun assimilation to the verb also recurs in the Ọṣun areas.

Negation

While negation is almost always expressed with the allomorphs of {kò} in NWY, some pronouns of CY and SEY have two forms each, one used in affirmative expressions and the other in negative expressions. We have in Ilesha (CY) for instance:

ó yún, 'he went'   éyún, 'he did not go'
mọ á, 'I came'   mẹ́á, 'I did not come'

that is, back vowels in the pronoun signal positiveness, while front vowels indicate negativeness. This feature recurs in some areas of SEY also. In Ondo we have:

wo yú, 'you went'   wé yú, 'you did not go'

We sketch here one more feature of divergence in the pronoun system of the dialects—the use of the pronoun as tense indicator in SEY areas. In Ondo for instance we have:

é lọ, 'he-she-it is going'
ó lọ, 'he-she-it went'
á lọ, 'he-she-it will go'

With noun subjects, the final vowel of the noun is assimilated to the he-she-it form for the particular tense.

'Olu went'	becomes	Ol'ó lọ
'Olu is going'		Ol'é lọ
'Olu will go'		Ol'á lọ

So also with Dele

Dél' ó lọ	'Dele went'
Dél é lọ	'Dele is going'
Dél' á lọ	'Dele will go'

Phonological Differences among the Major Dialect Groups

The lowest level of linguistic description is the sound system (phonology) and it is at this level that we find the most complex divergence among Yoruba dialects. We shall limit ourselves here to a discussion of only a few phonological features. We start with the consonants.

Many areas of SEY preserve the Proto-Yoruba voiced velar fricative gh i.e. /γ/, as in

oghó	'money'
àghọ̀	'skin, colour'
èìghọ̀	'taboo'
ghán	'dear, costly'
aghọn	'tortoise'

In all the occurrences of PY /gh/ in SEY above, the phoneme has been shifted to the bilabial semivowel /w/ in NWY and has been eliminated in CY. Thus we have

NWY	CY	
owó	eọ́	'money'
àwọ̀	aọ̀	'skin, colour'
èèwọ̀	ee-ọ̀	'taboo'
wọ́n	ọ́n	'costly, dear'
awun	aun	'tortoise'

It is to be noted that the area in which the prototype /gh/ is retained is not continuous. It is absent from both the Ijebu-Ode and Ijebu-Igbo dialects but preserved in Shagamu and Ikenne dialects. It is also the case that in the dialects where /gh/ is preserved, this phoneme is the only voiced fricative attested. Our structural evidence makes it probable that the shift of /gh/ to /w/ passed through the intermediate stage of /h/. The complex and multiple reflexes of NWY /h/ in both SEY and CY make this convincing. Moreover, all the dialects preserving the prototype

/gh/ lack /h/. It is also our guess that the shift of /gh/ to /w/ through /h/ predates all other consonant changes in NWY.

Another exciting consonant shift in our dialect area is connected with the confusion of the sibilants /s/ and /ṣ/ in NWY areas. A reconstructed proto-Yoruba consonantal system will probably reveal that /s/ and /ṣ/ have one prototype /s/ which has split into /s/ and /ṣ/ in SEY and many areas of CY but was changed to /s/ in NWY. Thus, we have

	Ondo (SEY)	Ibadan (NWY)	
/ṣ/	aṣọ	asọ	'clothing'
	uṣẹ́	isẹ́	'work'
	àṣà	àsà	'custom'
/s/	sá	sáre	'run'
	sùn	sùn	'sleep'
	sọ̀ọ̀ (to tell a lie)	sọrọ	'to narrate'

A subregional shift in Ikale dialects changes /ṣ/ to /s/ and /s/ to /h/ i.e.:

Ondo aṣọ becomes Ikale asọ 'clothing' and
Ondo sùn Ikale hùn 'sleep'.

Characteristic of NWY areas is the confusion of /s/ and /ṣ/ and this is due in part to contact of NWY speakers with SEY and to the introduction of the English language where the contrast between /s/ and /ṣ/ is functional. It is also to be observed that this sibilant confusion by NWY educated speakers is but a reflection of SEY use of those sibilants; to the NWY speaker, the distinctive separation of /s/ and /ṣ/ constitutes a list-learning problem.

Vocalism

In the vowel system of the dialects we have a number of complex but interesting differences. Only a few of the differences will be mentioned here. In the oral vowel system we note two major differences among our dialects:

(a) difference in inventory;
(b) difference in co-occurrence rules.

(a) while NWY and SEY have a seven oral-vowel system thus:

$$
\begin{array}{ccc}
i & & u \\
e & & o \\
ẹ & & ọ \\
& a &
\end{array}
$$

CY dialects make use of nine oral-vowel contracts:

(b) The exciting thing, however, lies in the difference between the co-occurrence of vowels in the two different systems. In all the dialects of Yoruba, there are co-occurrence limitations in the distribution of vowels, but these limitations differ. In all areas 'o' and 'ọ', 'e' and 'ẹ', and 'e' and 'ọ' do not co-occur in the same morpheme. In the CY areas, there are greater co-occurrence rules called vowel harmony. The vowels are divided into two groups— tense and lax:

Tense: i u   Lax: į   ụ
       e o   ẹ   ọ
       (a)   a

Tense vowels co-occur in the morpheme (word) and lax vowels co-occur but, except in the case of *a*, tense and lax vowels do not co-occur in the word. This vowel harmony has some effects on the morphology of those dialects in which it occurs.

We should also mention here that the vowel system of CY areas reflects more the earlier stage of the language. That is, at an earlier stage, all the dialects of Yoruba had this system of vowel harmony, relics of which are still preserved everywhere. Vowel harmony is being eliminated in all other areas (except CY) in the form of coalescence of certain phones.

Nasal Vowels

Nasal vowels are those vowels released while the nasal passage is open. In Yoruba orthography nasality of the vowel is shown by the presence of *n* immediately after the vowel. Thus the difference between tà — 'sell' and tàn — 'deceive' is that the first *a* is oral while the second *a* is nasal.

In the nasal vowel series we find a tripartite division of our area. Thus Ọyọ areas have three nasal vowels:

in un
ọn

while Ondo and Ijẹbu areas have four or five:

in   un

ẹn   ọn

(an)

Central Yoruba areas have either six or seven:

in   ụn

i̲n   ụ̲n

(ẹn) ọn

an

with ẹn being marginal to the system. There is also the co-occurrence restriction here: *in* and *un* are tense while all the others are lax.

Apart from these differences in the number of oppositions in the inventories, there are more exciting facts about the cross-dialect correspondences. Both SEY and NWY have undergone certain changes to arrive at their present systems. The more obvious changes are noted below:

CY		NWY		SEY		Gloss
in	rín	in	rín	in	rín	'laugh (n.)'
i̲n	ùri̲n	in	írìn	ẹn	ùrẹ̀n	'walk (n.)'
ẹn	—	in	—	ẹn	idẹn	'maggot'
un	ogun	un	ogun	un	ogun	'war'
ụn	ọdụ́n	un	ọdún	ọn	ọdọ́n	'festivity'
ọn	i̲bọn	ọn	ibọn	an	àban	'shotgun'

(ẹn is marginal to both NWY and CY systems. Except in Abẹokuta areas of NWY, it occurs only in a few words, one of which is iyẹn 'that').

From the discussion of Yoruba dialects above, an inevitable conclusion is that both CY and SEY dialects preserve an earlier stage of Proto-Yoruba than NWY. That is, the dialects of Ondo, Ọwọ, and Ekiti areas show more traces of antiquity than the Ọyọ Ọṣun, and Ẹgba dialects. (This is not the same thing as saying that settlements in the areas of dialect innovation, i.e. in Ọyọ for instance, are more recent than the settlements in the relic-preserving areas, though in the Yoruba case we have some reasons to believe this to be true.) Socio-cultural factors that are responsible for language change may affect different dialects at different rates of change. But on empirical evidence, we believe that SEY and CY areas have older settlements than NWY areas, for all over the world, areas of great antiquity are marked by the proliferation of dialects as we have, say, in the Ondo province, where every settlement, however small, can claim a dialect different from that of the next settlement.

A few other inferences may be drawn from our dialect study. What, for instance, and how long-lasting, was the effect of the Benin empire on SEY dialects? Can it be true that while in NWY areas, subjected to constant flux in populations and movements and migrations of peoples, a compromise dialect had to be arrived at (and this is probably partially responsible for the considerable homogeneity of the speech habits in this area), CY areas have had for some time a stable stock of peoples free from mixtures of the type posited for NWY areas and relatively insulated from such external influence as that exerted through the Benin Empire on SEY areas? Could this have been responsible for the comparative freedom of CY dialects from large innovations on the scale we have in NWY? We might also note that Ile Ifẹ, traditionally regarded as the cradle of the Yorubas and said to have been the cultural focus of Yoruba land, is on the borderline between CY and NWY. But we have not found any evidence that it exerted any worthwhile linguistic influence on other areas of Yoruba parallel to the much-talked-of influence in other spheres, otherwise we might have been able to discover concentric isoglosses with Ifẹ as the centre. Could Ifẹ's influence have been short-lived or of far less magnitude than historians have claimed?

Moreover, could the relic features in SEY dialects have given our historians the motivation for the division of Yoruba areas into two? Johnson and Lucas regard part of SEY–CY areas as peopled by aborigines while NWY is peopled by immigrants; Biobaku on the other hand, while recognizing the plausibility of such a division, posits an earlier date of immigration for SEY than for NWY.[1]

These are questions whose answers have immense implications for Yoruba origins and prehistory. More research in Yoruba dialectology is likely to bring us nearer to the solution of the problems.

---

[1] See S. O. Biobaku, 'An Historical Sketch of the Peoples of Western Nigeria', *Odu*, vi, 24–8. *The Origin of the Yoruba* (Lagos, 1955). J. O. Lucas, *Religion of the Yorubas* (Lagos, 1948). Johnson, *The History of the Yorubas*.

GLOTTOCHRONOLOGY AND YORUBA HISTORY

To many researchers into the history of non-literate peoples, glottochronology is the better-known aspect of historical linguistics because of its promises.

Glottochronology attempts to measure the degree of differentiation between two or more related languages as an index to the relative length of time that the languages have been diverging. When such index is calibrated along the time axis, it is hoped that the dating of the common ancestor—the proto-language—will be provided. Glottochronology then, as a historical linguistic technique, attempts to date when earlier dialect cleavages occurred and to provide the time-depth in the separation of related languages. As a dating technique, it thus parallels in historical linguistics what carbon 14 promises in archaeology. And since other historical linguistics techniques, like the comparative reconstruction technique, are inadequate models for dating the past, glottochronology has been sold easily without caveats to both historians and anthropologists alike. Glottochronology promises also, apart from the provision of time-depth estimates, implications for the subgrouping of genetically related languages, proof of genetic relationship among languages, and an estimate of the rate of lexical change within language. Unfortunately, glottochronology at the present stage of its development provides promises only; their fulfilment is beset with many problems. Even where it has been shown that glottochronology works (the control cases) there is still extreme scepticism among historical linguists as to the usefulness and empirical validity of extrapolating from this small number of control cases a theory to cover other cases of application.

Glottochronology operates with four basic assumptions:

1. That some parts of the vocabulary of any language are much less subject to change than other parts. This part of the vocabulary, the basic core vocabulary, is said to be assumed on empirical evidence and a test list of 200 such items is provided.

2. That the rate of retention of the items on this basic core vocabulary list is relatively stable and that it is constant through time. Using a thousand years as a unit of the chronological scale, it assumes that if in the first thousand

years a language retains 90 per cent of its basic vocabulary, in the next millenium, the language will retain 90 per cent of what is left. That is, if the language set out with say 100 core vocabulary items, at end of the first millenium it may have 90 items left. At the end of the second millenium it retains 90 per cent of the 90 items it started the second millenium with, that is 81 words.

3. That the rate of loss of items in the basic core vocabulary list is more or less the same in all languages, that is the rate of loss, under normal conditions, is the same in say, Chinese, English, Yoruba, and Egun, even though the number of speakers of these languages differs so widely: Chinese over 500 million and Egun less than a quarter of a million. This assumption is extrapolated from thirteen control cases, i.e. languages with historical records within the Indo-European language family, and the results range from a loss rate of between 13·6 per cent and 25·6 per cent per thousand years.

4. That if the proportion of cognates within the basic core vocabulary is found for any two languages, the time lapse since the two languages began to diverge from their common parent language can be computed 'provided that there are no interfering factors through migrations, conquests or other social contacts which slowed or speeded the divergence'.[1] A formula is then provided with three variables: rate of retention, r; period of time, t; and the fraction of the corresponding cognates from the diagnostic basic core vocabulary, c. The formula for finding the time-depth of separation is given by Swadesh as $t = \log c / 2 \log r$.

We may now briefly review the assumptions and see some examples of the application of glottochronology to Yoruba and related languages.

The establishment of the dichotomy between basic core or 'non-cultural' vocabulary as against cultural vocabulary is based on the criteria of frequency of the occurrence of items on the basic core list, their persistence and the universality of the concepts they denote as against the particular, culture-oriented

---

[1] S. C. Gudschinsky, 'The ABC's of Lexicostatistics', *Word*, xii (1956), 175–210.

denotations of the other elements in the lexicon of any language. But can this dichotomy be that sharp for any language, and if so, are the items on the diagnostic list universal? In our own work in Yoruba, for instance, we could not find single word glosses for the English 'green' and 'yellow', nor for 'freeze', 'dull', and 'ice'. And when the test list was used for the Badagry dialect of Egun, we found no single word glosses for 'cloud', 'because', 'if', 'lake', 'mountain', 'thin'. It seems that while the diagnostic word list meets the criteria of frequency, persistence and universality in Indo-European languages, further improvements are needed in its application to non-Indo-European languages. This finding led Hoijer to declare that 'there is, in short, nothing in lexico-statistic theory which enables us, once and for all, to establish a firm test list, translatable without difficulties into any language';[1] each language has not only its own peculiar structure but its own unique set of semantic patterns as well.

On the second assumption, we wonder whether the time span covered in control cases by glottochronology is not too short in language history to allow us to conclude that the retention rate of items of the basic vocabulary is constant through time. The control cases give us a time span of only about 2,500 years and language may be more than twenty times as old as that span. Complete empirical evidence of this basic assumption is not available and may remain so for thousands of years to come.

The third assumption is the most difficult to accept, that the rate of loss of the basic vocabulary is approximately the same for all languages, an assumption based on a test in fewer than twenty languages but with varying results of the rate of retention ranging from 86·4 per cent to 74·4 per cent per thousand years. Armstrong does 'not regard it as demonstrated that languages such as Arapaho and Cheyenne, with between 1,500 and 3,000 speakers, change at the same pace as Chinese'. But he is 'unable to say whether the rate of change is greater or less'.[2]

Our research in the Yoruba of Cuba, otherwise known as Lucumi, and the Ọyọ Yoruba negates the assumption of a constant rate of change for all languages. Perhaps a comparison of the two forms of Yoruba is not ideal owing to the chequered history of the

[1] Harry Hoijer, 'Lexicostatistics: A Critique', *Language*, xxxii, 49–60.
[2] R. Armstrong, 'Glottochronology and African Linguistics' *J.A.H.*, iii, no. 2 (1962), pp. 283–90.

Cuban Yoruba. Lucumi is now a cult language in Cuba, peculiar to the adherents of the San Tiera group and is preserved for worship. This form of Yoruba, and we insist it is Yoruba, has been subjected to much Spanish influence as a result of which it has lost its 'tonal' system to the Spanish 'stress' system and retains, by our own computation, less than 50 per cent of basic core cognates (47 per cent to be exact) with the Qyọ Yoruba. This gives us a time depth of between five and fifteen thousand years. And when we bear in mind that the actual historical separation between Lucumi and the Yoruba in Nigeria is only about 500 years old, the error range gains astronomical proportions. Olmsted[1] has found another development in Lucumi which negates even the second basic assumption of glottochronology: that the basic—root—morphemes change at the rate of 10 per cent faster than the 'cultural' vocabulary; but he excuses this deviation by pointing out 'that the social conditions incident to the formation of the Lucumi-speaking group were so special as to produce a language unclassifiable either as of genetic descent or as pidginized'. Such a case, he argues, might not be expected to conform to the assumptions underlying glottochronology.

Olmsted's argument derives from the fact that we know the history of the transplantation of Yoruba speaking peoples into Cuba. But what if the history were not known? And in any case how are we to be sure that in prying into the distant past for which written records are non-existent, we are not assuming a regularity in the development of languages, which in fact might have had as chequered a development as Yoruba in Cuba? Is there any language that may not have had a chequered history?

The final assumption deals with the computation of the time-depth of cleavage between languages derived from a common source. Here too, we find no agreement. Swadesh's formula has been given above as $t = \log c / 2 \log r$.

Hattori, on the other hand, on the basis of his study of Japanese dialects and comparing these with Germanic languages has given us another formula: $t = \log c / 1 \cdot 4 \log r$. The different yields from the application of these two formulae can be staggering. Armstrong's computation of the time-depth in the differentiation between Qyọ Yoruba and Edo gives us 3,200 years by Swadesh's

[1] D. L. Olmsted, 'Three Tests of Glottochronological Theory', *American Anthropologist*, lix, 839–42.

formula and 4,600 years using the Hattori formula, a difference of 1,400 years. Yoruba and Igbo have been separated for 4,000 and 6,000 years using Swadesh and Hattori respectively. Perhaps we may end up by having a different retention rate for African languages!

This critique of glottochronology is meant to point out the areas that need to be refined in the theory and to warn the unwary that computations arrived at through this theory should not be accepted without reservations. It has often been the case that the controversy which accompanies the introduction of new theories helps in the refinements of those theories.

Even with all these disagreements, glottochronology is not without its advantages. First, through the use of its basic core vocabulary list, it forces the ethnohistorian and the linguist alike to consider the cognate interrelations between languages. The establishment of sound-meaning correspondences within the basic core vocabulary among two languages is enough motivation for further investigation as to the closeness of the two languages. And where two languages are found to be related, it is worth the trial, however imperfect the methodology may be, to find out the time-depth in the separation of these languages. It should be borne in mind that the lapse of time established by glottochronology should not be regarded as absolute; a range of error can still be computed. It has been pointed out that in West African history the general tendency is to underestimate the depth of time involved and to posit migrations, if indeed there were mass immigrations of people into this region, within the Christian era, and that prior to these immigrations, this region must have been inhabited by faceless forms whose ways of life have since been lost to posterity. Glottochronology with its imperfections may then offer the essential and much-needed corrective. Whatever dating formula is used will not justify the historian's placement of the cleavage between Yoruba and Edo within the Christian era. We still await corroborative or corrective evidence from archaeology. A comparison of the historical, linguistic, and archaeological findings will be of immense advantage.

The second result of importance that glottochronology yields us is the realization that the curve that shows the loss in the basic core vocabulary is an exponential one. The percentage of loss remains constant no matter how many items of the core vocabulary are retained. It means that even where among languages we find a great number of cognates, the time-depth that separates these languages may still be great.

As has already been mentioned above, the glottochronological technique has been used by Armstrong to estimate the time depth in the separation of Yoruba on the one hand and some genetically related neighbouring languages such as Edo and Igbo on the other. Even though the evidence is not yet made public, it is reasonable to agree with Armstrong as to the time-depth he posits for the separation of Yoruba from these other languages. Armstrong goes a little further by treating Yoruba as a control case in one instance. Here he is concerned with the rate of change. Using a list of 132 words from Koelle's *Polyglotta Africana* published in 1853 he finds only three or perhaps four changes out of the 132 in their modern Ọyọ Yoruba forms. Since most of Koelle's informants had been away in Sierra Leone for upwards of twenty years, Armstrong's time-depth is given as 130 years and this yields an approximate rate of less than 20 per cent per thousand years.

ETYMOLOGY

Etymology is that branch of historical linguistics which deals with the history of a linguistic form, tracing this form back to its earliest determinable base and source in a given language or language group. Under etymology comes the discussion of place names, personal names, loan words, and loan blends. Etymology as a branch of historical linguistics must be distinguished from folk etymology. Etymology proper treats the history of a word with regard to the structure of which the word forms a unit and any phonetic changes posited for the word must be shown to be operative on other words of similar origin and similar phonetic structure. That is, if we posit that Yoruba *fèèlí* is derived from English *fail* [feil] we must be able to establish some phonetic laws whereby English [ei] in [feil] becomes Yoruba [ee] and how final consonant in English is made the onset of another syllable in Yoruba. We also have to state the conditions governing the choice of the vowel which forms the syllable peak of the consonant. We find many examples of English [ei] becoming Yoruba [ee]:

English	Yoruba
late [leit]	léèti

cake [keik]	kéèki
date [deit]	déèti
slate [sleit]	siléèti
brake [breik]	búréèki

That is the change of English [ei] to Yoruba [éè] is not unique to the word *fail* but almost universal to all words with [ei]. [ei] in English is a unit sound, a diphthong, and with its onset and coda forms a single syllable, defined by stress. In Yoruba, however, since the syllable is defined by tone placement, diphthongs are not made use of: a diphthong is therefore split into two unit sounds with two independent tones. Moreover, final consonants are not attested in Yoruba, therefore a final consonant of a borrowed word is usually made the beginning of a new syllable and a vowel is then appended to it. In the examples given the vowel is *i*. In other instances it could be *u* as in

English	Yoruba
shop:	ṣọọ̀bù
cook:	kúkù
record:	rẹ́kọọ̀dù

The choice of *i* or *u* as the final vowel depends largely on the vowel of the syllable preceding the final consonant in the donor language or its correspondence in Yoruba. If this vowel is a front vowel, the final vowel chosen is *i*; if on the other hand the vowel is a back vowel, the final vowel is *u*. Some other conditions are applicable, but this should not delay us here.

Etymology does not rest on positing phonetic laws only but insists on the correspondence in meaning also. All the forms cited above have retained in the recipient language similar meanings to what they had and still have in the donor language.

Folk etymology on the other hand is not concerned with rigorously establishing sound-meaning correspondences or accounting for the changes a word might have gone through to arrive at its present form and meaning. It is concerned with any change in the written form or pronunciation of words with little regard to their process of derivation or their place within the lexical structure of the language.

The etymology of loan words can be useful in indicating many types of historical relationship. First the existence of loan words in a language indicates that there might have been some contact either physical or cultural between the recipient language and the donor language, especially if both languages are not in a contiguous geographical area and are not demonstrated to be genetically related. The existence of Arabic loan words through Hausa in Yoruba is mostly in the area of trade and religion and this shows some cultural contact. Also the degree of assimilation of the borrowed words to the structure of the receiving language can indicate the relative chronology of the borrowing. Doublets are particularly useful in this sense, Yoruba *kọ́bọ̀* 'penny' and *kọ́pà* 'copper' constitute a doublet from the English *copper* and it is easy to show that *kọbọ* is the earlier borrowing of the two.

No work of any note has been done on Yoruba etymology but some has been done in Yoruba folk etymology. Folk etymology by its very nature contains the seeds of its own failure, and this is why Lucas's work *Yoruba Language: Its Structure and Relationship to other Languages* is most unreliable. We expand on this later on.

Place Names and Yoruba History

Place names within Yorubaland reflect more of their geographical locations, such as *Abẹokuta*—a place hidden away by rocks, *Okitipupa*—a place founded on a brown mound; wishes and states of mind like *Aiyesan*, 'may life be good' *Aiyetoro*, 'may there be peace', *Ilutitun*, 'new settlement', *Ilesha*, 'the grove of the gods', etc. The names of the streets and quarters within settlements, however, yield us some valuable historical information more than the names of the settlements themselves. Thus we have in Ibadan *Ekotẹdo*, a street founded by Eko people, *Inalende* ('fire drove me here'), a resettlement area after a former quarter had been razed. There are many place names whose derivations are obscure: Ondo is said to be a contraction of *idi edo* (a farm settlement) but how Ondo is derived, we are not told. The meanings of Ifẹ, Ijẹbu, Ọyọ are unclear to us. We find settlement and street names in Ondo province that reflect Edo influence. We have place names like Ado Ekiti (Ado is said to be derived from *ado*, the Yoruba name for Edo, and Ekiti is derived from *Okiti* 'hill'). In Ondo we have *Ogbodu* Street, traceable to the name of another street in Benin.

Personal Names:

Like place names, personal names in Yoruba reflect wishes and states of mind rather than the larger historical circumstances which might have occurred at the time of one's birth. Another disadvantage to the historian here is that the use of family names or surnames as an integral part of an individual's name must have been recent. Family names then as *Lalude* ('a profundity of wealth and prestige has arrived'), *Adebiyi* ('this is the offspring of royalty'), and *Kayọde* ('may there be joy') are limited in their scope of offering us any worthwhile historical information.

But we have some personal names which are derivations from loan words and show either the origin of their bearers or the religious affiliation of the bearers. Some of these names are very old and therefore have been assimilated into the Yoruba structure. Such names are *Gbadamọsi* and *Bademọsi* from *Badmus*. Again the usefulness of such names for historical study is limited.

FOLK ETYMOLOGY

We mentioned earlier that folk etymology is the preoccupation of the pseudo-linguist and therefore its results are almost worthless. It should, for that reason alone, not delay us here. But since it forms almost the whole basis of Lucas's claim that the Yoruba are Egyptian in race, culture, and language, we may as well say a word or two as applies to its use by Lucas.

The Egyptian origin posited by Lucas hinges on the identity in ancient Egyptian and Yoruba of such words as

Ancient Egyptian	Yoruba
rpa, rba	Yo-*ruba*—the living *rpa* (*rpa* being the name of a mythical king in North Africa)
Nimrod	Lamurudu
Horumla	Ọrunmila
Orion	Oro—an ancestral deity

and a host of others.

In a review article, 'Did the Yorubas come from Egypt?', Wescott shows Lucas to be deeply mistaken in his evidence. We quote Wescott in part:

Dr. Lucas's understanding of sound correspondences is as sketchy as his knowledge of phonetics. When he seeks to derive ordinary noun . . . in Yoruba from Egyptian proper names, Dr. Lucas strains all credulity. He relates Yoruba *ofu* 'waste' to the Egyptian Pharaoh *Khufu* by observing that Khufu's pyramid building was wasteful. He further suggests that Yoruba *aguton* comes from Greek *Aiguptos*, 'Egyptian' because sheep were so commonly depicted on Egyptian temple walls.

Wescott also takes Lucas to task as to the validity of his conclusion from West African/Egyptian cultural similarity: 'the cultural affinity which he, Lucas, sees as indicating a special Egyptian–West African nexus actually proved no more than that that Yoruba *may* have derived as much of their culture from Egypt as may many other peoples on their level of development.'[1]

We cannot agree more, and this also goes for the identification of place and personal names in Yoruba myths and folk lore with an origin outside the present home of the Yoruba.

It has been shown that language studies can aid ethnohistorical studies in many ways. The history of non-literate peoples can only be recovered through a co-operation among specialists in many fields, in history, anthropology, archaeology, and linguistics. The historian will be lucky if the evidence from these different fields is corroborative and complementary. In the Yoruba case, we are still a long way from establishing very reliable evidence from most of the fields relevant to history just because these disciplines are only beginning serious Yoruba studies. The essentially corrective or corroborative view from linguistics will emerge only after we are able to devote as much energy to Yoruba historical linguistics and dialectology as we are devoting to Yoruba grammar. Nonetheless the proof of genetic relationship that has been adduced shows that we may not view Yoruba origins in isolation from the origins of the Kwa peoples; that the time lapse that we posit for the migration of Edo peoples from Ifẹ, if indeed there was such a migration, is not deep enough is shown by glottochronology; Yoruba dialects probably provide the motivation for the recognition of a discontinuity between the Ọyọ peoples and the so-called aborigines, while we hold that the view that the historians postulate of a Yoruba origin different from their present home is probably based on folk etymology.

[1] R. Wescott, 'Did the Yoruba Come from Egypt?' *Odu*, iv, no. 10, 15.

The disadvantage inherent in our study cannot be over-emphasized. As more research is possible, more definitive conclusions may be arrived at.

CHAPTER XII
Political and Social Structure

P. C. LLOYD

ONE of the most striking features of the ethnography of the Guinea coast is the cultural uniformity within very large ethnic groups and the sharp cultural discontinuities between these groups. Thus, travelling eastwards through the forest areas one traverses in turn the land of the Akan, of the Ewe, of the Yoruba, Edo, and Igbo. Most certainly, man has lived in these areas for many centuries; a skeleton found in a cave near Akurẹ has recently been dated as being of a man living 11,000 years ago. The sharp cultural discontinuities suggest that each of these peoples has developed independently in recent centuries; there have been no large scale migrations of people from one area into a neighbouring one. The contrast here with Bantu-speaking Africa is very marked. The cultural uniformity which we see today is, of course, greater than at any time in the past. Samuel Crowther in passing in slavery from Ọyọ, through Ẹgba and Ijẹbu towns to Lagos, found the local dialects very strange to him; primary schooling today produces greater speech uniformity. The western-educated *élite*, drawn from all parts of Yoruba country but living predominantly in Ibadan and Lagos, set a common fashion. As these fashions spread to the margins of Yoruba country, so the dissimilarities with neighbouring peoples grow increasingly more marked.

When we speak of culture in this way we think of a large variety of discrete traits. Language, already mentioned, is important among these. So too are styles of dress, food habits, and the forms of ceremony and ritual connected with the life cycle—birth, marriage, and death—and with political festivals and religious observances. The study of these common traits is useful to the historian; though of greater significance are the traits shared with neighbouring peoples. A chief in a Yoruba town may hold a title which seems associated with Benin—*Ológbòṣẹ́rẹ́* for example, and his paraphernalia of office may include objects more commonly seen in Benin shrines than in Yoruba compounds. Does this suggest conquest, the migration of peoples, or merely the diffusion of ideas? The original *Ológbòṣèrè* may have been a Benin agent posted in the town; he may have been a Benin prince or warrior fleeing his kingdom who was accorded a title of his choice by his new host; he may have been a Yoruba man who had travelled in Benin and adopted its styles in order to enhance his prestige at home. The examination of the spread of such cultural traits provides an almost endless source of data for the historian but few easy solutions to his questions.

The cultural uniformity of the Yoruba people and the fascination aroused by the apparent discrepancies may nevertheless, detract from the study of another aspect of Yoruba society, its social and political structure, in which great variation exists. The institution of kingship seems common throughout most of Yoruba country, rituals of installation and paraphernalia of office follow remarkably similar patterns. From Kabba to Abẹokuta and Lagos one finds the same chieftaincy titles recurring, and, indeed, six of these—*Olisa, Ọdọfin, Ojọmọ, Aro, Ọsọlọ, Ọlọtọn*—are found, in recognizable form, in the highest grade of Benin titles.[1] Yet the structure of government in individual Yoruba kingdoms and communities is so diverse that one might, I feel, write a text book on African political structure drawing very many of one's examples from the Yoruba people. Thus the Kabba people in the extreme northeast of Yoruba country lack kingship in its usual form; the Ẹgba and Ekiti were organized in a number of very small kingdoms, the *ogboni* association being important in the former but absent in the latter. Ọyọ grew to be one of the largest of West African kingdoms with a most elaborate palace organization; after its collapse Ibadan rose to power with a political structure which was as simple as that of Ọyọ was complex. Ijẹbu and Ondo, as will be outlined below, had their own peculiarities. Such differences in political structure are apt to pass unnoticed among the Yoruba themselves; recognizing the same cultural traits in neighbouring kingdoms as they are familiar with in their own, they ascribe to these neighbours an identical form of government. Again, the uniformity of marriage ceremonies throughout Yoruba country suggests to most people a similar social structure. But whereas in most Yoruba societies we

[1] R. E. Bradbury, 'The Kingdom of Benin', in D. Forde and P. M. Kaberry (eds.), *West Africa Kingdoms in the Nineteenth Century* (Oxford, 1967).

find as the basic social unit the agnatic or patrilineal descent group, in Ijẹbu and Ondo cognatic groups are found, in which descent is traced from the apical ancestor in both male and female lines.[1] This distinction, may, of course, be little more than a terminological issue; for in Ijẹbu and Ondo most young men grow up with and succeed to the status of their fathers. Yet the difference between those Yoruba with agnatic and those with cognatic groups does seem to be correlated with marked differences in political structure, with differences in the status of wives, and, possibly, with differences in personality.

The study of these differences in political and social structure within Yoruba country constitutes one of the major fields of historical research. However, before examining some of the differences in greater detail, we ought perhaps to define our use of the term structure. To the sociologist a structure is a pattern of relationships between individuals and groups in society. When we speak of Yoruba social structure we mean, *inter alia*, that pattern of relationships between men and women of common descent which leads to our recognition of descent groups (or lineages) whose members corporately and variously hold rights in land, in political offices, and jurally over each other. The political structure similarly describes the relationship between members of the society in the sphere of government; it concerns the distribution of power between, in the Yoruba example, the ọba, their chiefs, and people.

The colloquial usage of the term structure often leads us to postulate a static pattern of relationships. The analogy which first comes to mind is that of a building. The organic analogy, that of a living body, is better in that it emphasizes the functional interdependence of the parts of the body, here the major units of the structure. But organisms though they grow and die do not radically alter their structure during their own lifetimes or between close generations. A mathematical model is more useful if perhaps rather more difficult to comprehend. The units are not bricks as in a building, or organs of a body, but variables which are so interdependent that a change in the value of any one of them leads to a corresponding adjustment in the values of the remainder. This analogy encourages us to see societies not as structurally static but in a continual process of change. An emphasis on the functional

[1] P. C. Lloyd, 'Agnatic and Cognatic Descent among the Yoruba', *Man*, n.s. i, (1966), 484–500.

interdependence of the parts of a structure may result in the attribution of all change to external causes. Few societies are so isolated one from another that the activities of one—territorial expansion, for instance—do not occasionally demand that the other make some adjustment to the new situation. And even the most isolated society is responsive to changes in the geographic environment. In seeing external factors as the prime agents of change we are apt to view the affected society as making the necessary adjustments and returning to a state of equilibrium. Such a viewpoint overlooks the dynamic processes which are going on within each society, an ever present stimulus to radical change.

In the descriptions which follow of the social and political structure of selected Yoruba societies our presentation must, perforce, be largely in static terms. But in the later sections an attempt will be made to offer a theory of change which illuminates the development of these structures.

KABBA[1]

The institution of sacred kingship is strictly speaking absent among the Kabba Yoruba. The supremacy of the *Ǫbaró* of Kabba seems to date from the nineteenth century Nupe conquest, and that of some other rulers now bearing the title *Olú* from the introduction of local government—a life president of the council assuming the title. The Kabba Yoruba constitute a number of independent groups—Yagba, Ijumu, Abunu, Ikiri, etc.; Kabba itself is the name of but one part of the Owé groups—the name assumed wider usage when this little settlement became an administrative centre, first for the Nupe overlords and then for the British administration. Each of these groups is relatively small; the Owe number 15,000 (1952) for example. The people of all these groups speak a dialect of the Yoruba language and culturally have many affinities with the rest of the Yoruba people. In lacking kingship and the pantheon of *orişa* associated with other Yoruba we may perhaps think of them—with some Itsekiri communities— as proto-Yoruba, unaffected by the immigration or conquest associated with Ǫranyan. This, is however, only a supposition and,

[1] P. C. Lloyd, 'The Traditional Political System of the Yoruba', *Southwestern Journal of Anthropology*, x, (1954), 366–84; E. Krapf-Askari, 'Time and classifications', *Odu*, n.s. ii, no. 2 (1966), 3–18.

even if itself plausible, cannot be taken to indicate that the social and political structure at present seen among the Kabba Yoruba was that of most Yoruba peoples a millenium or so ago.

In some Kabba groups, the Owe for instance, the whole freeborn community claims descent from a single ancestor. The Owe founder is said to have come from Ifẹ—though little significance should be attached to the place of origin beyond a desire of present-day Kabba people to be associated with other Yoruba. This founder had three sons who in turn founded the three settlements of the Owe people. This threefold division into sections, known as Ọna, the way; Ọtun, the right; Ohì, the left, recurs in other Kabba Yoruba communities, but has not been noticed elsewhere in Yoruba country, even in neighbouring Ekiti. These three sections are further segmented into patrilineages. These tend to vary in size of membership and generation depth but quite large groups are exogamous units, corporately holding rights to land and certain titles. A peculiar set of appellations is usually held by men and women of each group. Within the patrilineage the oldest male member is the olórí ẹbí; he is responsible for the administration of the group's internal affairs.

The Kabba Yoruba system of age grades resembles that of the neighbouring Ekiti, though differs from it in that it merges into a title-taking association. Men universally were initiated into the first age grade before the age of puberty and passed with little ceremony into the next grade either at puberty or on reaching marriageable age (opinions differ here). Most, but not all adult married men were admitted to the ìgemò grade upon payment of fees to and ceremonial acceptance by the existing senior chiefs. Men of this grade could use the ọpá staff and wear a red cap; they chose for themselves a title. By a similar process men could then enter the oróta grade when they might wear coral beads; but the number and designation of the titles in this grade were fixed and certain titles were reserved for members of specific patrilineages. The highest grade, that of olólú or ìwàrèfà, was comprised among the Owe of three titles only, one of which might be held by each of the three sections (though it would appear that before the mid-nineteenth century no section had a specific right to any one title). The Ọbaro was the most senior of these title holders, followed by the Ọbajẹmu and Ọbadọfin; he was, however, but *primus inter pares* and the olólú collectively could do little without the advice and consent of the *oróta*. The *ìgemò* were executors rather than makers of political decisions.

The Kabba Yoruba worship deities known as *èbòrà* variously identified with particular patrilineages and with hill spirits. Priestly functions were formerly attached to the higher chieftaincy titles; presumably, therefore, the decisions of the chiefs were sanctioned by fear of the supernatural or threat of excommunication.

EKITI AND ẸGBA[1]

Between the mighty empires of Ọyọ and Benin and the small but ancient kingdoms such as Ifẹ, Ilẹṣa, Owu, and Ijẹbu, was a zone of small states, collectively described in the east as Ekiti and the west as Ẹgba. The formation of the *Ekiti Parapọ* in the nineteenth century and the settlement of many Ẹgba in Abẹokuta has possibly given a more precise delineation to these groups than once existed. Here, again, one is tempted into postulating that these little kingdoms were similar in structure to others such as Ọyọ which later expanded in power. The hypothesis is plausible; but many of these kingdoms were relatively recent, their present dynasties being founded by refugee princes and warriors from the larger neighbouring kingdoms and empires. Their form of government cannot thus be taken for certain as illustrating an early Yoruba prototype.

Let us look first at the Ekiti kingdoms, for the traditional (or pre-1830) political structure of the Ẹgba is much more difficult to elucidate. The kingdom consists of a metropolitan town with, usually, much smaller subordinate towns; but the structure of both capital and subordinates is similar. Each town comprises a number of descent groups, the founders of each coming from a different place and often at a different period. The first ruler of the dynasty is thus the founder of the town. With their different origins, the individuality of each descent group, seen in its peculiar deities, appellations, and the like, is most marked. The members of a descent group corporately hold rights in land and chieftaincy titles, each of the larger groups usually holding one of the *ìwàrèfà* or most senior titles (the size of the group perhaps being the corollary of its political importance). The chiefs are elected by the members of their descent groups and the choice is ratified by the *ọba*.

The sacred kingship is hereditary within the royal descent group and passes only to sons born to reigning *ọba*. A rotation of the title

[1] P. C. Lloyd, *Yoruba Land Law* (Oxford, 1962).

between two, three, or four segments of the group is usual. Each new ruler is selected from among eligible candidates by the *iwàrèfà* chiefs. But in his installation ceremonies he assumes the supernatural powers accumulated by all his predecessors; he is, thus, a consecrated (or sacred) but democratically elected ruler. The political decisions of the kingdom are made by the senior chiefs; the *ǫba* merely ordains them. Junior chiefs, again often selected by and from among members of the descent groups, execute the decisions. Some of these chiefs seem, in the past, to have been responsible for organizing the public activities of the more senior of the five age grades (for men of eighteen to forty-five years of age). The *iwàrèfà* chiefs were, in addition, overlords for those subordinate towns which lay along the roads leading from their own quarter of the capital.

The power of the chiefs lay in their popular backing: that of the *ǫba* in the supernatural aura surrounding him and his independence from popular claims. For the *ǫba* had no personal control over any body of police with which he might enforce his orders; hidden in the palace he was isolated from the members of the royal descent group. This group was politically weak, for not only were its members unable to represent their own interests through the *ǫba*, but they were debarred from holding any other senior chieftaincy title conferring political power. The role of the *ǫba* was essentially that of an arbitrator between the chiefs, each competing on behalf of his own descent groups. His sacred status did however provide him with opportunities to increase his personal power.

The Ęgba kingdoms, though probably similar in size to those of Ekiti, differed in one important respect—the selection of chiefs. In fact, from a secular point of view the selection resembled more closely that of Kabba. The principal organ of Ęgba government was the *ogboni* association. Almost all men are believed to have entered its lowest grades but some rose to titled office through the payment of fees and with the consent of the members of the higher grades. The vacancies in the *iwàrèfà*, the highest grade of six chiefs, were filled by election by the remaining chiefs from among the members of the grade immediately below. It seems likely that the *iwàrèfà* titles were distributed equitably among the descent groups. Among the duties of the intermediate grades were the conduct of war—the *olorogun* chiefs, and the supervision of trade—the *pàràkòyí*.

Though many of the functions of the *ogboni* were those of secular government, it was closely associated with the earth cult. Its activities were highly ritualized and its meetings secret to non-members. The secrecy of the decisions, and particularly those resulting in the execution of an offender, preserved individual chiefs from the antagonism of their kin and members of their descent groups when the interests of these people were overridden; the chiefs' decisions were unanimous and the cohesion of the community was maintained.

It is believed that the *ọba*, or more usually his representative, sat in the *ogboni* meetings but did not hold any of the higher offices; the *ọba* might be impeached if he overreached his due powers.

Membership of the *ogboni* transcended individual kingdoms; its officers could pass with impunity through hostile Ẹgba territory.

OYỌ[1]

The early social and political structure of the kingdom of Ọyọ is not known to us and one would be rash in postulating that it closely resembled that of the Ẹgba or Ekiti. Nevertheless, in the structure of the kingdom at its height in the eighteenth century (known to us from contemporary research and from the descriptions of the Rev. S. Johnson, himself perhaps influenced by the nineteenth-century reconstruction of the Ọyọ kingdom by Atiba) we see a number of familiar features.

The *Alafin* was a sacred king, his status being very similar to that of other Yoruba *ọba*. His principal advisers were the *Ọyọmesi*—seven chiefs selected, as in Ekiti, by and from among the members of the leading descent groups. In Ọyọ Ile, the capital, being so much larger than any Ekiti town, the number of descent groups far exceeded the number of senior titles. The *Ọyọmesi* were therefore individually in charge of quarters, the smaller descent groups of which often held a chieftaincy title in respect of the quarter. A pyramidal system was thus developed. In addition the *ogboni* was an active association mediating, but with unknown effect, between the *Alafin* and the *Ọyọmesi*.

As the rule of Ọyọ extended in the sixteenth and seventeenth

---

[1] P. C. Lloyd, *The Political Development of Yoruba Kingdoms*, (in press); P. Morton-Williams, 'The Yoruba Kingdom of Ọyọ', in D. Forde and P. M. Kaberry (eds.), op. cit. (1967).

centuries from Ọyọ Ile over neighbouring towns of the savannah it seems likely that the political structure of *Alafin—Ọyọmesi—ogboni* was substantially maintained. But with conquest into the forest, resulting in the domination of the Ẹgba, and with the subjection of the neighbouring Fon kingdom of Dahomey followed in the mid-eighteenth century by the establishment of an independent trade route to the coast at Badagri, the *Alafin* was able to expand the palace organization. With the income derived from tolls and tribute he financed an administrative staff independent of the chiefs and descent group heads. This staff was headed by three titled eunuchs, the *iwẹfa*, whose spheres of competence were respectively religious, judicial, and political. (Their titles, *Ọna ẹfa, Ọtun ẹfa, Osi ẹfa*, remind one of the Kabba Yoruba tripartite division but here it is merely the palace organization which is so divided, not the Ọyọ community.) The palace staff commanded by these three eunuchs comprised the junior *iwẹfa*, the *ilari*—recruited usually from slaves and groups of artisans and professionals. Many of the senior *ilari* were given titles and held responsible positions as collectors of tolls or as royal agents in subordinate towns (a role fulfilled in other kingdoms by the senior descent group chiefs). At the height of Ọyọ's imperial power its palace organization must have numbered tens of thousands of individuals.

Through his ultimate personal control of his palace staff the *Alafin* achieved immense power. But this staff was, as we have said, recruited from slaves; it did not detach members from the descent groups of Ọyọ, led by the *Ọyọmesi*. These, in fact, profited too from the booty taken in war and from the prosperity of the slave-trade, then at its height. Both individually and collectively their corporate strength remained largely unimpaired. Tension between the *Alafin* and the *Ọyọmesi* during the eighteenth century is suggested in the very large proportion of *ọba* who lost their thrones by deposition, being obliged by the *Ọyọmesi* to commit suicide. For a period Ga, the *Baṣọrun*, and senior among the *Ọyọmesi*, was regarded as the virtual ruler of Ọyọ. *Alafin* Abiọdun restored the primacy of the throne in an allegedly peaceful and prosperous reign. But with his death tension again increased, people began to leave Ọyọ Ile, provincial rulers began to fight among themselves with the Fulani establishing themselves at Ilọrin and playing off the rivals until the whole structure of the empire collapsed, its major towns ruined and its people emigrating towards the forest.

IBADAN[1]

In the ruins of the Ọyọ empire Ibadan grew to be the major power in Yoruba country. One might have expected that this new entity would replicate many of the features of state organization seen at Ọyọ. In fact Ibadan's political structure is as simple, lacking specialized offices and structural differentiation, as that of Ọyọ was complex. Several reasons may be adduced. First, Ibadan was founded as a very large camp of warriors and refugees. Secondly, in its early decades these refugees still acknowledged the supremacy of the *Alafin* and supported the reconstruction of the *Alafin's* palace organization at the new capital, Ọyọ. Ibadan was seen as a military outpost of Ọyọ, defending the remains of the empire from further Fulani encroachments. Thirdly, none of the early military leaders of Ibadan was of sufficiently reputable royal blood as to claim kingship of the new town.

The initial settlers of the present Ibadan have completely obliterated the original Ẹgba town. Leading warriors built compounds for their kin and slaves and around these were grouped the compounds of their followers. Political power rested with the senior warriors, those with the largest followings; the councils of government lacked any elaborate structure. The hierarchy of chieftaincy titles which developed two or three decades after Ibadan's foundation, has persisted to the present day.

Unlike other communities where the chieftaincy titles tend to be held by descent groups (as in Ọyọ or Ekiti) or to be allocated in title associations (as among the Kabba Yoruba and the Ẹgba); the promotional system of Ibadan is unique. Basically two lines exist, those of the civil chiefs headed by the *Balẹ* (now the *Olubadan*) and of the war chiefs headed by the *Balogun*. There is also a line of junior warriors headed by the *Sẹriki*. Ranked below both *Balẹ* and *Balogun* are the *Ọtun*, *Osi*, *Ẹkẹta* (third), *Ẹkẹrin* (fourth), etc. Appointments are made to the lowest title in each line and, as vacancies occur through death higher in the line, those ranking below the deceased are each promoted one step. (Such regularity existed perhaps in theory only; leap-frogging by the more powerful was certainly not exceptional.) The *Balẹ* and *Balogun* were usually elderly men. Appointments to the lowest ranks of the title lines were

[1] P. C. Lloyd, *The Political Development of Yoruba Kingdoms*, (in press); B. Awe, 'Ibadan, its Early Beginnings', in P. C. Lloyd, A. Mabogunje, and B. Awe (eds.), *The City of Ibadan* (Cambridge, 1967).

made from among the *mǫgaji*. An important chief would, through his activities as a warrior or his patronage to immigrant groups, establish a large and thriving descent group and compound. Upon his death his title passed to none of his own descent group. The members of the group thereupon elected, as *mǫgaji*, a man of strong personality to head the group and its compound and to aspire to a titled office at least as influential as that of his predecessor.

The patrilineal descent groups of Ibadan, of diverse origin and with marked attributes of their individuality, corporately hold both town and farmland. Although they do not hold rights to specific chieftaincies, their support given to their *mǫgaji* is the basic element in their rise in the title hierarchy. Small descent groups with no hope of a titled leader ally themselves, as groups, to the more powerful ones, such bonds often transcending the division of Ibadan into quarters so that these are but geographic entities and not units of administration or alliances. Ibadan had no age grades; public work such as recruitment to the army was organized through the compounds, these being much smaller and more manageable units than would be an age grade in a town of such immense size. Few religious cults involved all Ibadan people; for most the deities of their own descent group were paramount. Thus, to an extent greater than in any other Yoruba town described here, the interests of the individual were represented through his descent group. This fact accounts for the heightened competition between descent groups in Ibadan, competition which is even further increased by the struggle for high titled office which itself brings further wealth and personal following to the successful chiefs and their groups. In this situation any attempt by a *Balę* or a *Balogun* to establish a more centralized form of government was seen by the other chiefs as constituting an attempt to promote the interests of the *Balę*'s (or *Balogun*'s) own descent group, and was thus resisted—as it happened with success as no such developments in the political structure of Ibadan were made in the nineteenth century.

IJẸBU AND ONDO[1]

In describing Ibadan we have seen that the highly corporate nature of the agnatic descent group in this community is the product of a particular set of historical factors and is closely corre-lated with the political structure of the state. In the other large

[1] P. C. Lloyd, *Yoruba Land Law* (Oxford, 1962).

towns of the forest margins, now forming Ọṣun Division, the agnatic descent groups are somewhat similarly structured, though these towns do not resemble Ibadan in their political structure. The contrast, however, with the kingdoms of Ijẹbu and Ondo is most marked. For here we find that the basic social units are cognatic descent groups—groups whose members trace descent from the founding ancestor through either male or female ascendants. Every man and woman thus belongs to a very large number of such descent groups; but the duties incumbent upon members permit their active participation in only a few, usually those in which parents and especially fathers have been active. Nevertheless a choice is open to the individual. The cognatic descent group usually has a residential 'core', members living in the village or compound of the founder, though others not so resident can well be active in the group's affairs. A system of chieftaincy titles, each hereditary within a descent group, is possible with unilineal descent but very difficult to operate with cognatic descent, though such groups may operate as pressure groups to confine certain titles to their own members. The choice of the individual as to which group he gives his prime allegiance is frequently affected by his desire to associate with the most influential group, the one which can offer him good land for farming, a suitable site for trading, patrons in striving for political office.

To what may one ascribe these differences between Ijẹbu and Ondo and the rest of Yoruba country? The myths and legends of both kingdoms can be interpreted as indicating that their present ruling dynasties came originally from Benin. Does this mean that their political structures are derived from Benin too and that these in turn produced an unusual social structure? (In Benin descent grouping has ceased to be a basis for social organization.) Or was the social structure of Ijẹbu and Ondo (and perhaps of all Yoruba if the evidence of their kinship terminology is to be accepted) originally based upon cognatic descent, the conquerors of Ijẹbu and Ondo devising a political system which reinforced this descent system, while other historical factors produced a dominance of the agnatic principle in the kingdoms to the north? These are questions to which we are unlikely to find ready answers. We may however note the apparent interdependence between political and social structure.

In Ijẹbu Ode, the capital, and in the dependent towns and

villages, the *ogboni* (here known as *oṣugbo*) is traditionally a major organ of government. Its constitution and mode of operation is similar to that in Ẹgba communities. Age sets were strongly developed though only their social functions persist to the present. In Ijẹbu Ode two palace associations offered political advancement to all Ijẹbu. The first, that of the *odì*, was restricted to the slaves of the *Awujalẹ* and constituted not only his palace attendants but also a variety of craftsmen and professionals. The second, the *ifore*, was open only to free-born Ijẹbu. The *ifore* association, with its hierarchy of grades, has much in common with the palace associations of Benin; yet the principle of promotion is not dissimilar to that of the *ogboni* or of the Kabba title grades. Two very important Ijẹbu titles, those of the *Olisa* and the *Egbo*, were hereditary in the descent groups of the first holders. These two chiefs, together with leading chiefs of the palace associations, formed the *ilámùrẹn*, the highest political council.

Titles whose holders may live in any part of the town cannot be vested with administrative responsibility over territorial units. In Ijẹbu Ode the quarter heads are the *olórítún*, the oldest men of each quarter—a unit comprising the compounds of one or more descent groups. Some of these descent groups do have minor hereditary titles but their functions are largely religious and succession from father to son, rather than rotation through several constituent segments of the group, seems more usual.

Ondo traditionally lacks the palace associations of the Ijẹbu. Its three grades of chiefs—the *Ìwàrẹ̀fà*, the *Ekulé*, and the *Ẹlẹ́gbẹ́*—invite comparisons with Kabba Yoruba and the Ekiti. But with a very few exceptions these titles are not hereditary. A man first takes an *elẹ́gbẹ́* title and then seeks promotion (by the *ọba* acting on the advice of his chiefs) to a title in the next higher grade and ultimately to an *ìwàrẹ̀fà* title. The *ìwàrẹ̀fà* and *ekulé* title holders and the most senior *elẹ́gbẹ́* have official residences to which they move with their kin on appointment. They are responsible for the administration of the quarters in which these compounds are individually located. Each such quarter head may himself appoint any number of junior *elẹ́gbẹ́* in his own quarter. In addition to these three title grades a number of other titles, many of them hereditary, existed; most of these can be seen as historical anomalies; their functions tend to be religious rather than political. The total number of chieftaincies in Ode Ondo, the capital, must in the past have numbered well over one thousand—enough for a high proportion of the adult men to have been entitled.

In both Ijẹbu and Ondo the attainment of high political office is an achievement resting largely upon the individual; he is not the elected choice of the members of his descent group. Yet his success does depend largely upon his mobilization of his kin and followers in support of his claims. He will seek the support of those descent groups with which influential patrons are associated. But, conscious of their power, the members of these influential cognatic descent groups may seek, as they have done in Ode Ondo in recent decades, to monopolize certain titles; in their corporate activities they begin to resemble the agnatic groups of other Yoruba kingdoms.

Where selection to titled office rests substantially with the king and not with the descent groups, the king's power becomes much more autocratic. But we cannot easily tell how autocratic the rulers of Ijẹbu and Ondo were in the past; for, as we have just seen, chiefs in these kingdoms were far from being solely dependent upon royal favours for their advancement—the support of their kin may well have been the major factor in their success.

COMMENTARY

What may the historian learn from these differences in the structure of government of Yoruba communities?

The first lesson is that the differences do exist. From contemporary documents or from oral history we may find a brief reference to or a broad hint of a civil war in a certain kingdom. It is tempting to clothe this bare fact with embellishments drawn from our knowledge of contemporary or recent Yoruba political structure, ascribing motives and roles to the postulated actors. Yet, as the above synopses have indicated, the relationship between *ọba* and chiefs is not uniform throughout each kingdom and thus a civil war in one kingdom may take a rather different form from that in its neighbours. Again, we may know from external evidence of an increase in the slave-trade, of the introduction of guns, of the development of a new trade route to the interior. Lacking any definitive evidence of the impact of such events upon Yoruba kingdoms we may postulate certain responses. But we should not expect each to respond in the same way; in fact the responses may differ widely.

A second approach lies in explaining the origins of the differences in social and political structure. Perhaps the differences which we perceive today have always existed. Informants, for whom myths of origin and much of oral history exist as a charter for present relationships, will stress that their community has always been governed in its present manner. In fact, changes in recent decades may well have been limited; and, in any case, there is a tendency for chieftaincy titles to be retained while their roles are altered, thus preserving an illusion of continuity. Yet there is little in the past two centuries of Yoruba history, for which our knowledge is considerable, to suggest that earlier centuries too did not witness many radical changes as kingdoms rose and fell in power and influence.

Alternatively we may postulate a period when a uniform social and political structure obtained throughout Yoruba country, present-day Kabba perhaps being the paradigm; from this base the differences we note today will have developed. But whilst we might safely postulate early structures which are less complex than the kingdoms of recent centuries, we have, in fact, no evidence of any original uniformity. Our earlier discussion of the cognatic descent groups of Ijẹbu and Ondo illustrates this point. They are clearly associated with a certain type of political structure, but we cannot say with any certainty whether they were antecedent to this form of government or consequent upon it.

Were we to have some verified hypotheses about the developmental process in African kingdoms such as those of the Yoruba we might be able to extrapolate their earlier social and political structures; there would be difficulties in this enterprise for we know little of the particular events of successive past periods which may have determined the actual course of development. In fact we do not have the verified hypotheses for these can be obtained only if we know of past social and political structures and can trace a course of development. We must beware of postulating an ethnographic base line solely from our knowledge of present-day societies and then claiming that a suggested political process is valid because it successfully accounts for the transition from this imaginary past to the present. Some will argue that such caution is unnecessary or unwarranted. It does seem plausible, for instance, to argue that the Ijoh states of the Kalabari developed from fishing villages structured similarly to those we see today on the Niger Delta coast; it seems reasonable to hold that the villages have remained substantially unaltered in the past few centuries. But it is not reasonable, in my opinion, to hold that the present-day communities of Kabba are a prototype of Yoruba social and political structure; nor can we postulate that the nascent Ọyọ kingdom resembled those of the Ekiti or Ẹgba. Neither Kabba, nor the Ekiti and Ẹgba have been so isolated in recent centuries as to warrant the assertion that their social and political structures have remained unchanged.

In short, we must remember that our knowledge of Yoruba kingdoms is confined to the very recent past and that extrapolation of earlier periods cannot necessarily be made from this evidence. Nor can we range these present societies along a single continuum —say from Kabba through Ekiti or Ẹgba to Ọyọ and thence to Ibadan—postulating a single course of evolution. We must presume that all of these societies underwent change in recent centuries; we cannot propose that each developed to the stage at which we know it, and then halted. The comparative study of Yoruba societies along these lines is bound to be unsatisfactory.

Fortunately these are not the only possible approaches and others exist which should prove more fruitful. Instead of looking directly for evolutionary sequences we should seek, in the comparison of contemporary societies, an understanding of their dynamic processes which seem most likely to produce structural change. Indeed the wide variety of social and political structures found within an area of such cultural homogeneity as Yoruba country, provides an excellent, though hitherto little exploited, opportunity for comparative study.

Sociologists stress the interdependence of the institutions of a society, yet the relationship is often implicit rather than explicit; nor is it often positively established. From cross-cultural surveys, however, we may establish that certain institutions recur together with a regularity greater than chance. We therefore presume them to be interdependent—a change in one will produce compensating changes in the other. But although such statistical procedures may provide the verification of hypotheses about social change they do not create the hypotheses. In other words, we can only begin comparing the political process in Yoruba societies if we have some initial hypotheses which direct our investigations. In the ensuing paragraphs I shall outline a process which I have described in greater detail elsewhere.[1]

In the first place we must examine the competition for wealth and power which exists between the individuals of any society. The uneven distribution of these scarce resources results in the stratification of society into strong and weak, rich and poor—the strong usually being rich, the weak poor. In the Yoruba situation land and rights to political office are often held, not by individuals, but by descent groups; it is the competition between these groups that constitutes much of the daily political process. The competition grows more intense as all the interest of an individual are expressed through a unilineal descent group; where he can articulate his interests through a number of cognatic groups or through other associations such as age grades, the competition between groups becomes more diffuse. Powerful groups may threaten to extinguish weaker ones by force. One system which ensures that they do not is the opposition of groups (or segments) which are approximately equal in strength. Another lies in the institution of an arbitrator. He may be a priest, perhaps even an alien in the society (such as the *laibon* of the Masai of Kenya). In the Yoruba situation the *ogboni* and the *ǫba* fulfil this role. The senior *ogboni* chiefs, though members of descent groups in competition, are so preserved by the collective secrecy of their meetings that they are not deemed personally responsible for decisions adversely affecting their own group. The *ǫba*, as a sacred king, is removed from the influences of his own group which is itself rendered politically weak.

Nevertheless, the attributes of sacred kingship are such that, although the *ǫba* is selected by the chiefs representing the descent groups and is constitutionally bound to accept their decisions, a strong ruler may exert considerable political power. A potential conflict thus exists between the *ǫba* and his council of chiefs. The *ǫba* attempts to weaken the chiefs by exploiting the competition between them and their descent groups; the chiefs, if united by the provocation offered by the *ǫba*, may depose him. In general, a balance of power exists between *ǫba* and chiefs; even the most adroit *ǫba* will surrender power to his chiefs in his senility and after his death the chiefs will choose a more pliant ruler.

[1] P. C. Lloyd, 'The Political Structure of African Kingdoms: an Exploratory Model', in M. Banton (ed.), *Political Systems and the Distribution of Power* (London, 1965), and *The Political Development of Yoruba Kingdom* (in press).

The contest between the ọba and his chiefs is fought not as a mere battle of words, for it attempts to gain favourable decisions; it concerns the control of wealth—the allocation of tribute, war booty and the like, and the allegiance of men—often attracted by the wealth at their patron's disposal. The principles governing the allocation of wealth and allegiance become institutionalized and then are not susceptible to rapid change. Thus an ọba who demands that all tribute be paid directly to him and not through individual chiefs (who keep a part as their perquisite) will generally arouse such opposition among his chiefs as to thwart his moves. However, new opportunities for the control of wealth and allegiance frequently arise. A new trade route offers a revenue in tolls, successful wars increase the scale of war booty, conquered territory yields new tribute and raises problems of administration, immigration adds to the following of the ọba and his chiefs. In so far as precedents for the allocation of these resources do not exist, ọba and chiefs will vie for the major share.

In general one expects that, as a kingdom grows in size and power, so will government become more centralized in the king and palace staff. The king exercises greater control over the appointment, promotion, and removal of his chiefs; more revenues flow directly to the king; state cults take precedence over those of individual descent groups and the descent groups themselves grow weaker in corporate spirit as members owe a competing loyalty to their ruler, seeking in him the means of social advancement or of protection. By virtue of his sacred status, of his independence, and of his ability to cause divisions among his chiefs, the king has some advantage in the struggle to control new resources; with each victory his position becomes stronger and further gains are easier to achieve. However, our brief studies of Ọyọ and Ibadan show that this evolutionary pattern is not necessarily followed in all cases. In Ọyọ the palace organization developed, but not at the expense of the descent groups; these remained powerful and the conflicts between the *Alafin* and his chiefs led to the collapse of the kingdom. In Ibadan the most senior chief, in a weak position since his office was not hereditary, could gain almost no power independent of that of the council of chiefs. The descent groups increased in strength and centralized government, denoted by a corps of highly differentiated and specialized offices, was almost non-existent. The reason for these developments in Ọyọ and Ibadan would seem to be in the precedents which existed when new resources of wealth and allegiance became available; control of these was gained by the descent groups and the increasing power of the state led, in the case of Ibadan, to a more intense competition between the groups.

One must recognize the differences in the social and political structure of Yoruba societies. But their comparison gives no easy answers to our historical problems. A neat pattern of evolutionary development is theoretically unlikely; and one would be unwise to place the societies, as we know them today, along a single continuum. Our hypotheses of the development of political structures are, as yet, most imperfect. We cannot establish any satisfactory ethnographic base line from which to measure change. Yet it is only through the comparison of societies that we can begin to understand these processes, and are better able to project our knowledge of Yoruba kingdoms into the past or to embellish with details the bare facts of past events.

Our interpretation of Yoruba history before the nineteenth century must still be largely speculative; and very many anthropologists would still object to exercises of this sort. Nevertheless, when the reconstruction of the past of African peoples are so often made by those who endow origin myths with a high degree of literality, or by those who postulate the migration of ethnic groups which maintain an unchanging culture over thousands of miles and through many centuries, the propositions of the scholar cognizant of the structural variety of societies and, in some measure, of their patterns of change must inevitably command respect.

CHAPTER XIII
Yoruba Warfare and Weapons

ROBERT SMITH

'The social history of nations is largely moulded by the forms and development of their armed forces.' (NAMIER)

THE ROLE OF WARFARE IN YORUBA HISTORY

In any study of the history of the Yoruba, warfare must play an important part. As with most peoples, much of what has happened in their past consists in a struggle for power, internally and externally, between factions and between states. War was a way of life, constructive as well as destructive, with its own customs, creeds, and artefacts. In the powerful Ọyọ kingdom and among other Yoruba, campaigns were launched at regular intervals as a part of the normal activity of the state, not necessarily as a consequence of political or other special motives. Apart from this, war was also undertaken in pursuance of national policy. The creation of the Ọyọ empire, for example, as well as the exceptional size of that kingdom, reflected the military predominance of its people, while the nineteenth century was a period of almost incessant war waged for political and economic motives among the older kingdoms and the new states which had emerged after the collapse of Ọyọ. Thus the object of the present chapter is to provide information about the basic conditions of warfare in Yorubaland the understanding of which is essential for the explanation both of shifts in military power and of the ensuing political changes.

A description of Yoruba warfare before about 1700 will be largely conjectural. But Dapper and Bosman, in their accounts of West Africa in the mid and late seventeenth century respectively, pay much attention to the warfare of the coastal peoples and, though they do not refer to the Yoruba, apart from a brief but pregnant mention of the Ọyọ army by Bosman, much of what they say is of general application to the whole area.[1] In the eighteenth

---

[1] Both O. Dapper (*Description de l'Afrique* (Amsterdam, 1686)) and W. Bosman (*A New and Accurate Description of the Coast of Guinea* (London, 1705)) deal

century Snelgrave, Norris, and Dalzel retail accounts, gathered at second hand (or more remotely) in Dahomey and on the coast to the south, of the famous Ọyọ cavalry. By the early nineteenth century, when Clapperton and Lander journeyed through Yorubaland, the Ọyọ empire and its armies were already far gone in their decline and the long wars which occupied most of the rest of the century had begun. For the latter part of the nineteenth century documentary evidence is increasingly abundant from official, missionary, and commercial sources, and descriptions at first hand occur of the armies and some of their engagements.[1]

Traditional history, as would be expected, is to a great extent concerned with wars and warfare. Johnson's *History of the Yorubas* is largely an account of campaigns. In his general introductory chapters he describes the government and household of the Alafin of Ọyọ, including the principal military officers of the kingdom, and outlines the organization and tactics of a Yoruba army, for which Ibadan appears to have provided the model.[2] Apart from this classic work, local histories abound,[3] and these are often equally devoted to accounts of wars. Descriptions of Yoruba society by anthropologists, concerned with the contemporary situation, are neglectful of military organization and warfare, though brief accounts have occasionally been given.[4] Doubtless much material remains uncollected, especially in the kingdoms other than Ọyọ—and time grows short as traditions are forgotten amid the preoccupations of the twentieth century.

Finally, supplementing the written record and tradition, are the physical remains of the warfare of past generations. These consist first in the weapons which are still scattered throughout the palaces, compounds, and shrines of the country and secondly

---

specifically and at some length with the army of Benin, but their accounts are contradictory: Bosman, for example, describes the Bini as cowardly and 'ignorant of the Art of War', whereas Dapper reports far more favourably. See also R. S. Smith, *Kingdoms of the Yoruba* (London, 1969), Chapter IX.

[1] For the nineteenth-century evidence, see J. F. A. Ajayi and R. S. Smith, *Yoruba Warfare in the Nineteenth Century* (Cambridge, 1964), *passim*.

[2] S. Johnson, *History of the Yorubas* (Lagos, 1921), Chapter IV, esp. pp. 70–5, and Chapter VIII, esp. pp. 131–7.

[3] See the general bibliography for these local histories.

[4] A. B. Ellis, *The Yoruba-Speaking Peoples of the Slave Coast of West Africa* (London, 1894), has some interesting, but unsubstantiated, passages on warfare. D. Forde's account (*The Yoruba-Speaking Peoples of South-Western Nigeria* (London, 1951), pp. 23–4) derives from Johnson.

in the mud-built fortifications which surround most towns and mark the sites of war camps, but whose traces are disappearing under the tropical rains, the advancing bush, and the new building on the fringes of the towns.

A basic factor affecting Yoruba warfare was the physical nature of the country. The Yoruba homeland comprises in the south the tangled swamps of the coast backed by high forest; further north the forest thins out and is replaced by woodland savannah (which, beyond the Yoruba country, shades into open or grassland savannah and, finally, on the further confines of Hausaland, into the desert). The Yoruba seem to have occupied approximately their present area for many hundreds of years. The migrations which are described in their traditions of origin are likely to refer only to small-scale movements from the savannah into the woodland and forests as the latter became capable of supporting a larger population with the introduction of new food crops and the spread of iron-working and thus more efficient cultivation. Ile Ifẹ, whence came the royal dynasties which ruled the major kingdoms and which is the centre of religion, lies deep in the forests of central Yorubaland. Ọyọ, the kingdom which attained the greatest territorial extent and political power, and for a time was mistress of an empire which included as tributaries other Yoruba kingdoms and also Dahomey and parts of Nupe and Borgu, lay until the nineteenth century almost wholly within the woodland savannah. The other kingdoms lay either wholly in the forest, like Ẹgba and Ijẹbu in the south, or straddled the division between the zones, as did Ketu in the west and Ekiti in the east.

Savannah and forest called for their own methods of warfare. In the former, the relatively open countryside made possible swift movement, the deployment of large bodies of men, and the use of weapons—bows, slings, javelins, and clubs—at long range: above all, this was cavalry country where horsemen could range freely and their mounts were less exposed to the tsetse which infested the south. In the forest, as the Fulani cavalry were to discover in the nineteenth century,[1] movement was restricted and there was visibility over only a short distance. Horses were

---

[1] The Fulani of Ilọrin's first encounter with the Yoruba in forest warfare was against the Ijẹṣa in the Pole War, about 1830 (Johnson, op. cit., p. 222). The Ọyọ had a similarly disastrous experience against the Ijẹṣa during the reign of *Alafin* Ọbalokun, probably about two hundred years earlier (Johnson, op. cit., p. 168).

impeded by the dense undergrowth and soon sickened under the attacks of the tsetse. Weapons had to be used at short range and men were forced to move in single file. This was ideal country in which to ambush an enemy and to attack him at short range or in hand-to-hand combat with sword and spear. The general introduction of fire-arms into Yoruba warfare took place only in the first part of the nineteenth century, apparently between the 1820s and the 1840s. Guns had been owned and used by the Yoruba long before that time, and their adoption as a mass weapon seems curiously belated when it is remembered that the Ekiti had encountered Bini soldiers using guns in the sixteenth or early seventeenth century and that the neighbouring Dahomean and Ashanti armies had guns probably before the end of the seventeenth century.[1] Even near the end of the nineteenth century fire-arms had not entirely displaced traditional weapons in the Yoruba armies. But now the demand for the new weapons had many repercussions, political and economic as well as military, and the character of the wars of the nineteenth century, especially their scale and duration, led to other innovations. Of the two following sections of this chapter, the first will attempt a general description of the warfare of the Yoruba as it seems to have been in the period before about 1850 while the second will mainly concern the changes which took place in the latter part of the century.

WARFARE AND WEAPONS BEFORE c. 1850

While the decision to make war or undertake a campaign was vested in the ruler of a kingdom or town, the command of the armies belonged to his war chiefs: it was unusual for the ruler to take the field himself although in times of crisis he might be expected to do so. Like other chieftaincies, the war titles were hereditary within certain families or groups of families. In Ọyọ the army of the capital was commanded by the Başọrun, the leading member of the central council known as the Ọyọ Mesi and the most powerful of the Alafin's officials. There was also a military corps d'élite known as the Ẹşọ. This was a group of seventy noble captains who were all required to live in the capital. Each of the sixteen senior Ẹşọ bore special titles, of which the first was that of

[1] A. Oguntuyi, A Short History of Ado-Ekiti (Akurẹ, n.d.), pp. 27–8; W. J. Argyle, The Fon of Dahomey (Oxford, 1966), pp. 9–10; K. Arhin, 'The Structure of Greater Ashanti', J.A.H. vii, no. 1 (1967), p. 68.

Gbǫnka. Some might be appointed as *Balogun* ('war lord'), commanding an army in the field, and it was from their ranks that the *Alafin* chose the highest military officer of all, the *Arę Ǫna Kakanfo*. This general (usually termed either the *Arę* or the *Kakanfo*) was responsible for the conduct of specific military operations, offensive or defensive, in any designated area of the kingdom. He was accordingly expected to establish his base near the frontiers and was not usually allowed to visit the capital. Johnson ascribes the creation of this office to the reign of *Alafin* Ajagbo, but as Afǫnja, the famous *Kakanfo* at Ilǫrin early in the nineteenth century, was accounted only the sixth to hold the rank, it seems either that the office was not held continuously, appointments being made only in times of crisis, or that it dates from a later period, perhaps from the south-western expansion of Ǫyǫ in the late seventeenth or early eighteenth century.[1]

The *Ęşǫ* was a body created to serve the *Alafin* and his central government. The rest of the military organization of the capital was repeated on a diminishing scale in the other towns of the Ǫyǫ kingdom, every subordinate ruler being expected to be able to put into the field an army appropriate to his resources which might on national occasions be required to serve alongside the army of the capital. Even the *Balę*, or rulers of the smaller towns in Ǫyǫ, were supported by a group of war chiefs with titles based on those of the *Alafin*'s army. The system reached its highest point of development in the military state of Ibadan, which had been founded about 1830 and succeeded to much of Ǫyǫ's political power and territory. The over-all command of the army was exercised by the *Balogun*, who took up his position in the centre. Under him came the *Ǫtun* and *Osi Balogun*, commanding the right and left wings respectively, then the *Ękęrin*, *Ękarun*, and *Ękęfa Balogun* (fourth, fifth, and sixth). The young warriors, who bore the brunt of battle, were commanded by the *Seriki* with *Ǫtun*, *Osi*, *Ękęrin*, *Ękarun*, and *Ękęfa Seriki* as subordinates. There were similar grades for the vanguard, under the *Asaju*, and the cavalry, under the *Sarumi*. Another title was that of *Aręagoro* (a young chief who was *alter ego* of a senior), while mounted warriors in the service of a great chief were called *Bada*.

[1] For the *Ęşǫ* and other military chieftaincies of Ǫyǫ, see Johnson, op. cit., pp. 73–4; for the *Arę*, see P. Morton-Williams, 'The Yoruba Kingdom of Ǫyǫ', in *West African Kingdoms in the Nineteenth Century*, D. Forde and P. Kaberry (eds.) (Oxford, 1967), p. 57.

Less information is available about the armies of the other Yoruba kingdoms. One important feature which apparently differentiated them from Qyǫ and Ibadan was the absence of a cavalry arm. In the nineteenth century horses were used in the south only by chiefs and their immediate followers, and this was probably also the case in earlier times.

The embodiment of the armies seems to have followed the same principles throughout Yorubaland, including Qyǫ, though there were many local differences between the kingdoms in organization and nomenclature. In theory, all able-bodied freemen were liable for service under the chief appropriate to their family or the quarter of the town where they lived, and were expected to bring a weapon with them; this obligation normally extended only to the current seasonal campaign. In any event, those who enrolled were nearly all part-time soldiers called up from their farms, though the slaves and other household dependants of the chiefs formed the nucleus of the army. A possible exception to this situation obtained in Ijębu where, according to one account, a standing force, the *omodogwa*, was in existence in the early nineteenth century. When not on campaign the *omodogwa*, who in the capital numbered about 1,000 men, performed police duties. The main Ijębu army consisted of a militia commanded by the *olorogun* or war chiefs, each of whom brought to the field a company of 50 to 100 men made up of his kinsmen, slaves, and other followers. The whole force was divided into three regiments under generals known as the *Oloukongbon*, the *Ade Chegou*, and the *Ade Kola*. The *Awujalę* had his own bodyguard, the *agoune*.[1] But apart from the *olorogun* (or *ologun*), these titles are unknown in Ijębu Ode today; they were apparently not in use in the latter part of the nineteenth century nor was there any standing army then except in so far as this term can be applied to the 'war boys' (slaves and other household retainers) of the war chiefs. The Ęgba either had no military organization before Lişabi's day or (more likely) had been required to disband it during the Qyǫ ascendancy. But in the eighteenth century Lişabi, their national hero and liberator from Qyǫ, formed a militia, the *Ęgbę Olorogun*. When this took the

---

[1] M. D'Avezac, in P. Curtin (ed.), *Africa Remembered* (Ibadan, 1967), pp. 217–88. But d'Avezac's informant, Osifekunde, had been absent from his native Ijębu for about twenty years.

field, the centre was commanded by the *Jaguna*, the right wing by the *Lukotun*, and the left by the *Lukosi*.[1]

It seems impossible to estimate the average size of the armies in the period before 1850. Snelgrave wrote vaguely of an Ọyọ army sent against the Dahomeans in the early eighteenth century as consisting of 'many Thousands' of horsemen.[2] Later in the same century Norris wrote:

The Dahomans, to give an idea of the strength of an Eyoe army, assert, that when they go to war, the general spreads the hide of a buffaloe before the door of his tent, and pitches a spear in the ground, on each side of it; between which the soldiers march, until the multitude, which pass over the hide, have worn a hole through it; as soon as this happens, he presumes that his forces are numerous enough to take the field. The Dahomans may possibly exaggerate, but the Eyoes are certainly a very populous, warlike and powerful nation.[3]

At the end of the century, when the Ọyọ were raising a numerous army for what proved to be an unsuccessful invasion of Nupe, the Alafin ordered this buffalo hide to be 'twice trodden'.[4] Clapperton's account in 1826, at a time when the decline of Ọyọ was already well advanced, is hardly more precise:

The military force consists of the caboceers and their own immediate retainers, which, allowing one hundred and fifty to each, will not give such immense armies as we have sometimes heard stated; that of Yourriba is perhaps as numerous as any of the kingdoms of Africa.[5]

The Ibadan army, as appears from the system of ranks and titles outlined above, was differentiated according to the roles of its several elements, and this presumably reflects the position in the Ọyọ armies of earlier times. According to the order of battle given by Johnson, the vanguard included all the *Bada* and must therefore have been essentially a mounted force. The main body consisted of the younger warriors under the *Seriki* and in the rear

[1] A. K. Ajiṣafẹ, *A History of Abẹokuta* (London, 1924), pp. 30–2; S. O. Biobaku, *The Ẹgba and their Neighbours, 1842–1872* (Oxford, 1957), pp. 9–10. Ajiṣafẹ fails to differentiate between the military organization of Liṣabi and that at Abẹokuta.

[2] W. Snelgrave, *A New Account of Some Parts of Guinea and the Slave Trade* (London, 1734), p. 56.

[3] R. Norris, *Memoirs of the Reign of Bossa Ahadee, King of Dahomy* (London, 1789), pp. 11–16.

[4] A. Dalzel, *The History of Dahomy* (London, 1793), p. 229.

[5] H. Clapperton, *Journal of a Second Expedition into the Interior of Africa* (London, 1829), p. 57.

the rest of the troops, as a reserve, under the *Balogun* and his subordinates; this was an infantry force although the chiefs and their *aides* were normally all mounted. Finally, the cavalry under the *Sarumi* reconnoitred and skirmished in advance or on the wings of the army.

It was almost certainly their ability to maintain their cavalry arm which enabled the Ọyọ to attain their commanding position among the peoples of Guinea. Tradition relates that under Ọrọmpọtọ, the second of the four *Alafin* who reigned at Ọyọ Igboho, the rearguard of the army consisted of a thousand footsoldiers and a thousand horsemen, a *gbaju* leaf being tied to the tail of each horse to obliterate its hoof marks,[1] which suggests that the Ọyọ cavalry was already in existence in the late sixteenth century. In an apparent reference to an attack on Allada by the Ọyọ in 1698, Bosman wrote that their army was 'all Horsed' and added that 'This Nation strikes Terror into all the circumjacent Negroes'.[2] It is clear from this, and from references by Snelgrave, Norris and Dalzel in the eighteenth century, that the long-range military expeditions mounted by the Ọyọ were undertaken at this time entirely by cavalry.[3] This would have given them great mobility and striking power, at least so long as they were fighting in the savannah. That they were able to operate so far to the south-west as to reach Allada and its port of Whydah is explained by the break in the forest belt at this point which allowed the cavalry to follow a route along which savannah conditions prevailed down to the coast.

The horses for the Ọyọ cavalry were obtained from the less heavily tsetse-infected countries to the north of the kingdom. There are indications in tradition that the main supply came from the Nupe, horse fairs being held in towns near the Niger, while Borgu was another source. The Ọyọ do not seem to have been able to breed replacements for their mounts, probably because of the prevalence of the tsetse combined with the long gestation period of the horse. When the Nupe and Borgu provinces broke away from the empire during the latter part of the eighteenth century, the consequent interruption to the supply of horses may have

---

[1] Johnson, op. cit., p. 161.
[2] Letter xx, pp. 397–8.
[3] See especially Snelgrave, op. cit., p. 56, where he writes that the Ọyọ 'never use Infantry'. This presumably refers only to the Ọyọ expeditions against Dahomey.

accelerated the decline of Ọyọ's military power. The horses which Clapperton and Lander obtained without much difficulty during their journey through Yorubaland in 1826 seem to have been usually of poor quality.[1]

The primary armament of the Yoruba armies before the general introduction of fire-arms consisted of swords, spears, and bows and arrows.[2] Swords were of two main types: the *agẹdẹngbẹ*, the heavier weapon, curved, with a single outer blade, and the *ida*, which was double-bladed and either based on the slightly tapering European swords of the sixteenth century or more often of an elongated leaf shape (resembling those of the Hallstatt period of the European Iron Age). Other types were the short *jomo*, the inward curving *tanmogayi* or sabre, and the *ada*, *ogbo*, or *ele*, a short sword often called a cutlass. These were all designed for cutting or slashing, while for stabbing at close quarters a dagger (*ọbẹ*) was used. Spears were known as *ọkọ* when used for thrusting and as *esin* when thrown; in either case they carried narrow iron heads socketed onto the shaft, often barbed, and flat rather than trilobate. Broader-headed spears, akin to those used in the Sudan, were called by a Hausa word, *mashi*. The points of the spears were dipped before battle into poisonous brew. The bows (*ọrun*) were between four and five feet in height, the stave being of one of several kinds of pliant wood and the string of twisted leather, antelope's hide, or hemp, threaded at one end and tied frontally at the other. The force at full draw was about forty pounds and the range about 100 yards. A hinged form of crossbow (*akatanpo*) with a divided wooden stock was in use during the nineteenth-century wars and doubtless earlier, probably deriving from a Portuguese or other European prototype.[3] Lander claimed that 'The Yaribeans [Ọyọ] have the reputation of being the best bow-men in Africa'; their young men engaged in such frequent practice that they often succeeded in sending their arrows through a small hole in a wall used as a target, distant 'upwards of a hundred

---

[1] For examples, see Clapperton, op. cit., (1829), p. 34, and R. Hallett (ed.), *The Niger Journal of Richard and John Lander* (London, 1965), p. 58.

[2] This and the following five paragraphs are based on R. S. Smith, 'Yoruba Armament', *J.A.H.* viii, no. 1 (1967).

[3] Bishop Crowther recorded a Yoruba aphorism: *akatanpo ko to ija, ta li o mu igi wa ikoli oju* ('A crossbow is not enough to go to war with; whom do you dare face with a stick?'). Crossbows are preserved, for example, at Ikonifin (near Iwo) and Ọwọ.

yards'.[1] Arrows (ọfa) carried iron heads, varying in pattern in much the same way as the spearheads and often barbed, but they were usually attached to the shaft by a tang rather than socketed. The shafts were of palm, reed, or savannah grass, nocked and sometimes fletched with paper or dried leaves. Crossbow bolts were usually indistinguishable from arrows. Like spears, arrows were dipped into poison before use.

A variety of weapons was used as secondary armament. The club, probably the oldest and simplest of all weapons, had evolved into several forms, from the basic kondo, a knobbed stick for throwing or striking, cut and trimmed from the forest,[2] to the mallet-like olu, the larger kumọ, and the orokumo with nail-studded head, and in iron the gaman, ogolo, and ogo or ogbo, some of these having iron coils spiralled round the body. The double-headed mace (ọṣe), though principally a ritual instrument, occasionally formed part of a warrior's fighting equipment. Small missiles were hurled by the sling (kannakanna), still used for hunting in the countryside. Throwing knives (asa) and spiked fighting bracelets (gbunnu or gunna) are also said to have been used, though no Yoruba examples have been traced. Of the other weapons, examples abound, most probably dating from the last century. In addition, ceremonial and symbolic versions of all the major weapons occur: swords with elaborate metal hilts and decorated, though blunt-edged, blades, spears, carved maces, and miniature models of bows and arrows in decorated brass, are used as symbols of office and honour and of membership of societies and guilds.

The origins of these weapons can only be a matter of surmise, and it is impossible to determine whether the sword, spear, and bow, for example, evolved independently into their present forms among the Yoruba or were based on prototypes imported from other peoples. But most of the weapons used by the Yoruba were widespread in Africa, and it seems beyond doubt that weapons featured in the trade of the continent from early times. In the nineteenth century sword-blades were brought from North Africa

---

[1] R. Lander, Records of Captain Clapperton's Last Expedition, ii (London, 1830), p. 222. See also Crowther in Curtin (ed.) (1967), p. 301, and Ajayi's footnote 26 to this.

[2] G. J. A. Ojo, Yoruba Culture (London, 1966), p. 34, illustrates the ease with which a man could arm himself by quoting an aphorism: a ki nja nigbo, raun ọpa ('It is ridiculous to complain of having no weapon in a fight in the forest').

across the desert to the Hausa emporium of Kano and thence were traded further south, a pattern which had probably endured for centuries. The importance of Ọyọ in the savannah of northern Yorubaland partly derived from its commercial links with the north, while Ijẹbu merchants from the forests were accustomed to travel with their cloth as far as northern Nupe. But from about 1500 onwards this commerce was rivalled, and then surpassed, by the trade with Europeans on the coast. Weapons, mostly 'cutlasses', became prominent among seaborne imports into Guinea. Thus it came about that European swords, with their prized steel blades and of varying patterns, including the sabre, became known to the Yoruba, whose cutlers—the blacksmiths—occasionally attempted to copy them in local materials and with local variants of style.

By far the greater part of the weapons of the Yoruba must have been of home manufacture. Their wood carving is an ancient art, and the craft of the bowyer, practised by certain families within each town, is a branch of this. The smelting of iron from local ores was also known, and may date back to about A.D. 500. But this production was so inefficient that before 1500 the output of metal weapons, such as swords and spear- and arrow-heads, can only have been on a small scale,[1] and implements of sharpened wood or stone would have predominated. After 1500, iron (at first in 'wedges' and 'pieces', and later in the ubiquitous bars and rods) was being imported into West Africa by sea from Europe in increasing quantities, and the war industries of the Yoruba must have been revolutionized thereby. The principal craftsmen concerned were the blacksmiths who were responsible (sometimes with the help of the brass-casters) for the manufacture of swords, spear- and arrow-heads, and iron clubs; after the introduction of fire-arms they still played a considerable role in forging ammunition and assembling and adapting guns from imported parts. But the local metal-workers never succeeded in producing steel, and the iron blades of their swords were always liable to break or bend.[2]

There does not seem to have been any concept of uniform in the

[1] D. Williams, 'Iron and the Gods: A Study of the Sacred Iron Figurines of the Yoruba', Staff Seminar Paper, University of Lagos (1967).

[2] S. A. O. Babalọla, 'Rara Chants in Yoruba Spoken Art', Staff Seminar Paper, University of Lagos (1966), quotes a *rara* chant by Baba Nino of Iwo which refers to the twisting and spoiling of a sword-blade in battle.

Yoruba armies, at least until the nineteenth century, though friend could be distinguished from foe at close quarters by his facial scarifications. There are indications that metal armour was occasionally used: two shirts of chain mail are preserved in the palace of the Ọlọwọ of Ọwọ, for example, and Johnson recounts that in the reign of Alafin Ofinran Baṣọrun Sokia wore an 'iron coat' (ẹwu irin).[1] Some protection was afforded by the padded and many-pocketed jackets (gberi or lenku), sewn over with charms, which were worn by warriors (and are still used by hunters). Presumably all wore one or other type of the usual Yoruba head-gear, but no helmets either of metal or leather, such as were worn by the warriors depicted in the Benin plaques, seem to have been known. Shields (apata) were described by informants who had seen examples which were of either hide or wood; presumably they were used by most warriors before the introduction of fire-arms. Chiefs were distinguished by their war aprons (wabi), covered with cowries and charms, while bowmen wore an iron finger- or thumb-guard (ifarun) and a leather guard or bracer (ijasan) on the left arm for protection against the bowstring; they carried a tubular quiver (apo), containing about twenty arrows and made of leather or bamboo.

The equipment of the Ọyọ horses, so far as the mounts of the chiefs were concerned, was of some elaboration and also reflected the influence of the kingdom's northern neighbours[2] and, remotely, of the Arab and Berber worlds across the Sahara. Saddles were usually of the Oriental type with high protective pommel and cantle. Bits (ijanu) consisted of a U-shaped unjointed bar, usually of brass and iron. The brass stirrups were of the Arab and Hausa shape, narrow and curved at each end like a fire shovel;[3] they were known in Ọyọ as lekafa (cf. Hausa likafi which derives from the Arabic rikab) or as oko aṣa ('flying hawk', from a supposed resemblance). A horse might also be fitted with a brass headband

---

[1] K. C. Murray, personal communication; Johnson, op. cit., p. 160. Ellis writes (op. cit., p. 171) that among the Yoruba 'Shirts of mail and breast-plates were sometimes seen, and appear to have been obtained from the natives of West Soudan', and H. Baumann and D. Westerman, Les Peuples et les Civilisations de l'Afrique (Paris, 1957), p. 354, makes a similar claim. Neither gives any references.

[2] As was noticed by Clapperton 1829, p. 2; more modest equipment in the Ijẹbu kingdom is described by Osifekunde in Curtin (ed.) (1967), p. 287.

[3] The comparison was made by H. Barth, Travels and Discoveries in North and Central Africa, ii (London, 1857), p. 46.

(*igbamu, ikomu*), possibly an embryonic piece of horse armour to protect a vital part. All this metal equipment was handsomely decorated in geometric patterns, the base of the stirrup being pierced with an open-work rosette. More modest equipment in less durable material was in everyday use, such as stirrups of leather or wood. In Ẹgbado in 1830 Lander was able to obtain an 'English saddle' (by which he must have meant a flat hunting saddle).[1]

The Yoruba paid considerable attention to defence. All towns and even some larger villages were surrounded by a roughly concentric 'wall' of dumped earth or, less often, by a stockade. Capitals and other important towns sometimes had two or even three walls, the interval between the circuits being usually upwards of a hundred yards. As well as providing defence in depth, this system gave protection to an army forming up for attack between the walls (as at Ọṣogbo in 1838/9). Exceptionally, in country such as the Oke Ogun where the material was at hand, a wall was constructed of large stones, something like the dry-stone walls of the Cotswolds or northern England. There was an outer ditch to each earth wall, from which the wall itself had been quarried and whence mud for repairs could be taken. The ditches provided an additional obstacle; they were planted with thorns and in the wet season the rains converted them into partial moats. Near the walls (usually on the outside) the land was left uncultivated for some distance so that the dense forest and undergrowth impeded an aggressor who left the narrow paths leading to the gates. These gates were sometimes complex structures with angled entries, heavy wooden doors, and gatehouses which could be defended by bowmen.[2] The Ẹgba and Ẹgbado in the nineteenth century built wooden watch-towers on stilts above the walls; more usually, sentries were posted in high trees.

Two main types of earthen city wall are found in Yorubaland. The first were massive earthworks of some twenty feet in height and correspondingly broad, fronted by a ditch of almost equal depth. Remains of walls, of these dimensions are to be seen at, for example, Ketu, Igboho and Owu, and also encircling the kingdom

---

[1] R. and J. Lander in Hallett (ed.) (1965), p. 69. In Borgu in 1827 Richard Lander had a narrow escape from drowning when his foot became entangled in his leather stirrups while he was crossing a river near Kaiama: see Lander (1830), p. 178.

[2] See Ajayi and Smith (1964), pp. 142–3, for plans of the gates at Ketu and Ado.

of Ijẹbu Ode—the Eredo; the walls of Old Ọyọ seem also to have been on this scale. The second type was a lower and less substantial construction, only some four to five feet in height. The tops of these walls were sometimes thatched to prevent erosion by rain. This type was built, for example, at New Ọyọ, Ijaye and Ibadan, and around many older towns and also the camps of armies in the field, and it has been suggested[1] that it was designed as a breastwork over which the recently introduced guns could be fired. Almost certainly the walls were occasionally used in this way, but they are unlikely to have originated for the purpose since towns were provided with them before the general spread of fire-arms and in some places, moreover, the height of such walls was increased by a wooden or bamboo palisade.

In a recent article on the walls of Benin, Graham Connah has distinguished between city walls which were 'freestanding mud-built walls' and those which were 'earthen ramparts'. The former, he claims, occurred most frequently in the savannah while the latter were associated with the high forest.[2] This generalization is not borne out in Yorubaland where both types of wall are found in both the forest and the savannah. Earthen ramparts (whether of the massive or the low types described above) are by far in the majority, though free-standing mud-built walls are also found, usually in the vicinity of gate-houses (as at Kiṣi and Igboho) where slits for archers were inserted. Connah makes a further distinction between 'a city wall, that is to say a defensive structure, and a linear earthwork concerned more with the delineation of boundaries'. So far as Yoruba walls are concerned—and it is convenient to continue to call them 'walls' rather than 'earthen ramparts' or the archaeologists' rebarbative 'dump ramparts'—the distinction is not of much significance for the historian. It is true

---

[1] By J. Omer-Cooper in a paper presented to the Congress of the Historical Society of Nigeria in 1960. See Ajayi and Smith, op. cit., p. 25, for a fuller discussion of the point.

[2] G. Connah, 'New Light on the Benin City Walls', *J.H.S.N.* iii, no. 4 (1967), pp. 593–6. For a detailed description of a famous city wall in the savannah of Northern Nigeria, see H. L. B. Moody, 'Ganuwa—the Walls of Kano', *Nigeria Magazine*, xcii (1967). The Kano Walls are for the most part free-standing. Connah's attempt to answer the question 'What is a wall?' was anticipated in the eighth century by Bede, who distinguished between an earthen rampart made of bonded sods and a wall of stones (*Eccl. Hist.* i, 5). The word 'wall' was also applied to the earthen ramparts of Liverpool which withstood five days' bombardment and several assaults before the city fell to Prince Rupert during the Rebellion in England.

that many Yoruba towns do not appear particularly well sited
for defence, and doubtless many other considerations entered into
the choice of site. Once a town was founded, however, it needed
walls both to give protection to the inhabitants and to mark the
boundary between the town proper and its home farms (*oko etile*).
The military purpose must certainly have been foremost in
troubled times. When Clapperton was journeying up to Old Oyọ
in 1826 he found that the inhabitants of 'Assulah', disturbed by
reports of the spreading wars around them, had recently surrounded their small town by a ditch, and presumably also a wall,[1]
and several examples of fighting along the walls of towns can be
cited later in the century, especially at Abẹokuta.

This emphasis on fixed defences might suggest that the Yoruba
had an entirely static concept of warfare. This would be misleading.
Despite poor communications and consequent difficulties in
appreciating the factors involved in any war, the leaders of Oyọ at
any rate must have been far from lacking in strategy. Tradition
claims that during the reign of *Alafin* Ojigi (probably in the late
seventeenth or early eighteenth century) the army made a circuit
of the whole Yoruba country.[2] Whether or not such a formidable
enterprise was really accomplished, there is little doubt that by the
eighteenth century the Oyọ had brought parts of the the neighbouring Nupe and Borgu under their control and had established their
ascendancy over Yoruba kingdoms to the south and west. Even
more impressive was their defeat of the Dahomeans in the course
of numerous expeditions by their cavalry and the control which
they exercised over the important trade route leading south-west
from Oyọ to the coast, a distance of some 200 miles. These achievements all required the planning of military operations on a grand
scale, together with an appreciation of the tactical and logistical
problems which they entailed.

The conduct of military operations, apart from the employment
of cavalry, was probably much the same in the armies of all the
kingdoms. After the muster of troops, a campaign opened with
sacrifices to the war standard (*ọpa ogun*, *ọpaga*, a wooden or iron
staff to which a cloth was usually attached). The army then moved
to the vicinity of the enemy, and a walled camp would be built.
Siege warfare ensued, occasionally brought to a pitched battle and

[1] Op. cit., p. 20.
[2] Johnson, op. cit., p. 174.

varied by ambushes on the lines of communication. Commissariat problems were reduced to a minimum as troops were expected to live off the country (*piyę*, or foraging) and, when sieges were protracted, to raise crops within the camps. During an engagement, provided that the country was reasonably open, the infantry moved forward carrying their spears in bundles and throwing them as javelins, to be retrieved later by other footsoldiers coming up in the rear. Bows provided the 'artillery'. They were primarily a weapon of the footsoldiers, as elsewhere in West Africa,[1] though Snelgrave writes that in an eighteenth-century expedition against Dahomey the Ọyọ cavalry were armed with bows (perhaps for dismounted action) as well as javelins and 'cutting swords'.[2] Crossbows were probably used normally from the ground, being spanned from a sitting or lying position, and would have been primarily of use in defensive action. After exhausting the contents of their quivers, bowmen could draw arrows from a reserve placed in baskets on the battle-field. This, together with the method of firing in line adopted when guns were introduced, suggests that the use of the bow as a mass weapon to provide a barrage of fire may have been evolved. Once battle had been joined, the subsequent operations could to some extent be controlled by beating out the chief's commands on his war drums, which could similarly be used to mislead or to transmit information about the enemy. In the forests of the south, ambushes and close fighting prevailed. Johnson describes the Owu, for example, as preferring to engage their enemies at close quarters using their *agędęngbę*.[3]

Warfare in West Africa was conducted on conservative lines. Thus the foregoing description of the armies and weapons of the Yoruba as they were in the eighteenth and early nineteenth centuries may be assumed to apply generally to earlier times, going back, possibly, to the arrival of the Portuguese on the coast or to the formation of the present kingdoms. Yet this conservatism must not be overstated. Human ingenuity and inventiveness could always play a part. Two curious examples of this were used in war not by but against the Yoruba, but are worth quotation. The first occurred during the attack on Dahomey by an Ọyọ cavalry force in the early eighteenth century which is referred to above. The Dahomean

---

[1] Barth, op. cit., iv, pp. 231–2, remarks on this.
[2] Op. cit., p. 56.
[3] Op. cit., p. 206.

infantry were armed with muskets, the noise of whose discharge so alarmed the horses of the Ọyọ that they were unable to charge. Nevertheless, it seems that the Ọyọ would eventually have won the battle had not the Dahomeans, after the fighting had lasted four days, resorted to a stratagem. They retreated from their camp, leaving behind a great quantity of imported brandy. As expected, the Ọyọ fell upon this unaccustomed treat. The Dahomeans soon returned and, finding their enemy in a drunken stupor, were able to dispatch them without further trouble.[1] The second, and rather taller story was related to Clapperton, who was shown a group of villages near Old Ọyọ which had been destroyed by the Fulani in an aerial incendiary attack. His informants

pointed out a rock close to the south side of the town, from whence the Fellatas flew the pigeons to set fire to it. The mode of doing it was, by making combustibles fast to the tails of the birds, which on being let loose from the hand, immediately flew to the tops of the thatched houses, while the Fellatas kept up a sharp fire of arrows, to prevent the inhabitants extinguishing the flames.[2]

The Yoruba seem to have been in origin, and for most of their history, an inland people, and their wars were fought mainly on land. But some of the southern kingdoms, notably Lagos, maintained fleets of war canoes on the lagoons and rivers which served not merely as a convenient means of transporting troops to military objectives on land but were also battle units which engaged in an authentic, albeit miniature, form of naval warfare.[3]

The Yoruba canoes, like those elsewhere in West Africa, were 'carved' or 'dug' and burnt out from the trunks of single trees. The largest were capable of carrying, in calm waters, up to about 100 men. The builders were specialists, living usually in the forests behind the coast, though 'Boughiye', a famous centre of boatbuilding in the Ijẹbu kingdom in the early nineteenth century, was situated somewhere on the sandy spit of land between the sea and the lagoon and was presumably dependent on timber imported from the mainland.

The armament carried by the warriors in lagoon warfare probably differed little if at all from that in land warfare. There are

[1] Snelgrave, op. cit., p. 57.

[2] Clapperton (1829), p. 62.

[3] This section is based on Robert Smith, 'To the Palaver Islands: war and diplomacy on the Lagos lagoon in 1852–1854', *J.H.S.N.* v, no. 1 (December, 1969), and 'The canoe in West African history', *J.A.H.* xi, 4 (1970).

indications that engagements on the lagoon were usually fought at a distance (though hand-to-hand combat would have been feasible in the shallow waters) and that the throwing spear was the predominant weapon before the introduction of fire-arms. From the late eighteenth century the characteristic armament of the war canoe came to be a small brass or iron cannon in the bows, either lashed into position or mounted on a swivel, while an increasing proportion of the warriors was armed with muskets.

The earliest reference to the lagoon warfare of the southern Yoruba is Dalzel's description of the blockade of Badagry by the war canoes of Lagos in 1784. A missionary account of an attack on Badagry by Ọba Kosọkọ of Lagos in 1851 shows that fire-arms were used in much the same way as in land battles; the engagement lasted about five hours, during which the Lagos warriors 'loaded their swivels and guns, pulled inshore, fired and quickly returned to reload, and so they continued'. Other descriptions of lagoon warfare are to be found in British consular and missionary papers dealing with the hostilities conducted against Lagos in 1853 by Kosọkọ, by now deposed as ọba by the British and living in exile at Ẹpẹ.

Fortifications were as important for waterside as for inland towns. British accounts of Lagos after its capture in 1851 and of Ẹpẹ under Kosọkọ's rule show that stockades were preferred to the more familiar mud-built walls; these extended into the water and were covered by fire from guns concealed in trenches to the rear.

WARFARE AND WEAPONS IN THE SECOND HALF OF THE NINETEENTH CENTURY

During the first half of the nineteenth century a number of forces were at work which from about the middle of the century were to change the character of Yoruba warfare, disturbing a pattern which had probably endured for centuries. From the military point of view the most important of these forces was the introduction, long-delayed, of fire-arms as a mass weapon. But there were others, political and economic, of equal significance, and though it would be beyond the scope of this chapter to deal with these at length, they must be mentioned since in many ways they too affected the conduct of war. There was, first, the disintegration, followed by the collapse, of the empire and kingdom of Ọyọ, due partly to a combination of internal weaknesses and partly to the attack launched upon the Ọyọ by the warriors of the Hausa-Fulani *jihad* in whose path they found themselves. Even before the final abandonment of the capital at Old Ọyọ in or about 1835, the political heritage was being parcelled out. New states had arisen, notably Ibadan and Ijaye, both in origin military camps to which refugees from the towns and armies of Ọyọ flocked together for protection, and Abẹokuta, the composite town in which the inhabitants of the Ẹgba forest sought shelter. The withdrawal of the Ọyọ to the protection of the forests in the south and the redisposition of resources in the new states enabled the Fulani drive to be held, though even as the threat from the north subsided another came from the west whence strong Dahomean armies began to raid deep into Yorubaland until almost the end of the century. Meanwhile a fierce struggle for predominance was developing among both the new states and the old kingdoms, into which eventually almost all the Yoruba were drawn. The situation was exacerbated by the growing demand, both external and internal, for slaves, a demand which could most conveniently be satisfied by taking captives in war. Finally, the extension of trade between the interior of Yorubaland and the coast, stimulated by British efforts to replace the Atlantic slave-trade by legitimate trade in palm products and by the desperate need of the combatants to obtain fire-arms and powder, greatly enhanced the importance of communications and the value of local tolls, so that there was constant dispute between the states demanding access to the coast and those which stood athwart the roads. Thus, for nearly a century, the Yoruba country was convulsed by war.

Since these factors, which all contributed to change the character of Yoruba warfare, operated to differing degrees and over differing periods of time, the change did not come about in any sudden or dramatic way nor can it be said to have taken place in any particular year or even decade. By about 1850, however, the change had become apparent, and the mid-century makes a convenient dividing line. There was another development around this time, greatly affecting the historian's task. From the 1840s onwards, the wars and politics of the Yoruba were subject to careful and increasingly interested scrutiny by outsiders, and written sources of information become ever more abundant. Systematic reporting by officials began with the establishment of the British Consulate of the Bights of Benin and Biafra in 1849, which was followed by active British intervention in Lagos affairs in 1851 and the annexation of 1861. Soon other countries came to be represented in Lagos as trade there expanded. From the military point of view, probably the most valuable document in the official category is the report which Captain A. T. Jones of the West India Regiment prepared on the Ẹgba army and its operations at Ijaye in 1861.[1] The second main source of information consists in the publications, correspondence, and other documents of the Christian missions, the first of which began work in Yorubaland in the early 1840s. Though often partisan, these papers are at least as valuable as the official records and sometimes show a greater understanding of the local situation.[2] Finally, there are the archives (still somewhat neglected) of the trading companies which established themselves in increasing numbers at Lagos in the wake of the consular and colonial administrations and had the best of reasons to pay attention to the changing fortunes of the 'interior wars'.

Fire-arms seem to have been introduced into Yorubaland at first in small numbers. Their first appearance at Ọyọ may have been as part of the annual tribute rendered by the Dahomeans under an agreement of 1747, which is said to have included 40 guns,[3] and the first reference to their use there occurs in Johnson's account[4] of the struggle which overthrew Baṣọrun Gaha, in or about 1774. According to Johnson, it was the Ijẹbu who during their war against the Owu about 1820 first used guns on any scale; he writes that 'being nearest to the coast, they had the advantage of obtaining guns and gunpowder from Europeans in exchange for slaves', and he remarks on their marksmanship and 'steady fire'.[5] Yet the use of these new weapons spread only slowly, partly because of difficulties in obtaining both the guns and the powder and partly because the cheap and primitive muskets supplied by the traders were far from ensuring victory over an enemy armed with the old

---

[1] Printed as an appendix to Ajayi and Smith (1964), pp. 129–40. Captain Jones's report may be compared to the famous description of the Zulu army of Cetshwayo which H. B. Fynney submitted to Lord Chelmsford.

[2] For an illustration of the use of missionary sources, see Ajayi and Smith, op. cit., *passim*. See also a review of this book in *Ibadan*, xxi (1961), pp. 93–4, by E. A. Ayandele, who draws attention to other important missionary sources.

[3] E. G. Parrinder, *The Story of Ketu* (Ibadan, 1956), p. 28 (based on a tradition recorded in Abomey in 1911); Argyle op. cit., p. 25. Parrinder also refers to the use of fire-arms in Ketu in the eighteenth century (op. cit., pp. 33–4).

[4] Op. cit., pp. 184–5.

[5] Ibid., pp. 208–9.

conventional weapons; though the noise of their discharge was alarming, they were slow to fire, wildly inaccurate, and sometimes more dangerous to the musketeers than to their adversaries. Lander, describing what he had seen in Ọyọ in 1826 and 1827, wrote that 'Quantities of muskets are procured from the coast, but they are of comparatively little use to the people, who know not how to handle them with effect'; they often carried them into battle without either powder or shot and threw them away when they retreated.[1] The victory of the Ibadan over the Ilọrin at Oṣogbo in 1838/9 was achieved without the help of fire-arms, which were apparently not used by either side. By 1851, however, the Ẹgba had numerous guns with which they succeeded in beating back a desperate attack on Abẹokuta by a Dahomean army which was similarly armed. As Jones's report shows, of their warriors at Ijaye ten years later, all but an 'infinitesimal proportion' had guns.

The guns supplied for the West African market by European traders were primitive smoothbore muzzle-loaders, the most common being flint-locks. The best known were of Danish manufacture, and hence the name 'Dane gun' or 'Long Dane' came to be applied to all muskets. Locally made wooden stocks were sometimes fitted to the imported barrels and mechanism. The ammunition consisted of bullets or bolts of bar-iron, forged by local blacksmiths into varying sizes. Sometimes several of the smallest bullets were loaded and discharged together. The recoil was violent, so that the muskets were fired from the hip or at arm's length. The rate of fire was naturally slow; at Ijaye the Ẹgba musketeers fired their guns and then retired to reload while others took their place. Banana fibre was used as wadding and with the powder produced a dense cloud of smoke, fatal to any attempt at concealment.

Dane guns continue to be used by Yoruba hunters to the present day. But by the end of the Ijaye war the Ẹgba had obtained a number of the new breech-loading rifles. These were in every way greatly superior to the Dane guns: they were more accurate, had a greater range, and could be loaded more quickly and more safely. They were in great demand during the Sixteen Years War (1877–93), when they were used to particularly good effect by the Ijẹṣa troops. The Ijẹbu army which contested the advance on Ijẹbu-Ode of the British-led force from Lagos in 1892 was equipped with

[1] Lander ii (1830), p. 222.

many Snider rifles as well as Dane guns, but apparently had not learnt to fire these from a prone position. In 1883 the Ibadan complained that the Ijẹṣa were even using a Gatling machine gun against them. Artillery played no real part in the wars. It appears, however, that the Ijẹbu about 1820 were using 'cannon (akka); that is, small bronze pivot guns which they aim from behind the palisades of their fortified towns',[1] and the Ẹgba chiefs at Ijaye had a number of one and a half inch pieces which were fired from rests, though the seven howitzers which the British Government presented to Abẹokuta in 1851 for defence against the Dahomeans seem never to have been used in action.

It remains to examine in what ways the various new elements, political, military, and economic, which had made their appearance in Yorubaland by mid-century, altered the character of the wars. In the first place, the collapse of Ọyọ and the abandonment of much of the northern part of the kingdom led to a strategic retreat by the armies and many of the peoples into the shelter of the forests in the south. The Ọyọ were compelled to adapt their method of fighting to the new environment, and they succeeded so well that by 1840 the armies of Ilọrin were ceasing to be a major threat. A second fundamental change was in the duration and extent of the nineteenth-century wars. Before the Owu war, seasonal campaigns provided the pattern for Yoruba warfare. Now a war would last for years, interrupted but not broken off by the rains, drawing in allies to either side so that it attained a far greater scale than in previous centuries, and was fought with a bitterness all too characteristic of fratricidal strife—since these wars were largely waged among the Yoruba themselves with the Ilọrin and Dahomeans in alliance with any side as opportunity offered. War was now a more complicated undertaking: the obtaining of fire-arms and the supply of powder and shot, and later of cartridges, constituted a major logistical problem in itself and moreover entailed the maintenance of trade with suppliers at the coast. The larger armies could no longer live entirely off the country and the provision of food-stuffs from the home farms and from allies had to be ensured. Thus the safeguarding of lines of communication, or 'keeping open the roads' as it was called, became as important for belligerents far from their bases or from the coast as for traders, missionaries, and

[1] Osifekunde in Curtin (ed.), op. cit., p. 287.

officials. Conversely, states such as Ijẹbu and Ẹgba set great store by their control of access to the coast and constantly resorted to the blocking of roads and rivers as a means of asserting this.

Wars of the type fought in the nineteenth century by the Yoruba called for larger armies than heretofore. This demand was met partly by the coalition of allies and partly by calling on more men; the latter was facilitated by the increased population in many of the belligerent towns where refugees had flocked, Ibadan and Abẹokuta being like states in themselves. The composition of the armies reflected the new conditions and new weapons. Footsoldiers were now musketeers instead of bowmen, swordsmen, and spearmen, and horsemen sometimes carried pistols. There seems to have been no real attempt, except perhaps in Ibadan, to emulate the cavalry of Ọyọ, but the titles were maintained and chiefs and their retainers in most armies were mounted. Jones writes that the Ẹgba horses were 'numerous and hardy, requiring little attention and feeding on grass';[1] another European observer was struck by the high prices— three to seven young slaves or from £30 to £70—which chiefs and other wealthy men were prepared to pay to the dealers haunting the war camps for horses from the north, always more esteemed than the Yoruba ponies.[2] Meanwhile, the military organization of the states was expanding to meet the exigencies of the wars. A feature of this was the adoption of the military grades of the Ọyọ (or Ibadan) by other kingdoms whose armies had previously been less highly developed; the Ẹgba, for example, on forming their state at Abẹokuta felt the need for commands and titles which would apply to the whole people rather than to their many sections and so created a *Balogun* of the Ẹgba, a *Seriki*, and other chiefs, and even a *Sarumi* with his lieutenants,[3] though it is unlikely that the last acted on cavalry principles. Another development was the growth of a greater measure of military professionalism, a reflection both of the technical and manpower demands of the new warfare and weapons and of the displacement of a large part of the population from their farms and normal occupations. Many of the outstanding warriors of the nineteenth century were men who owed little to their birth and had come to the fore by their talents as war leaders,

---

[1] Ajayi and Smith, op. cit., p. 134. Cavalry mounts in England were rarely taught to support themselves by grazing.

[2] A. Millson, 'Yoruba', reprinted from the *Journal of the Royal Geographical Society* (1891).

[3] Biobaku, op. cit., pp. 14, 32.

YORUBA WARFARE AND WEAPONS

and they maintained their positions by enrolling numerous personal followers, their 'war boys', as full-time soldiers. This was particularly the case in Ibadan, a town which retained its original military character, but examples of professional warriors can be taken from any part of the land.[1] The Ọyọ army itself was no longer of much importance (it played only a minor role in the Ijaye war, for example), but an interesting development among the Ọyọ Yoruba was that after the death of Oluewu on the battle-field of Ilọrin it was decreed that in future no *Alafin* should accompany his troops to war.

Tactics in these wars changed only slowly. Siege warfare still predominated and many Yoruba retained their faith in the efficacy of their earth-built defences, a factor noted as late as 1892 when the author of a British intelligence report wrote of the Ẹgba of Abẹokuta that they had—

implicit faith in the impregnability of their wall and ditch. . . . As a rule they never venture out into the open when *attacked*, not even to resist small parties of raiders from other countries. Hitherto this system has been completely successful[2]

presumably a reference to the repulse of repeated Dahomean attacks on Abẹokuta. The long campaigns, during which an army might spend years in the field, led to the construction of elaborate camps whose fortifications enclosed stoutly built houses, with earthen or bamboo walls and roofs of thatch, and well-cultivated farms. From such bases an army would sally forth from time to time, either to attack the walls of an enemy's town or to meet his army in the field. In the forests the ambush was still much practised, and at the end of the period the Ijẹbu chose to defend their kingdom against the British-led expedition from Lagos by a series of surprise attacks along the path taken by the invaders, culminating in a stand at a river-crossing six miles south of their capital.[3]

When an action began, the troops spread out in open order and fired away in the direction of the enemy so long as their ammunition lasted. Occasionally a feigned retreat was made, but (according

[1] See J. F. A. Ajayi, 'Professional Warriors in Nineteenth Century Yoruba Politics', *Tarikh*, i, no. 1 (1965).

[2] P. R. O., CO 147/88: printed intelligence report of 15 July 1892.

[3] Robert Smith, 'Nigeria—Ijebu', in *West African Resistance* (ed. Crowder), (London, 1971), pp. 170–204.

to Captain Jones) tactical manœuvre went no further than this. The principles of covering fire, fire and movement, and flanking attacks were hardly developed, and night attacks were rare. Ground was won by superior fire-power and frontal movement, and was frequently lost again when the soldiers retired to replenish their ammunition. Johnson's account of the Ijaye war does, however, distinguish the Ibadan from the Ẹgba in this respect since the former had learnt to hold their gains 'until their own relieving company came up'.[1] Hand-to-hand fighting in the field seldom took place after the introduction of fire-arms; one of the last occasions was in the Gbanamu ('grasping fire') war in the early 1830s when the Ibadan swordsmen overcame their Ifẹ and Ijẹbu opponents by lifting or thrusting aside the barrels of their muskets.

Information about an enemy was much sought in the Yoruba armies. Before hostilities began, agents were sent out to gather intelligence and also to spread misleading reports about their own side. In the field, chiefs were equipped with 'reconnoitering glasses or telescopes', as Jones noted, and sentries continued to be posted in high trees or on the wooden watch-towers.[2]

The impact of the nineteenth-century wars on Yoruba life is still somewhat difficult to assess. Clearly they greatly hindered the growth of that legitimate trade in palm products which the British—abolitionists, officials, and traders—wished to foster. At the same time the dislocation of the life of the country as a whole was probably exaggerated by contemporaries. Vast areas lay remote from the scenes of battle and the narrow lines of communication, and here the wars can have had little effect upon the traditional patterns of society. Many captives were taken in the wars, but just as the view, propagated by European observers like Burton, that the wars were undertaken almost solely for this purpose must be abandoned, so must its corollary, that all captives were sold into slavery. Some were imprisoned, the least fortunate were executed in reprisals, some were redeemed by their families or friends or even released freely after a short time. Certainly many, probably the majority, of those taken, were ultimately sold as slaves, though, as the century wore on, an increasing proportion went to the local rather than the export market. With regard to casualties, there is a conflict of evidence. Some observers, notably Captain Jones,

[1] Op. cit., p. 340.
[2] Ajayi and Smith, op. cit., pp. 137–8.

thought that the number of dead and wounded after a battle was derisorily low, while the reports of the missionaries, some of whom did valiant service in tending the wounded, are at variance with this. It seems that the introduction of fire-arms did not at first lead to any increase in casualties and perhaps they even decreased in the long-range field warfare. Yet in the close fighting necessitated by an attack upon the walls of a town or camp there could be many dead, as was shown in the Dahomean attacks on Abẹokuta. Moreover, the replacement of muskets by rifles was leading to more accurate shooting and a greater number of fatal and dangerous wounds, and warfare seems to have been waged with increasing bitterness on the Kiriji battle-field during the Sixteen Years' war.

The inter-Yoruba wars were brought to an end by a peace treaty signed at Lagos in 1886, followed by the breaking-up of the camps at Kiriji under the supervision of commissioners appointed by the Governor of Lagos and by the operation of a cease fire at Modakẹkẹ. But on the north-eastern front the Ibadan and the Ilọrin still engaged in their hostilities, and the account of a joust, reminiscent of Ariosto, which took place at Ilobu between two picked lancers from the armies should not obscure the seriousness of this final phase of the wars. At last, in 1893, after the expedition from Lagos against the Ijẹbu the previous year had demonstrated both the determination of the British authorities and the superior armament and discipline of their force, Governor Carter was enabled to convert the precarious peace of 1886 into a reality, and then to persuade the Ibadan and the Ilọrin to agree to a demarcation line, break up their camps, and withdraw the armies to their capitals. The peace which at long last had come to the country did not reflect a decision reached militarily between the combatants; to some extent it was occasioned by their exhaustion, but mainly it was the result of British intervention. A completely new phase now opened: the phase of the West African Frontier Force, the Nigeria Regiment, and the campaigns against the Germans in two world wars, in all of which Yoruba soldiers played an honourable part. Unlike the arbitrary dividing line of 1850 on which this chapter hinges, the *Pax Britannica* of 1893 made a clear break in the slow evolution of Yoruba warfare from what may be called a medieval into a modern form.[1]

---

[1] The author is grateful to Mr. Denis Williams and Mr. R. C. C. Law who read the draft of this chapter and made many helpful suggestions.

Bibliography

The bibliography which follows is not intended as an exhaustive catalogue of all the published material available on Yoruba history, but as a guide to the *primary* material and its character. The distinction is not easy to sustain with consistency, since secondary sources, such as scholarly works, frequently include citations and quotations from primary evidence which may not be available elsewhere in published form. But in spite of its necessary incompleteness, it is hoped that this bibliography will prove of value to those engaged in the study of Yoruba history.

WRITTEN SOURCES

No list is offered here of the numerous published works by European traders, missionaries, explorers, and other travellers which make some reference to the Yoruba and their history. Few appraisals of the value of the testimony of individual writers have been published. There is, however,

LAWRENCE, A. W., 1961 'Some Sources Books for West African History', *J.A.H.* ii, no. 2.

which examines O. Dapper, *Naukeurige Beschrijvinge der Afrikaensche Gewesten* (Amsterdam, 1668), W. Bosman, *Nauwkeurige Beschryving van de Guinese Goud-Tand-en Slave Kust* (Utrecht, 1704), and J. Barbot, *A Description of the Coast of North and South Guinea* (London, 1732), though without particular reference to their testimony on Yoruba history. In addition,

WALDMAN, L. K., 1965 'An Unnoticed Aspect of Archibald Dalzel's *The History of Dahomey'*. *J.A.H.* vi, no. 2, and
AKINJOGBIN, I. A., 1966 'Archibald Dalzel: Slave Trader and Historian', *J.A.H.* vii, no. 1.

throw some light on A. Dalzel, *The History of Dahomy* (London, 1793). For the unpublished archival material, an excellent bibliography of the English, French, Portuguese, and Brazilian records relevant to the study of Yoruba history in the eighteenth century is to be found in I. A. Akinjogbin, *Dahomey and its Neighbours, 1708–1818* (Cambridge, 1967). For the nineteenth century the most important official documents are those in the Public Record Office in London classified under F.O.84 (Slave-Trade), F.O.2 (Africa, Consular), and C.O. 147 (Lagos Colony, after 1862). A bibliography of the missionary records will be found in J. F. A. Ajayi, *Christian Missions in Nigeria, 1841–1891* (London, 1965).

ORAL TRADITION

Valuable general appraisals of the value of oral testimony and the techniques to be employed in recording oral traditions are:

VANSINA, J., 1961 'De la tradition orale', *Annales du Musée Royal de l'Afrique Centrale*, Sciences Humaines, no. 36: trans. by H. M. Wright as *Oral Tradition* (London, 1965).

CURTIN, P. D., 1968 'Field Techniques for Collecting and Processing Oral Data', *J.A.H.* ix, no. 3.

Studies with particular reference to the field of Yoruba history are:

BEIER, H. U., n.d. 'The historical and psychological significance of Yoruba myths', *Odu*, no. 1.

BIOBAKU, S. O., n.d. 'Myths and oral history', *Odu*, no. 1.

—— 1956 'The problem of traditional history, with special reference to Yoruba tradition', *J.H.S.N.* i, no. 1.

LLOYD, P. C., n.d. 'Yoruba myths—a sociologist's interpretation', *Odu*, no. 2.

VERGER, P., 1962 'Oral tradition in the Cult of the Orishas and its connection with the History of the Yoruba', *J.H.S.N.*, ii, no. 3.

For the problem of chronology in oral history, see:

ALAGOA, E. J., 1966 'Dating Oral Tradition', *African Notes*. iv, no. 1.

LOCAL HISTORY

The following is an attempt to present as complete a listing as possible of the published local histories for towns and areas in Yorubaland. A complete list is virtually impossible, since most of them are printed on ephemeral local presses and published privately, so that they quickly become impossible to obtain and difficult to trace.

ABIQLA, J. D. E. and others, 1932 *Iwe Itan Ileṣa*, Ileṣa.

ADEDEJI, S. O., n.d. *Brief History of the Owa of Ijeshaland Chieftaincy Title*, Ibadan.

—— 1961 *Itan Kukuru Nipa Ilu Ileṣa*, Ileṣa.

ADELAGBE, D., n.d. *Iwe Itan Ore, Qtun, ati Moba*.

ADEMAKINWA, J. A., 1953 *Ifẹ, Cradle of the Yorubas*, Parts 1 and 2; published in both English and Yoruba versions, Lagos. Part 3 was published in Lagos (1960), in Yoruba only.

ADENIJI, D. A., 1958 *Itan Ilu Tonkere*, Iwo.

ADEWOYIN, A. A., n.d. *Itan Eṣindalẹ Awọn Ile Qba Qni Ifẹ*, Ile Ifẹ.

—— n.d. *Itan Idasilẹ Ile Aiye, Oduduwa ati Oriṣa Pẹlu Qlọfin Osangangan Qbamakin*, Ile Ifẹ.

ADEYẸMI, M. C., 1914 *Iwe Itan Qyọ-Ile ati Qyọ isisiyi*, Ibadan.

AJIṢAFẸ, A. K., 1924 *History of Abẹokuta*, Bungay.

—— 1931 *Abẹokuta Centenary and its Celebration*, Lagos.

AKINDOJU, S. A. and QLAGUNDOYE, M. O., 1962 *The History of Idanre*, Ibadan.

AKINYẸLE, I. B., 1911 *Iwe Itan Ibadan ati Iwo. Ikirun at Oṣogbo*, Ibadan (3rd edn. Exeter, 1950).
—— 1946 *The Outlines of Ibadan History*, Lagos.
ALADE, S., 1950 *The Awakening of Akurẹ*, Akurẹ.
ALUFA, J. M. F., 1954 *Itan Ajero ati Orilẹ-ede Ijero*, Ijero.
AROJOJOYE II, *Ọba* of Ijẹbu-Jẹṣa, 1959 *Itan Kukuru fun Iṣẹdalẹ Ilu Ijẹbu-Jẹṣa*, Ijẹbu-Jẹṣa.
ASHARA, M. B., 1951 *The History of Ọwọ*, Ọwọ.
AVOSEH, T. O., 1960 *A Short History of Ẹpẹ*, Ẹpẹ.
DINA, J. L., 1944 *Iwe Itan Yemetu*, Ibadan.
DUROJAIYE, P. L., 1955 *Awọn Idile Yoruba ati Orilẹ Wọn*, Apa Kini, Ibadan.
EPEGA, D. O., n.d. *Itan Ijẹbu ati awọn ilu miran*, Lagos.
FỌLARIN, A., 1931 *A Short Historical Review of the Life of the Egbas*, Abẹokuta.
GBỌLAHAN, D., 1951 *Iwe Itan Aha*, Ibadan.
GEORGE, J. O., 1895 *Historical Notes on the Yoruba Country*, Lagos.
JOHNSON, S., 1921 *The History of the Yorubas*, O. Johnson (ed.), Lagos.
KẸNYỌ, E. A., 1956 *Iwe Awọn Ọba Ile Yoruba*, Lagos.
—— 1959 *Founder of the Yoruba Nation*, Lagos.
—— 1962 *Itan Iṣẹdalẹ Iwo*, Ibadan.
—— 1964 *Yoruba Natural Rulers and their Origin*, Ibadan.
KUKURA, IBN, n.d. *Ta'lif akhbar al-qurun min '-umara' bilad Ilurun:* See B. G. Martin, 'A New Arabic History of Ilorin'? *Research Bulletin* of the Centre of Arabic Documentation, University of Ibadan, i, no. 2, (1965).
LAOYE I, *Timi* of Ẹdẹ, 1956 *The Story of my Installation*, Ẹdẹ.
LOṢI, J. B. O., 1913 *Iwe Itan Eko* Lagos: trans. as *History of Lagos* (Lagos, 1914) (reprinted Lagos, 1967).
—— 1923 *History of Abeokuta*, Lagos.
LUCAS, J. O., 1949 *Oduduwa*, Lagos.
ODUTỌLA, O., 1946 *Iwe Kini Ilọsiwaju Eko Itan Ijẹbu*, Ijẹbu Ode.
OGUNRINDE, S. O., 1962 *Olusanta ati Ikẹrẹ*, Ikẹrẹ.
OGUNSHAKIN, P., 1967 *Olumọ*, Lagos.
OGUNTUYI, A., n.d. *Itan Kukuru Nipa Ado-Ekiti*, Apa Keji and in English as *A Short History of Ado-Ekiti*, Part 2, Akurẹ. (Part 1 seems not to have been published.)
—— n.d. *Aduloju Dodoundawa Oko Ekiti Oko Akoko*, Ibadan.
OJO, S., n.d. *Iwe Itan Yoruba*, Apa Kini, Ibadan.
—— n.d. *Iwe Itan Oyọ, Ikoyi, ati AFIJIO*, Ọyọ.
—— n.d. *A Short History of Ilọrin*, Ọyọ.
—— n.d. *Iwe Itan Ṣaki*, Ọyọ.
—— 1953 *The Origin of the Yorubas*, Part 1, Ibadan; Part 2 was published at Ọyọ (n.d.).
OJO, W., n.d. An unpublished work on Imesi Ile, which was the basis of Anon., 'Folk History of Imesi Ile', *Nigeria Magazine*, no. 42 (1953).

Ọkẹ, M. O., 1969 *Itan Ilẹ Ijẹṣa*, Ibadan.
OKUBOTE, M. B., 1937 *Iwe Ikekuru ti Itan Ijẹbu*, Ibadan.
ỌLAFINMIKUN, J. B., 1950 *Iwe Itan Ọfa*, Ọfa.
OLUGANNA, D., 1959 *Oṣogbo*, Oṣogbo.
OLUNLADE, E., 1961 *Ẹdẹ, A Short History*, trans. I. A. Akinjogbin, ed. and annot. H. U. Beier, Ibadan.
OLUṢỌLA, J. O., 1968 *Ancient Ijẹbu-Ode*, Ibadan.
OMIDIRAN, D. F., 1955 *Itan Ogún Ekiti-Parapọ*, Okemesi.
ONOTELUWO, A. A. and others, 1960 *Iwe Itan Abijaparako*, Ijẹbu Igbo.
OYERINDE, N. D., 1934 *Iwe Itan Ogbomọṣọ*, Jos.
PAYNE, J. A. O., 1893 *Table of Principal Events in Yoruba History*, Lagos.
WOOD, T. B., 1878 *Historical Notices of Lagos, West Africa*, Lagos.

In addition to such works, traditional material can be found in records of the accounts of missionaries and other travellers, and in government records, for example the *Intelligence Reports* in the National Archives at Ibadan. A substantial collection of traditional histories is also preserved in the files of the Yoruba Historical Research Scheme, which are at present (1969) in the School of African and Asian Studies of the University of Lagos.

NON-YORUBA TRADITIONS

Information on Yoruba history is often preserved in the traditions of neighbouring peoples. These can be found in the following works:

Badagry:
AVOSEH, T. O., 1938 *A Short History of Badagry*, Lagos.

Benin:
EGHAREVBA, J. U., 1960 *A Short History of Benin*, 3rd. edn. Ibadan (First published 1934).

Borgu (Bariba):
DUFF, E. C., 1920 *Gazetteer of Kontagora Province*, London.
HERMON-HODGE, H. B., 1929 *Gazetteer of Ilọrin Province*, London.

Dahomey:
DUNGLAS, E., 1957 8 'Contribution à l'histoire du Moyen-Dahomey', 3 vols, *Études Dahoméennes*, xix–xxi.
LE HERISSÉ, A., 1911 *L'ancien royaume de Dahomey*, Paris.

Igala:
BOSTON, J., 1962 'Notes on the origin of Igala kingship', *J.H.S.N.*, ii, no. 3.

Nupe:
ELPHINSTONE, K., 1921 *Gazetteer of Ilọrin Province*, London.
HERMON-HODGE, H. B., 1929 *Gazetteer of Ilọrin Province*, London.
NADEL, S. F., 1942 *A Black Byzantium*, Oxford.

Porto Novo (Allada):
AKINDELE, A., 1914 *Iwe Itan Ajaṣẹ*, Porto Novo.
AKINṢQWQN, A. and AGUESSY, C., 1953 'Contribution à l'étude de l'histoire de l'ancien royaume de Porto-Novo', *Memoires de l'I.F.A.N.*, no. 25.
DUNGLAS, E., 1967 'Origine du royaume de Porto-Novo', *Etudes Dahoméennes*, n.s. nos. 9–10.

ORAL LITERATURE

For studies of various categories of oral literature among the Yoruba, see:
ABIMBQLA, 'W., 1964 'The Odù of Ifá', *African Notes*, i, no. 3.
—— 1965 'Yoruba Oral Literature', *African Notes*, ii, no. 3.
BABALQLA, S. A. O., 1966 *The Content and Form of Yoruba Ijala*, Oxford.
An analysis of the value of the Ifà divination corpus for the historian is provided by
ABIMBQLA, W., 1967 'Ifà Divination Poems as Sources for Historical Evidence', *Lagos Notes and Records*, i, no. 1.
Texts are available in
ABIMBQLA, W., 1968 *Ijinlẹ Ohun Ẹnu Ifà*, Apa Kiini, Glasgow.
—— in press *Awọn Oju Odu Mẹrẹẹrindinlogun*, Ibadan.
ATILADE, E. A., 1963 *Iwe Oriki Awọn Orilẹ Yoruba*, Lagos.
BABALQLA, S. A. O., 1967 *Awọn Oriki Orilẹ*, Glasgow.
YEMITAN, O., 1963 *Ijala—Arẹ Ọdẹ*, Ibadan.

CEREMONIES

For general studies of Yoruba ceremonies, see:
ADEDEJI, J. A., 1966 'The place of drama in Yoruba religious observance', *Odu*, n.s. iii, no. 1.
OGUNBA, O., 1967 'Ritual drama of the Ijẹbu people—a study of indigenous festivals', Ph.D. Thesis, University of Ibadan.
Descriptions of individual festivals, usually with some commentary on their purported historical reference:
AJAYI, A., 1965 'Olusanta Festival' (Ikẹrẹ), *Nigeria Magazine*, no. 84.
AKEREDOLU, J., 1963 'Igogo Festival' (Qwọ), *Nigeria Magazine*, no. 77.
AKINRINṢQLA, F., 1965 'Ogun Festival' (Ondo), *Nigeria Magazine*, no. 85.
BEIER, H. U., 1954 'Festival of the Images' (Ilobu), *Nigeria Magazine*, no. 45.
—— 1956 'Oloku Festival' (Okuku), *Nigeria Magazine*, no. 49.
—— 1956 'The Ọba's Festival, Ondo', *Nigeria Magazine*, no. 50.
—— 1957 'Obatala Festival' (Ẹdẹ), *Nigeria Magazine*, no. 52.
—— 1957 'Oshun Festival' (Osogbo), *Nigeria Magazine*, no. 53.
—— 1958 'Ori-oke Festival, Iragbiji', *Nigeria Magazine*, no. 56.
—— 1959 *A Year of Sacred Festivals in One Yoruba Town* (Ẹdẹ), Lagos.
—— 1964 'The Agbegijo Masqueraders' (Oṣogbo) *Nigeria, Magazine*, no. 82.

CROWDER, M., 1959 'A new Emir turbanned' (Ilọrin), *Nigeria Magazine*, no. 63.
LLOYD, P. C., 1961 'Installing the Awujale' (Ijẹbu-Ode) *Ibadan*, no. 12.
MacRow, D. W., 1953 'Shango Festival at Oshogbo', *Nigeria Magazine*, no. 40.
MURRAY, K. C., 1951 'The stone images of Ẹsiẹ and their yearly festival', *Nigeria Magazine*, no. 37.
OKESOLA, E., 1967 'The Agbo Festival in Agbọwa', *Nigeria Magazine*, no. 95.
ODUKOYA, M. A., 1959 'Okosi Festival at Ẹpẹ Town', *Odu*, no. 7.
PARRINDER, E. G., 1951 'Ibadan Annual Festival', *Africa*, xxi, no. 1.
STEVENS, P., 1965 'The Festival of the Images at Esie', *Nigeria Magazine*, no. 87.
—— 1966 'Orisha-nla Festival' (Ile Ifẹ), *Nigeria Magazine*, no. 90.
VERGER, P., 1961 'Ejigbo Festival', *Nigeria Magazine*, no. 70.
WALSH, J. M., 1948 'The Edi Festival at Ile Ifẹ, Nigeria', *African Affairs*, no. 47.
WESCOTT, J. A. and MORTON-WILLIAMS, P., 1958 'The Festival of Iya Mapo' (Igbẹti), *Nigeria Magazine*, no. 58.

ARCHAEOLOGY

ADERẸMI, SIR ADESỌJI, the Ọni of Ifẹ, 1937 'Notes on the city of Ifẹ', *Nigeria Magazine*, no. 12.
ALLISON, P. A., 1963a 'Newly discovered stone figures from the Yoruba village of Ijara, Northern Nigeria', *Man*, lxiii. 115.
—— 1963b 'A terracotta head in the Ifẹ style from Ikirun, Western Nigeria', *Man*, lxiii. 194.
—— 1964 'A carved stone figure of Eshu from Igbajo, Western Nigeria', *Man*, lxiv. 131.
ARRIENS, C., 1930 'Die heilige Steinfiguren von Ifẹ', *Der Erdball*, iv. 333–41.
BARKER, H., 1965 'Examination of the Ifẹ bronze heads', *Man*, lxv. 10.
BASCOM, W. R., 1938 'Brass portrait heads from Ile Ifẹ, Nigeria', *Man*, xxxviii. 201.
—— 1939 'The legacy of an unknown Nigerian "Donatello"', *Illustrated London News*, 8 April 1939, pp. 592–4.
BERTHO, J. and MAUNY, R., 1952 'Archéologie du pays Yorouba et du Bas-niger', *Notes Africaines*, lvi. 97–114.
BRAUNHOLTZ, H. J., 1940 'A bronze head from Ifẹ, Nigeria', *British Museum Quarterly*, xiv. 75–7.
CARTER, G. F., 1963 'Maize to Africa', *Anthropological Journal of Canada*, i, pt. 2, pp. 3–8.
—— 1964 'Archaeological maize in West Africa: a discussion of Stanton and Willett', *Man*, lxiv. 95.
DENNETT, R. E., 1910 *Nigerian Studies*, London.

DUCKWORTH, E. H., 1938 'Recent archaeological discoveries in the ancient city of Ifẹ', *Nigeria Magazine*, xiv. 101–5.

ELGEE, C. H., 1908 'Ifẹ stone carvings', *Journal of the African Society*, vii. 338–45.

ELISOFON, E. and FAGG, W. B., 1958 *The Sculpture of Africa*, London.

EYO, EKPO, 1968 'Ritual pots from Apomu Forest: Ondo Province, Western Nigeria', *West African Archaeological Newsletter*, viii. 9–15.

—— 1970a '1969 Excavations at Ile Ifẹ', *African Arts*, iii. 2, pp. 44–7, 87.

—— 1970b 'Ife so Far', *Black Orpheus*, ii, no. 4.

—— 1972 'New Treasures from Nigeria', *Expedition*, xiv no. 2, pp. 2–11.

FAGG, BERNARD E. B., 1949 'New discoveries from Ifẹ on exhibition at the Royal Anthropological Institute', *Man*, xlix. 79.

—— 1953 'Some archaeological problems at Ifẹ', *Conférence Internationale des Africanistes de l'Ouest, Vᵉ Réunion, Abidjan, Compte rendu*, pp. 125–6.

—— 1956 'Caribbean treasure hunt', *West Africa*, 6 October 1956.

—— 1959 'The Nok culture in prehistory', *J.H.S.N.*, i. 288–93.

FAGG, B. E. B. and FAGG, W. B., 1960 'The ritual stools of ancient Ifẹ', *Man*, lx. 155.

FAGG, WILLIAM B., 1949 'The antiquities of Ifẹ', *Image*, ii. (reprinted in *Magazine of Art*, xliii Washington, 1950, 129–33).

—— 1950 'A bronze figure in Ifẹ style at Benin', *Man*, l. 98.

—— 1951 'De l'art des Yoruba', *L'Art Nègre*, Présence Africaine, x–xi. 103–35.

—— 1963 *Nigerian Images*, London.

FAGG, W. B. and UNDERWOOD, LEON, 1949 'An examination of the so-called Olokun head of Ifẹ, Nigeria', *Man*, xlix. 1.

FAGG, W. B. and WILLETT, FRANK, 1960 'Ancient Ifẹ, an ethnographical summary', *Odu*, viii. 21–35. (Reprinted in *Actes du IVᵉ Congrès Panafricain de Préhistoire*, Tervuren, Section 3, pp. 357–73.

FROBENIUS, LEO, 1912 *Und Afrika Sprach*, 3 vols. Berlin.

—— 1913 *The Voice of Africa*, 2 vols. London.

—— 1923 *Das unbekannte Afrika*, München.

—— 1949 *Mythologie de l'Atlantide*, Paris. (Original edition: *Atlantis X, Die atlantische Götterlehre*, Jena, 1926.)

GOODWIN, A. J. H., 1953 'The origin of maize', *South African Archaeological Bulletin*, viii, no. 29, 13–14.

—— 1958 'Walls, paving, water-paths and landmarks', *Odu*, vi. 45–53.

HAMBLY, W. D., 1935 *Culture Areas of Nigeria*, Field Museum, Publication 346, Anthropological Series, Chicago, xxxi.

JEFFREYS, M. D. W., 1963 'How ancient is West African maize?', *Africa*, xxxiii. 115–31.

KRIEGER, K., 1955 'Terrakotten und Steinplastiken aus Ifẹ, Nigeria', *Berichte aus den ehemaligen Preussischen Kunstkammer*, Neue Folge, Berliner Museen, Berlin, pp. 32–9.

LANDER, RICHARD and JOHN, 1832 *Journal of an Expedition to Explore the Course and Termination of the Niger*, London.

LOMBARD, J. A., 1955 'A propos des pierres sculptées d'Ifẹ', *Notes Africaines*, lxviii. 1.

MAUNY, RAYMOND, 1962 'A possible source of copper for the oldest brass heads at Ifẹ', *J.H.S.N.*, ii. 393–5.

MEYEROWITZ, H. and V., 1939 'Bronzes and terracottas from Ile Ifẹ', *Burlington Magazine*, lxxv. 150–5.

MOSS, A. A., 1949 'Further light on the Olokun head of Ifẹ', *Man*, lxix. 159.

MURRAY, K. C., 1941 'Nigerian bronzes: works from Ifẹ', *Antiquity*, xv. 71–80.

—— 1943 'Frobenius and Ile Ifẹ', *The Nigerian Field*, xi. 200–3.

[MURRAY, K. C. and FAGG, B. E. B.] 1955 *An Introduction to the Art of Ifẹ*, Lagos.

MURRAY, K. C. and WILLETT, F., 1958 'The Ore Grove at Ifẹ, Western Nigeria', *Man*, lviii. 187.

MYERS, O. H., 1967a 'Excavations at Ifẹ, Nigeria, Obameri's Shrine', *West African Archaeological Newsletter*, vi. 6–7.

—— 1967b 'Excavations at Ifẹ, Nigeria, Oduduwa College Site', *West African Archaeological Newsletter*, vi. 8–11.

NIGERIA 1946 etc. *Annual Report on Antiquities for the Year 1946* etc. Lagos.

OZANNE, P. C., 1969 'A new archaeological survey of Ifẹ', *Odu*, n.s. i. 28–45.

READ, C. H., 1911 'Plato's "Atlantis" rediscovered', *Burlington Magazine*, xviii. 330–5.

STANTON, W. R. and WILLETT F., 1963 'Archaeological evidence for changes in maize-type in West Africa', *Man*, lxiii. 150.

TALBOT, P. A., 1926 *The Peoples of Southern Nigeria*, 4 vols., London.

UNDERWOOD, LEON, 1949 *The Bronzes of West Africa*, London.

WILLETT, F., 1958 'The discovery of new brass figures at Ifẹ', *Odu*, vi. 29–34.

—— 1959a 'A terracotta head from Old Oyo, Nigeria', *Man*, lix. 286.

—— 1959b 'Bronze figures from Ita Yemoo, Ifẹ, Nigeria', *Man*, lix. 308.

—— 1959c 'Bronze and terracotta sculptures from Ita Yemoo, Ifẹ', *The South African Archaeological Bulletin*, xiv. 135–7.

—— 1960 'Ifẹ and its archaeology', *J.A.H.*, i. 231–48.

—— 1961a 'Recent archaeological discoveries in Ilesha', *Odu*, viii. 4–20.

—— 1961b 'Investigations at Old Ọyọ, 1956–57, an interim report', *J.H.S.N.*, ii. 59–77.

—— 1961c 'The ritual stools of ancient Ifẹ', *Man*, lxi. 187.

—— 1962a 'The introduction of maize into West Africa: an assessment of recent evidence', *Africa*, xxxii. 1–13.

WILLETT, F., 1962b 'The microlithic industry from Old Qyǫ, Western Nigeria', *Actes du IVᵉ Congrès Panafricain de Préhistoire et de l'Etude du Quaternaire*, Tervuren, ii. 261–72.

—— 1965a 'Spectrographic analysis of Nigerian bronzes', *Archaeometry*, vii. 81–3.

—— 1965b *Council for Old World Archaeology Surveys and Bibliographies*, West Africa Area 11, no. 3, pp. 6–7.

—— 1966 'On the funeral effigies of Qwǫ and Benin, and the interpretation of the life-size bronze heads from Ifę', *Man, Journal of the Royal Anthropological Institute*, n.s., i. 34–45.

—— 1967a *Ifę in the History of West African Sculpture*, London.

—— 1967b 'Pottery classification in African archaeology', *West African Archaeological Newsletter*, vii. 44–55.

—— 1969 'Archaeology in Africa', *Expanding Horizons in African Studies*, ed. G. M. Carter and Ann Paden, Evanston.

—— 1970a 'New light on the Ifę-Benin relationship', *African Forum*, Vol. 3 no. 4/Vol. 4 no. 1, pp. 28–34.

—— 1970b Revised version of Willett 1960 in *Papers in African Prehistory*, ed. R. Oliver and J. D. Fage, Cambridge.

—— 1970c 'Excavations at Ita Yemoo, Ifę, Nigeria, 1957–63', *Proceedings of the VIth Congress of Prehistoric and Protohistoric Sciences, Prague, 1966*.

—— 1971a *African Art: An Introduction*, London.

—— 1971b 'Nigeria', *The African Iron Age*, ed. P. L. Shinnie, Oxford.

—— 1971c 'A Survey of Recent Results in the Radiocarbon Chronology of Western and Northern Africa', *J.A.H.* xii (pt. 3), pp. 339–370.

WILLETT, F., and DEMPSTER, A. N., 1962 'Stone carvings in an Ifę style from Eshure, Ekiti, Western Nigeria,' *Man*, lxii. 1.

INDEX OF SITES OF ARCHAEOLOGICAL IMPORTANCE DESCRIBED IN THE BIBLIOGRAPHY
Most of these sites are described also in Willett 1960 and 1970b to which separate references are not included here.

Ilesha	Nigeria, 1958–62, pp. 20, 65; Willett, 1961a; 1967a, pp. 179–80, pl. 107.
Ita Yemoo	Nigeria, 1957–8, p. 3, figs. 2A, B; 1958–62, pp. 4, 54; Willett, 1958; 1959b; c; 1967a; b; 1970c.
3, Iyekere Street	Willett, 1967a, pl. 90.
Iwinrin Grove	Bertho and Mauny, 1952, fig. 13; Fagg, B., 1953; Hambly, 1935; [Murray and Fagg], 1955, pp. 6, 19, 21, 22; Nigeria, 1952–3, p. 10; 1958–62, p. 4; Willett, 1967a, pp. 60–1 and *passim*, pls. 23, 25, 27, 28, 30, 36, 37, 76.
Kubolaje	Bertho and Mauny, 1952, fig. 7, no. 4; Willett, 1967a, pp. 59, 64, fig. 35.
Lafogido	Willett, 1967a; Eyo, 1970a; b.
Obaluru	Willett, 1967a, p. 65, pl. 13, 14.
Odo Ogbe Street	Eyo, 1970a; b.
Obameri Grove	Myers, 1967a; Willett, 1967a, pp. 61, 79, 101, 156, pl. 67, fig. 5.
Oduduwa College	Myers, 1967b.
Ogbon Oya Quarter	Goodwin, 1953; Nigeria, 1952–3, p. 9; 1953–4, p. 14; Willett, 1967a, pp. 64–5, pl. 92.
Ogún Ladin	Fagg, B., 1953; Frobenius, 1912, 1913; Goodwin, 1958; Nigeria, 1952–3, pp. 8–9; Willett, 1967a, pp. 80, 101, pl. 72.
Old Ọyọ	Frobenius, 1949; Nigeria, 1956–7, p. 3; Willett, 1959a; 1961b; 1962b.
Olokun Grove	Fagg, B., 1953; Fagg, W. B. and Underwood, 1949; Frobenius, 1912; 1913; 1949; Moss, 1949; Nigeria, 1952–3, pp. 9–10; 1953–4, p. 14; Willett, 1967a, pp. 24–6 and *passim*.
Olokun Walode	Fagg, B., 1953; 1959; Nigeria, 1952–3, pp. 9, 13; 1953–4, pp. 13–14; Willett, 1967a, pp. 25, 59, 101, pl. 31.
Opa Oronmiyon	Bertho and Mauny, 1952, fig. 1; Fagg, B., 1953; Frobenius, 1912, 1913; Nigeria, 1953–4, pp. 7–13; Talbot, 1926, fig. 89; Willett, 1967a, pp. 79–80, pl. 73.
Ore Grove	Arriens, 1930; Bertho and Mauny, 1952, figs. 5, 8, 9, 10; Dennett, 1910; Elgee, 1908; Frobenius, 1912, 1913; Lombard, 1955; Murray and Willett, 1958; Nigeria, 1956–7, p. 3 and plate; Talbot, 1926, pp. 339–40, figs. 83–6, 88, 90; Willett, 1967a, pp. 79, 80, 120, pl. 74.
Orun Oba Ado	Nigeria, 1958–62, pp. 39, 54, 59; Willett, 1965b; 1967a, p. 132.
Osongongon Obamakin	Fagg, B., 1953; Goodwin, 1958; Nigeria, 1952–3, p. 8.
Owo	Eyo, 1972.
Wunmonije Compound	Barker, 1965; Bascom, 1938; 1939; Braunholtz, 1940; Duckworth, 1938; Fagg, W. B., 1949; 1950; 1951b, pp. 112–15; Mauny, 1962; Meyerowitz, 1939; Murray, 1941; [Murray and Fagg], 1955; Nigeria, 1949–50, p. 6; 1950–1, p. 1; Underwood, 1949; Willett, 1966; 1967a.

ART

Art in Wood:

BEIER, H. U., 1957 *The Story of the Sacred Wood Carvings from One Yoruba Town* (Ilobu), Lagos.

—— 1958 'Gelede Masks', *Odu*, no. 6.

—— 1963 'Three Igbin Drums from Igbomina', *Nigeria Magazine*, no. 78.

CARROLL, K., n.d. 'Yoruba Masks', *Odu*, no. 3.

—— n.d. 'Ekiti Yoruba Woodcarving', *Odu*, no. 4.

—— 1967 *Yoruba Religious Carving*, London.

LAOYE I, *Timi* of Ẹdẹ, 1959 'Yoruba Drums', *Odu*, no. 7.

WESCOTT, J., 1958 *Yoruba Art in German and Swiss Museums*, Ibadan.

—— 1962 'The Sculpture and myths of Eshu-Elegba, the Yoruba trickster', *Africa*, xxxii, no. 4.

WILLETT, F., 1966 'On the funeral effigies of Ọwọ and Benin. . .', *Man*, n.s., i, no. 1.

Art in Metal:

For the metal sculpture of Ile Ifẹ, see the works cited under *Archaeology*.

KRAPF ASKARI, E., 1966 'Bronze objects from the Owe Yoruba, Kabba Province, Northern Nigeria', *Odu*, n.s. iii, no. 1.

WILLIAMS, D., 1963 'Lost Wax Brass-casting in Ibadan', *Nigeria Magazine*, no. 85.

—— 1964 'The iconology of the Yoruba *Edan Ogboni*', *Africa*, xxxiv, no. 2.

—— 1966 'Two brass masks from Ọyọ-Ile', *Odu*, n.s. iii, no. 1.

—— 1967 'Bronze casting moulds, cores, and the study of Classical techniques', *Lagos Notes and Records*, i, no. 1.

Art in Stone:

For the stone sculptures of Ile Ifẹ, Ijara, Igbajọ, and Ẹsure, see works cited under *Archaeology*.

CLARKE, J. D., 1938 'The stone figures at Ẹsiẹ', *Nigeria Magazine*, no. 14.

DANIEL, F DE F., 1939, 'Stone sculptures in Nigeria' Ofaro and Ẹfọn, *Nigeria Magazine*, no. 18.

MILBURN, S., 1936 'Stone sculptures at Ẹsiẹ (Ilọrin Province)', *The Nigerian Teacher*, no. 8.

MURRAY, K. C., 1951 'The stone images of Ẹsiẹ and their yearly festival', *Nigeria Magazine*, no. 37.

STEVENS, P., 1965 'The Festival of the Images at Ẹsiẹ', *Nigeria Magazine*, no 87.

Architecture:

This subject has not been much studied. See, however,

BEIER, H. U., 1954 'The palace of the Ogogas at Ikerre', *Nigeria Magazine*, no. 44.

—— 1958 'Changing face of a Yoruba town' (Erin), *Nigeria Magazine*, no. 59.

MURRAY, JACK W., 1955 'Old Houses of Lagos', *Nigeria Magazine*, no. 45.
OJO, G. J. A., 1966 *Yoruba Palaces*, London.
Wall-paintings:
BEIER, H. U., 1960 'Yoruba wall paintings', *Odu*, no. 8.

LINGUISTICS

For the general position of Yoruba among African languages, see
GREENBERG, J. H., 1966 *The Languages of Africa*, Indiana University.
On the value of linguistic evidence for the historian, see
ARMSTRONG, R. G., 1964 'The use of linguistic and ethnographic data in
    the study of Idoma and Yoruba history', in Vansina, J., Mauny, R.,
    and Thomas, L. V., (eds.) *The Historian in Tropical Africa*, Studies
    presented at the Fourth International African Seminar, Dakar, 1961,
    Oxford.
For the attempt to connect Yoruba with the language of Ancient Egypt,
see
LUCAS, J. O., 1948 *The Religion of the Yorubas*, Lagos.
and for its refutation,
WESCOTT, R. W., n.d. 'Did the Yorubas come from Egypt?', *Odu*, no. 4.

SOCIAL ANTHROPOLOGY

The relevance to historians of the Yoruba of the data of social anthropology
is discussed in
BRADBURY, R. E., 1964 'The historical uses of comparative ethnography,
    with special reference to Benin and the Yoruba', in Vansina, Mauny,
    and Thomas (eds.), *The Historian in Tropical Africa*, Oxford.
LLOYD, P. C., 1968 'Conflict Theory and Yoruba Kingdoms' in Lewis,
    I. M., (ed), *History and Social Anthropology*, London.
Historical reconstructions of political structures of Yoruba states are:
BIOBAKU, S. O., 1952 'An historical sketch of Ẹgba traditional authorities',
    Africa, xxii, no. 1.
MORTON-WILLIAMS, P., 1967 'The Yoruba Kingdom of Ọyọ', in Forde,
    D., and Kaberry, P. M., (eds.), *West African Kingdoms in the Nineteenth
    Century*, Oxford.
Descriptions of social and political organization not orientated specifically
towards historical questions may be found in:
ADEGORIOLA I, *Ogoga* of Ikẹrẹ, n.d. 'A note on the administration of
    Ikerre before the advent of the British', *Odu*, no. 3.
BIOBAKU, S. O., 1956 'Ogboni, the Egba Senate', in *Proceedings of the
    Third International West African Conference, Ibadan, 1949*, Lagos.
FỌLARIN, A., 1934 *Ogboni ati awọn oye miran ni Abẹokuta*, Abẹokuta.
KRAPF ASKARI, E., 1965 'The social organization of the Owe—a prelimin-
    ary report', *African Notes*, ii, no. 3.
——— 1966 'Time and classifications—on ethnographical and historical
    case studies of the Kabba Yoruba, *Odu*, n.s. ii, no. 2.

LLOYD, P. C., 1954 'The traditional political system of the Yoruba', *South-Western Journal of Anthropology*, x, no. 4.

—— 1955 'The Yoruba Lineage', *Africa*, no. 3.

—— 1960 'Sacred kingship and government among the Yoruba' Ado Ekiti, *Africa*, no. 3.

—— 1962 Yoruba Land Law, Oxford (includes detailed descriptions of Abẹokuta, Ijẹbu Ode, Ondo, and Ado Ekiti).

MORTON-WILLIAMS, P., 1960 'The Yoruba Ogboni Cult in Ọyọ', *Africa*, xxx, no. 4.

—— 1964 'An outline of the cosmology and cult organisation of the Ọyọ Yoruba', *Africa*, xxxiv, no. 3.

SCHWAB, W. B., 1965 'Kinship and lineage among the Yoruba' Oṣogbo, *Africa*, xxxv, no. 4.

Index